Making the Immigrant Soldier

MAKING THE IMMIGRANT SOLDIER

HOW RACE, ETHNICITY, CLASS, AND GENDER INTERSECT IN THE U.S. MILITARY

Cristina-Ioana Dragomir

UNIVERSITY OF ILLINOIS PRESS
Urbana, Chicago, and Springfield

Library of Congress Cataloging-in-Publication Data
Names: Dragomir, Cristina-Ioana, author.
Title: Making the immigrant soldier : how race, ethnicity, class, and
    gender intersect in the US military / Cristina-Ioana Dragomir.
Description: Urbana : University of Illinois Press, [2023] | Includes
    bibliographical references and index.
Identifiers: LCCN 2022045651 (print) | LCCN 2022045652 (ebook) |
    ISBN 9780252045035 (cloth) | ISBN 9780252087165 (paperback) |
    ISBN 9780252054303 (ebook)
Subjects: LCSH: United States—Armed Forces—Noncitizens—Case
    studies. | Noncitizen soldiers—United States—Case studies.
Classification: LCC UB418.N66 D73 2023 (print) | LCC UB418.N66
    (ebook) | ddc 355.2/2362—dc23/eng/20221025
LC record available at https://lccn.loc.gov/2022045651
LC ebook record available at https://lccn.loc.gov/2022045652

To my mother, Viorica Andree,
whose resilience, humor, and sharp wit inspire me every day

Contents

Preface

"I Am Light Green"

For those who regularly travel by New York City subway, it will not come as a surprise that getting out of the underground at a new stop often results in geographical confusion. The New York City landscape changes rapidly, and it never ceases to amaze me how this diversity keeps even old-time New Yorkers on their urban toes. This was my feeling when I got out of my train on the upper side of Harlem, where it was hard to grasp my bearings. Here, the city landscape was airy, the sky was visible to the naked eye, and the wind traveled fast through the field in front of me. This was my first trip for my new research project in which I engaged as a doctoral student. I was writing a research paper for my exciting Ethnography class, and, as the professor suggested upon hearing that I work on immigrants in the American military, I embarked on my first field visit to the National Guard station.

While I was aware of the historical process of naturalization of immigrants in the American armed forces, I knew little of the contemporary U.S. military and of its recruits. I was fascinated by the vision of unity, equal treatment, and meritocratic creed that the military exudes. I wanted to see how it was all possible. At face value, the American military was able to perform the ultimate citizenry ideal: treat all its members equally, respect their diversity, and allow their mobility among its ranks. It seemed to me the embodiment of the American citizenship ideals. The American dream.

Emboldened by this vision, I embarked on this journey on a windy fall day. My disorientation of coming out of the subway into an unknown station was not my only confusion. I was not sure where to go, whom to ask, or how to proceed with all this. So, I took long strides to what my map was indicating was the National Guard building and found myself at its entrance. The building was old, with high walls and empty hallways. All seemed foreign and cold. The guard smiled benevolently and asked how he could help. I explained that I was a graduate student doing research and that I would like to speak with someone. He promptly called an officer. This juxtaposition was one that would grow familiar to me over the years: the buildings and the environment were cold and unfriendly, while the people were polite and welcoming.

A tall, dark officer in fatigues came and walked me in. He patiently listened to me, asked me a few questions, and then asked a few recruits if they would like to talk to me. A few volunteered, and they were eager to share their experiences. Among them was a tall, slim Dominican soldier who was telling me about her journey that led her to the National Guard, and she referred to herself as "light green." She was jovial, energetic, and of good humor. I asked her what that meant. She laughed loudly and said: "It is like that. I am fair skin, so I am 'light green.'" Seeing my puzzled look, she continued, "He is dark green," and pointed to her African American colleague, who smiled and nodded. She explained that that is how they referred to one another, while alluding to their shared military identity: green.

Her words stayed with me. They made me wonder: Why was "color" present in the military? How did it translate? What did it mean? If "color" was still pertinent within military dynamics, did ethnicity, class, and gender play any role? If so, what roles were they? How did they interact with the meritocratic, equalitarian ethos of the U.S. military?

With all these new questions swirling in my mind, I found my way to the subway station and took the train home. For the months to come, I pondered these questions, and in trying to answer them I engaged in this research. Thus, the kernel of this book came into existence.

Acknowledgments

This book took a number of years to write, and it has been the collaborative work of many people whose efforts, time, and dedication could never be repaid. In what follows, I could bring to view only a few of the ones whose support directly shaped my work. In particular, I would like to thank my three main participants, Lily, Alexa, and Vikrant. Throughout the years, they let me enter their world, sharing with me their time, desires, and frustrations, as well as the details of their lives. Their support was invaluable and a tremendous epistemological journey.

This project started during my graduate studies, and there have been mentors along the way who shaped this work from the very beginning. Special thanks to David Plotke, whose mentorship and support have been relentless. David has been always there for me, during the pits of writing despair, when my research was awarded, and when I received my doctoral degree. I could not have written this book without his generosity, kindness, sharp interrogations, and solid support. Many thanks to Terry Williams, who inspired my writing and gave me insight into research methodologies that were pioneering in the social science field. Terry's openness to everyone he comes in contact with is contagious, and while working with him in the field I was encouraged to relate with my participants in ways that led to new avenues of knowledge. Also, my work was shaped by the late Aristide

Zolberg, whose intellectual support and expertise in the field of migration never ceased to amaze me. Ari's kindness, insights, and advice helped me pursue my work; the memory of our lengthy conversations about this book still nurtures my academic quest for meaning and truth.

This work was completed while I was at Queen Mary University of London, and I would like to send many thanks to the School of Politics and International Relations staff, especially to Kimberly Hutchings, whose support empowered me to finalize this work. I would also like to thank my reviewers, the editor, and many colleagues who read this work, whose dedication, support, and advice helped me rearticulate my work and produce a more insightful book.

There have been many people who were there with me throughout this long journey. They are both colleagues and friends who listened to me, read drafts, or simply stood by me when times were difficult. While it is hard to mention them all, I would like to send special thanks to Hadas Cohen, Ana Cristea, Marina Kaneti, Adam Joyce, Veronica Zebadua, Cristina Bugnaru, Camilo Godoy, Adina Calugaru, Dana Bucur, Denise Dallmus, and Daniel Najouks.

The completion of this book would not have been possible without the support of the Rockefeller Institute at the State University of New York in Albany, where I was a postdoctoral fellow, and the Center for Advanced Study of India, at the University of Pennsylvania, where I was a visiting fellow. I am specifically grateful for the encouragement of Rey Koslowski and Devesh Kapur.

My work was further sustained by a Die Zeit—Bucerius Fellowship, "Settling into Motion" (special thanks for their support to Anna Hoffman and Petra Borchard), and also by the Global Fellow Open Society Foundation, among many others. Last but not least, I am deeply grateful to Sadhguru Jaggi Vasudev, whose support and guidance have been immensely transformative. Finally, my deepest reverence to all those who came to the United States of America with a dream, who were relentless in pursuing it, and who were willing to work for the goodwill of all to make it happen.

Making the Immigrant Soldier

Introduction

Becoming an American:
Naturalizing in the United States

> Like previous generations of immigrants, there is one trait you all share
> in common: courage. It takes courage to get up and leave everything you
> know and go to another place, no matter where it is. You know, the only
> homes you've ever known, the lives, the loved ones who weren't able to
> come—for a new start in the United States of America.
> —President Joseph R. Biden, July 2, 2021

This is a book about immigration in the United States. It is a book that tells
three life stories of immigrants who enlisted in the American armed forces
before they were American citizens. Their stories show how they occupy
multiple spaces and inhabit diverse (and not always convergent) identities
and how this gives them different (and unequal) access to the institution
of the military and to the host country. Their stories also reveal the role
played by race/ethnicity, class, and gender in the naturalization process and
in the military service.

For many decades, U.S. citizenship has symbolized freedom and democracy and held out the promise of a good life. Migrants eagerly undergo a

process of "naturalization," learning the new country's norms, standardizing their behavior, and adjusting to fit in,[1] while hoping for a better life. All of this in spite of the fact that the reality of their new life differs greatly from their typical expectations. As we will see in the following pages, U.S. citizenship is in fact stratified, precarious, and often unable to fulfill its promises to the most vulnerable of its members.

Countries have different rules about their naturalization process. In the United States, it is typically assumed that newcomers first become "permanent residents" (or "green card" holders), then lawfully reside and work for a period of minimum five consecutive years to qualify to apply for U.S. citizenship, and then complete their naturalization process. Thus, the time needed for a permanent resident to become "naturalized"[2] is usually at least five years.[3] However, these years of residency typically come after a period of time—an estimated three years—that immigrants have spent living on a visa (as a student, worker, diplomat, and so on). Hence, through regular and lawful means, it usually takes a *minimum* of eight years for an immigrant to the United States to transition from being a foreigner to being a citizen. This period is deemed necessary for one to become part of the new country, to learn its rules, and to adjust.

Many countries around the world require an extended period of residency as proof of good moral standing before granting citizenship rights and privileges to their migrants. These requirements are not surprising and are accepted as a given by immigrants (like myself). So, when I learned that by enlisting in the U.S. armed forces, one can go from being a foreigner to being a citizen—bypassing the "permanent resident" status—in as little as five months, I became curious about this alternative "naturalization" path,[4] and about the transformation that immigrants undergo while serving in the U.S. armed forces. I wanted to see how immigrants' diversity in terms of race/ethnicity, gender, and class impacted this process and whether the military was acting as a social equalizer and superimposed a unique military identity on immigrant recruits. In other words: I wanted to understand how and if service in the U.S. armed forces would create a national and military identity capable of superseding other aspects of immigrants' identity, or whether the immigrants' race/ethnicity, gender, and class define their naturalization process.

This question is not new, but one that in different forms has preoccupied many scholars. For example, referring to immigrants' identities in public spaces such as subways, Tonnelat and Kornblum state that "in some 'zones' the usual categories can be 'relatively irrelevant'; such differentiation is a characteristic trait of the subway's social order. That is, people on trains are riders before they are women, black, young, Hispanic, or rich. As a result, what one ought to do as a rider takes precedence over the discriminating features of fellow passengers" (2017, 7). Thus, while one's racial or gender identity is important, in specific circumstances it can be superseded by other forms of public identity, such as that of a subway rider. Following this logic, we can then expect immigrants serving in the U.S. military to be both soldiers and men, Romanian, rich, and white. However, Tonnelat and Kornblum continue, "this does not mean that diversity is of no consequence. Women, for example, do not have the same subway experience as men, adolescents do not behave like older adults, and people of different racial and ethnic groups do not feel they are treated in the same way as white, middle-class New Yorkers are" (7). But would the same logic reproduce within the military? Should we expect civilian power hierarchies to persist, in spite of military superimposed identities? Should we expect—for example—that the experiences of female Latina immigrant soldiers differ greatly from those of Indian male immigrant soldiers of the same rank? Pursuing this line of inquiry, this book uncovers if (and how) race/ethnicity, gender, class, and their intersection play a role in immigrants' "naturalization" via military service or whether the superimposed military identity obliterates all other categorization and the hierarchies they embody.

It is important to underline that each American branch of service has a distinct military subculture. These differences further reverberate into everyday gender dynamics and structures, making these distinctions crucial in understanding one's identity transformation. While sharing a common historical starting point and considering that "while the U.S. military today has never had a higher fraction of women, they remain just 16 percent of the total force,"[5] each branch of the armed services has developed differently with respect to the integration of women within their ranks. For example, the Army began training men and women together on an experimental basis in 1977. The Air Force accepted its first female member in 1948; however, "the women of the WAF didn't see the same kind of action as Air Force men: they were generally relegated to clerical and medical tasks."[6] The Marine Corp started female integration in the 1990s. Moreover, the

Marines, who long relied on the slogan "A Few Good Men," as of December 2019 had only 231 female Marines serving in combat, 52 officers and 179 enlisted women.[7] It is therefore not surprising that masculinity (and femininity) is expressed and experienced quite differently within the U.S. military branches.

These differences play an important role in shaping one's identity, and it is therefore expected that the experiences of immigrant recruits might differ accordingly. In this book, I have been mindful of these variances across the institution. However, the people I worked with also shared with me experiences that highlighted the commonalty of their process of transformation via the military service.

While the people presented in this work are American immigrants serving in the host country's military, the process of naturalization that they undergo is not unlike that of many civilian folks. Immigrants, just like anyone else, navigate multiple identities, take on different positions, and are often placed at the crux of competing identities: being women/men/trans, they are racialized, nationalized, and part of the global class structures. The process of navigating these multiple intersectionalities becomes ever more pertinent when looking at those who are a part of well-defined institutions, like the military. Thus, working with migrant soldiers exposes the dynamics of this process of naturalization, while allowing us to see our own—at times—contradictory ways of being in the world and the various sites of oppression we occupy.

Not Yet Americans: Foreign-Born Soldiers in the U.S. Military

For those born in the United States, the "American dream" of social mobility, of opportunities for prosperity and success, might have been weakened over the past decades, but its legacy still stands tall in many hopeful immigrant eyes. In spite of its outdated immigration policies and draconic detention practices, America is still seen by many as "a country of immigrants," a land of wealth, freedom, and individual success. This America is diverse—but equalitarian, filled with difficulties—but generously offering ways to overcome them. Immigrants come to America hoping to access this life. While this "American dream" might become a reality for some newcomers, for many it does not materialize. For some immigrants, the (estimated) eight years of U.S. residency might have passed without their being "naturalized." Others might find that the legal immigration process is too strenuous to undergo and decide to return to their home country. For these reasons (and often more), hoping to better their lives and rapidly streamline their immigration status, approximately eight thousand newcomers join the U.S. armed forces every year.[8]

This book presents the stories of three immigrants who came to America ready to embrace its well-known dream, but found themselves in dire situations. All three were unable to make ends meet, to support their families back home, and to travel outside of the country. Not unlike their native-born peers (Mittelstadt 2015), to incur the social and economic mobility that was not accessible to them in the civilian realm, they looked to the military, the state organization[9] that proclaims equality and success based on individual merit for all its members, and they decided to enlist in the U.S. armed forces. All three aimed to achieve a better life.

The three immigrant soldiers are Lily from Romania, Alexa from South America, and Vikrant from India. Their names have been changed, and so were a few details about their lives, to ensure their privacy. Although they come from different parts of the globe and they have never met, their lives are strikingly similar. As all three came to the United States to better their socioeconomic conditions, the academic literature would label them "economic migrants." However, highlighting the tension between how immigrants see themselves and how immigration specialists describe them, when I asked them why they immigrated, all three responded that they came because they wanted to explore the world. Honoring their views, while acknowledging their economic aspirations, in the following pages I suggest a different understanding of their coming to America: the three participants were young—in their twenties and early thirties—so searching for economic improvement blended with their curiosity and sense of adventure. Alexa and Lily were undergraduate students, and Vikrant had just received his master's degree. Lily and Alexa originally arrived in the United States on "cultural exchange programs," and Vikrant came as a graduate student, so all three entered on temporary nonimmigrant visas, which presumed that they would go back home when they completed their programs and their visas expired.

Immigrant-receiving countries often assume that temporary workers and students/visitors come in only to do the assigned activity and then gracefully leave the scene, leaving no trace of their presence. Aristide Zolberg (1997) labeled immigration policies that treat immigrants based on this assumption as "wanted but not welcome," showing that states envisioned newcomers to be temporary settlers arriving to satisfy a particular and temporary need of the host country, willing to retreat back home once their tasks have been accomplished. However, year after year, immigrant after immigrant, they have been proven wrong. From the Bracero program,[10] whose legacy the United States still feels today, to the irregular migrants who cross the borders and work in agricultural jobs, the history of American immigration is filled with stories of those who came, worked, and did not return to their home countries. The immigrants I speak about in this book took a similar route. For them, the "land of opportunity" was not "paved with gold," and maybe it was not even paved. They share a longstanding gray immigration status,[11] which they tried to adjust, and when they did not fully succeed, they took a path less traveled: they enlisted in the U.S. military.

This book presents how they came to America, their life before and during military service. To understand their "naturalization" process, much of my research rests on the shoulders of immigration scholars who have examined the role that race/ethnicity, gender, and class play (Alba 1999; Alba and Nee 1997; Cornell and Hartmann 1998; Hirschman 1983; Portes and Rumbaut 1990, 2001; Silberman, Alba, and Fournier 2007; Waters 1999; Zolberg 2006a). I rely heavily on their work, at times engaging critically with it, and I apply it to the experiences of the three immigrant soldiers to see how the dynamics and power within the U.S. military resemble or diverge from those of civilian society. Because of the great work that precedes me, I focused this book on the three participants and compare their experiences to the civilian experiences studied by those scholars, to further critical reflection on migration and naturalization in the contemporary United States. Additionally, the work with African Americans (Bussey 2002; Merhson and Scholssman 2003; Shaw and Donnelly 1975; Wakin 1971) and women in the U.S. military (MacKenzie 2013, 2015; Van Creveld 2000; Kamarck 2015; Elshtain 2000) guided and empowered my analysis of how race and gender impact one's experience of military service. Inspired by these diverse bodies of work, I show here that even if the participants did not enter the military considering identity and class politics, identity and class politics met them and structured their experiences.

Three Immigrant Soldiers: Lily, Alexa, and Vikrant

This book presents the life stories of Lily, Alexa, and Vikrant, but my own story of immigration is also woven throughout the text. Through auto-ethnographic snippets,[12] I further explore the impact of gender, class, and ethnicity/race in today's "naturalization" process. Moreover, these references are meant to place the participants in conversation and to ground my research by revealing my (limited) positionality. While I never served in the U.S. or any other military, I came to the United States in the same way Lily and Alexa did, and just like them I searched for opportunities to better my life. We are of similar age, and I also came to America in my early twenties. Like both women, I came with a "cultural exchange program"[13] that allowed me to work in a job that not many natives wanted; like Vikrant, I completed my graduate studies in the new country and was on a student visa for a number of years.

Alexa, Lily, and I arrived in the late 1990s, when America was experiencing an economic boom. The country had many low-paying jobs that required medium education and good language skills, for which it was difficult to find workers. One of the industries in dire need of qualified and semiqualified labor force was the (summer) camp industry. Hardly considered a serious immigration source or a field facing labor shortages, summer camps are glorified, with many Americans sharing nostalgic memories as participants or camp counselors, or both. But working in camps is not an easy job. It requires a lot of responsibility, long hours, commitment, and drive. Not many Americans are willing to work for a high-demand, long-hours, and low-paying job, in spite of its emotional rewards, so employers have to look abroad to ensure a full staff ready at the start of their season. This demand for temporary staff opened the door for many international youths to visit America. The countries and regions favored for recruitment were the United Kingdom, New Zealand, and Australia (for camp counselors, because of their language skills) and eastern Europe (for eastern Europeans' willingness to work as support staff, primarily in maintenance and hot kitchens).

Lily, a fellow Romanian, is a half decade older than me. We did not know each other prior to this study, but we found we shared a great deal: memories of communism and of our country's transition to democracy, the image of America as the "land of opportunity," and an eagerness to visit a country that would (probably) not even grant us a tourist visa. For both of us, working in a camp for a few summer months seemed to be a good opportunity to make money and to travel to the United States. So, a few years before me, Lily joined one of the many American companies with recruitment offices in eastern Europe and became for the summer a member of the support staff in an American camp for children with disabilities.

I found Alexa in a similar situation. She was from South America, but came to the United States from the Czech Republic, where she was an undergraduate student, which allowed her to participate in the "cultural exchange program" that gave her a temporary work visa. In contrast to Lily and myself, Alexa came not to work in a camp but for a family. Even years after this first employment in the United States ended, Alexa recalled it as the most lucrative job she had had. She and her boyfriend at the time worked for a family in New Jersey; Alexa took care of the home, and her boyfriend was the family's driver. I met her as she arrived in the United States and was going to her new job. Because of shared experiences, we quickly became friends.

Vikrant I met years later, in 2009, when I was already working with immigrants in the U.S. military. I read about his military enlistment in the newspaper. I contacted the reporter who wrote the article, and he connected me with Vikrant, who readily agreed to be a part of my study and later allowed me to use his online posts for this research.

While we all share common points in our immigration story, the immigration paths of Lily, Vikrant, and Alexa, as well as their experiences of America, differ from mine. Alexa and Lily fulfilled their original contracts and went back to their home countries—as I did. But, unlike me, when they returned to the United States the following year, they took a chance, stayed in the new land, and later on enlisted in the armed forces. My participants found their own paths to America, worked, and experienced the gray area of the immigration limbo. After years of hardship, they had a hard time streamlining their social mobility, so they joined the U.S. armed forces. While our paths diverged, these common experiences created a bridge between the respondents and me, allowing us to connect and through this connection create the stories presented in these pages.

Book Structure and Outline

This research project did not start from the hypothesis that race/ethnicity, gender, and class shape the experience of immigrants in the military. The conversations I had with the participants were open and did not follow a precise script. Throughout the interviews, the themes of race/ethnicity, gender, and class came to the fore and shaped my analysis. Rather than following a unidirectional, linear path, either deductive or inductive, in line with Schwartz-Shea and Yanow, my work follows an "abductive" process. Thus, I start from the premise that "there is no end point in abductive reasoning as in a 'circular-spiral' pattern" (2011, 28), in which "one 'discovery' leads to another" (32).

Because the work seeks to examine a puzzle I encountered working "in the field," I have attempted to balance academic rigor with a style that allows the life stories to flow. This task at times felt like a graceless dance, so I decided to tilt the balance toward the participants' narratives—and focus on telling their life stories. To ensure that their voices are heard and to create more vivid images of Lily, Alexa, and Vikrant, I insert long quotes and even reproduce dialogues. This endeavor, as everything else in life, comes with a price—namely, the truncating of academic discourse and a limited use of its jargon. However, to respect the social science standards, and to create a sharp and in-depth study, I decided to place most of the academic references in footnotes.

The book is designed to be read from start to finish, while allowing for the possibility that a reader will engage with one or more chapters at random. To this end, I have kept chapters on theory, methodology, or a particular life story separate. I start by outlining the current and historical situation of immigrants in the U.S. armed forces and next highlight scholarship on the intersectionality of race, gender, and ethnicity in the context of both military and immigration research.

The following parts, except the conclusion, follow a parallel structure. To ensure coherence and to allow for the life stories to be read both independently and in tandem, each follows the same organization. They begin with a vignette that aims to introduce a vivid image of the person and then continue with an overall assessment of either Lily, Alexa, or Vikrant, outlining the main line of development of their life story, showing how these immigrants decided to move into a new country, and how imprecisely contoured their decision was. The narrative then presents their life before entering the military: their home country and their coming to America; it details their enlistment and military experience/training, showing the obstacles they faced once they decided to join the host country's armed forces. Next, while recognizing that in practice these categories work in tandem, to devolve into analysis each section separately considers the impact of class, race/ethnicity, and gender on the three immigrant soldiers' lives. Each story ends by outlining a conclusion, delineating within the framework of intersectionality the obstacles faced by Lily, Alexa, and Vikrant throughout their naturalization process within the military. It explains how their identities were shaped within the institution of the military, both allowing and creating obstacles one their way to accessing social justice.

In the last part of the manuscript, I further interrogate how the three immigrant soldiers, who often find themselves at the margins of the societies that they protect, access social justice while having a dignified use of their gender, race/ethnicity, or class. Overall, through this book, I bring into view that in spite of the uniformity of military training, immigrants' "naturalization" shapes different paths, depending on one's gender, accent, class, and country of origin.

As the methodology used for this book is qualitative/interpretative, bridging academic and nonacademic work, a thorough explanation is needed to highlight the novelty of the approach and the benefits—as well as the limitations—of such a method. Thus, in the appendix, a through explanation of the methodological tools used is presented.

CHAPTER 1

Conceptual Work

Foreigners in the U.S. Military

Many people find it surprising when foreigners—by definition outsiders in a community—enlist in the host country's military and potentially sacrifice their lives (Amaya 2007a) for a cause and a people to which they do not belong. However, the recruiting of foreigners into a country's armed forces is not rare. For example, the French Legion and British armies have been accepting foreign nationals since World War I (Barkawi 2017; Ware 2012), and the contemporary Israeli military service[1] has an institutionalized process for transforming foreigners into citizens.

In the United States, from the Civil War onward, groups of newcomers—including Irishmen, Germans, eastern European Jews, and Italians—enlisted in the armed forces and used military service to become naturalized (Dragomir 2012). Currently, about 5–7 percent of the country's military personnel are foreign nationals,[2] and in 2019 "the number of veterans who were born outside the United States [was] approximately 530,000, representing 3 percent of all 18.6 million veterans nationwide."[3]

To recognize immigrants' contributions to the U.S. armed forces, changes to the Immigration and Nationality Act have streamlined the naturalization process. On July 3, 2002, President George W. Bush signed an executive order providing "expedited naturalization" for noncitizen men and women serving on active-duty status since September 11, 2001. The order granted the right to apply for citizenship to around 15,000 members of the U.S. military who had served fewer than three years. In return for their military service, immigrant soldiers can acquire citizenship in as little as three months.

Additionally, in February 2009, the Military Accessions Vital to the National Interest scheme was launched.[4] MAVNI is a pilot recruitment program that has been allowing noncitizens who have lived[5] (mainly on temporary visas) in the United States for at least two years to apply for military enlistment.[6] The existence of programs like MAVNI—which allow foreigners with special skills to join its forces and, in return, get American citizenship within three months—seems to create a win-win situation. The American armed forces become more heterogeneous, and the United States benefits from the settling of new, highly skilled immigrants, who are willing to risk life and limb for their new country. At the same time, foreigners swiftly become citizens and gain legal and formal access to economic resources and political and civil rights.[7] This rapid legal naturalization raises the following questions: How are the immigrant soldiers becoming U.S. citizens? And is this process meritocratic, or do categorizations such as race, ethnicity, and gender play a role? In other words, if, as immigration scholars like Portes and Zhou (1993a, 1993b,) tell us, immigrants' (civilian) identity plays a crucial role in their naturalization in (civilian) America, do these markers play a similar role in the military, or is the military able to offer a different path to citizenship?

Intersectionality Studies Impacting Migration Studies

To answer these questions, I turned to intersectionality studies (Cho, Crenshaw, and McCall 2013; Craven and Davis 2014; Davis and Craven 2016; D. King 1998; Crenshaw 1989; Guy-Sheftall 1995; Hawkesworth 2006, 2016a, 2016b). These studies, which focus on exposing power dynamics, provide sharp tools to carry out an in-depth analysis of immigrant soldiers' experience, by highlighting the impact of the categories that shape one's experience in institutionalized settings. Intersectionality scholars have shown how "multiple axes of oppression challenge the whiteness of women, the maleness of all people of color, and the heterosexuality of all" (Sanchez-Hucles and Davis 2010, 175) and call for research that does not focus on only one aspect of a person's life, because "simple categorizations along a single dimension do not capture the dynamics of [their] experiences" (176). They argue that an intersectional approach does not treat race, class, gender, ability, and sexuality as autonomous categories, but rather seeks to "examine their interaction in understanding leadership identity, behavior, and effectiveness" (176–77), showing how "multiple aspects of identity yield different workplace experiences and connections to the organization" (177).

Following Crenshaw's (1991)[8] seminal intersectionality theory, throughout three individual narratives I expose how intersectionality operates on the ground and in doing so reveal the systems that produce them. This approach highlights how the categories of race/ethnicity, gender, and class operate as tools of analysis to identify the place that the three participants in this work occupy and how they try to access the institution of the military and implicitly their host country. This work is also rooted in what McCall (2005) names the "intra categorical complexity"[9] approach to the study of intersectionality, by analyzing how individuals are excluded from previous analysis.

While these tools have been available for decades, within military studies they have often been ignored by scholars engaging in analysis (Mettler 2005) or had limited (while important) "thinking through intersectionality," "exploring how institutionalized hierarchies are naturalized by feminization and thus are effectively depoliticized," and who "appli[ed] the insights gained to the problematics and war" (Peterson 2007, 11).

Looking at the three U.S. immigrant soldiers to see how their race/ethnicity, gender, and class lead to practices of inclusion and exclusion within the military and the host country shows how social groups "negotiate both context and symbolism simultaneously" (Few-Demo 2014, 172).

In line with Lorde and Clarke (2007) and McCall (2005), I argue that life stories are the optimal method for drawing out processes and examining how change occurs in the life of immigrants who join the U.S. military. In the following pages, this understanding of intersectionality highlights how the three immigrants who participated in this research occupy multiple spaces and inhabit diverse and not always convergent identities and how this gives them different (and unequal) access to the institution of the military and to the host country. Thus, this conceptual framework informed my exploration of how come Lily is successful in accessing the military programs, but at the same time fails to be promoted and to climb the social hierarchy. It enabled an understanding of how Alexa's ethnic identity and gender work together in limiting her longed-for integration, and how while Vikrant's gender works well in his accession to the military, his ethnicity and race mark his daily interactions and place him in a marginal position that he continuously needs to (re)articulate and define.

Finally, while the intersectionality framework is typically used to explain how minority women face different and taxing challenges in performing their identity (Sanchez-Hucles and Davis 2010; Hesse-Biber 2014), this work could also be employed to reflect on the privileged role that one's gender and race/ethnicity can play in accessing power structures. Thus, in this book, I engage intersectionality in its traditional manner and analyze how being a woman and Latina (for example) in the U.S. military might place folks in a disadvantageous place within power dynamics, and thus work against their ability to access justice. In addition, I use the intersectionality framework to show how gender can act as a privilege within institutional settings. Thus, Vikrant's use of masculine gender pronouns is seen as a form of empowerment and a way of "fitting in" the new environment, which also leads to his naturalization.

While it is clear that race/ethnicity, gender, and class work in tandem on the ground, in the following pages they will be presented as analytically distinct in order to better recognize their role and their implications. Class, gender, and race/ethnicity are powerful tools of identification, but if they are used distinctly in social analysis, their precariousness is quickly revealed. While here race/ethnicity, gender, and class are separately analyzed, this is a mere analytical distinction used to illuminate different structural political aspects, when in practice these categorizations work in tandem to create the specific systemic hierarchies in which the three participants find themselves.

A Not So Classless Host Country and Military

In spite of the myth of America being the land of immigrants (Hingham 2002), studies of American immigration reveal how ethnicity, race, class, and gender play an important part in determining both who enters the country and, once they are inside, whether they become an integral part of its political, cultural, social, and economic communities. For example, Portes and Zhou (1993b) emphasize that immigrants coming to the United States enter a stratified—not a classless—society, and their assimilation also means *class* assimilation. While some immigrants succeed in entering the middle or upper class,[10] at times they also "assimilate down," losing their middle-class status, and are absorbed into the host country's lower class.

When this happens, immigrants—just like natives—look for opportunities to transgress this social order.[11]

As with natives, for immigrants, enlistment in the military is not necessarily motivated by national zeal or eagerness to protect the "homeland" (Appy 1993), but is often connected to accessing social and economic resources. Thus, because becoming a part of the U.S. armed forces is perceived as an opportunity to access social and economic resources that are seldom available in the civilian realm (MacLeish 2013; Mittelstadt 2015), immigrants—just like natives—decide to enlist.

There are strict rules governing how one joins the U.S. labor force. A foreign education degree is often of little help in finding suitable "white-collar" employment, and domestic education is often privileged. Accessing support to continue higher education in the host country by means of military service (for example, through the GI Bill) becomes an attractive incentive for immigrants. This, in tandem with embracing a new military identity that gives immigrants (at least visual) recognition as an integral part of American citizenry, fuels their desire for social mobility (Bacevich 2013). Alexa, Lily and Vikrant saw the prospect of being socially accepted through military work and the possibility of following domestic education programs as worth pursuing—and they decided to enlist in the U.S. armed forces.

Race and Ethnicity in the U.S. Immigration System

So far, I have been using "race/ethnicity" generally and in tandem, but it is necessary to explain the terms further in the immigration context. There is an overlap between the concepts of "race" and "ethnicity": their extensive usage across U.S. history "reinforces a perception of them as natural, scientific entities, rather than as humanly created, social (arti)facts" (Yanow 2003, 17). Embedded in our social life, "race" and "ethnicity" have broad use, but their exact meaning is not clearly defined (24). It is, rather, changing, evolving, including and excluding groups, making and remaking identities. For example, "The Irish, Italians, Jewish and other non-Anglo Saxon, non-Protestant European immigrants identified as races in the 1800s to mid 1900s only when their designation as distinct racial groups had been lost from public discourse, where they are subsumed under 'White'" (19). "Race" and "ethnicity" are social categories created and used for population management, and they share a changing and interlinked history. I will use the categorization of "race/

ethnicity." Other studies of migration often use the terms separately, but the approach I am adopting is better suited to explaining how ethnic differences in the United States have been racialized. This is because the United States went through several periods of accepting and denying naturalization of immigrants based on categorizations of "race" and "ethnicity."[12]

The preference for white European immigrants, unquestionable from the very beginning (Zolberg 2006b), became obvious with the passing of the Chinese Exclusion Act of 1882, which made the exclusion of immigrants based on their race official (Yin 2012). The act stated that "in the opinion of the Government of the United States the coming of Chinese laborers to this country endangers the good order of certain localities within the territory."[13] As a result, immigrants of Chinese origin were legally and formally excluded from American citizenship. From this point onward, the relevance of race and ethnicity in immigration policies openly gained currency and culminated with the infamous Johnson-Reed Act of 1924, which limited annual immigration from particular countries based on one's "birth or ancestry."[14] With this act, ethnic and racial selection became an open and integral part of the U.S. immigration system. The act led to the creation of new categories of racial difference and national ideas, and as a result it enabled "the identification of immigration with both non-whiteness and illegality" (Ngai 2014).

Four decades after the passing of the Johnson-Reed Act, the 1965 Immigration Act abolished the quota system and at a stroke dramatically changed the racial composition of American immigrants.[15] While early immigrants were of European descent and as result mostly white, starting in the second part of the twentieth century, immigrants diversified the racial composition of the American population.

One's country of origin is important not only in determining whether one is allowed entry in a destination country, but also in the naturalization process. As we have seen, immigrants do not automatically assimilate into the middle class or naturalize into a nonethnic unified American core; they enter "a stratified system of social inequality, in which different social categories—whether birth-ascribed or not—have unequal access to wealth, power and privilege" (Barth and Noel 1972). Consequently, the benefits of "becoming American" depend largely on what stratum of American society absorbs the new immigrants. Hence, immigrants naturalize into an American society that is not only economically stratified but also one in which class intersects with race/ethnicity.

Thus, as Waters (1994) and Portes and Sensenbrenner (1993) attest, ethnicity and race have become key markers in the contemporary waves of migration politics. While emphasizing the role played by race and ethnicity in deciding who can enter the country and who can acquire citizenship (Gerber 2011; Hoeder 2014),[16] we need to explore how education, economics, and religion, as well as the interplay between individual motivation and network capital, shape the naturalization process (Portes and Rumbaut 1990, 2014).

For the participants in this study, race and ethnicity prove to be significant markers in their naturalization process—mostly unbeknownst to them. Lily is white, and the privilege of her whiteness (DuBois 1962; Baldwin 1996; T. Allen 2012; Frankenberg 1993; Roediger 2007) made it possible for her to keep her foreignness (mostly) invisible, so that it did not affect her place in the military hierarchy. Thus, Lily didn't tell me or reflect upon unjust daily military racial scrutiny. But Alexa—a Latina—felt she was often closely watched by her superiors. In contrast to Lily, Alexa perceived her ethnicity to be a burden, something immediately noticeable that deterred her from pursuing the career of her dreams. Her ethnic heritage highlighted the intersection of race and ethnicity: she was ethnically South American, but her presence was racialized. In spite of her vehement opposition to her racialization as someone who was not "white," she was seen as a Latina or Hispanic. Alexa attested that she felt that this identification placed her close to other minorities, such as Mexicans, and as a result she was often seen as a lesser immigrant. Alexa's understanding reflects the ethnic and racial inequalities that exist in American society: Latino/a/x immigrant children suffer a high rate of poverty (Landale and Oropesa 1995; Amaya 2007b), while nonwhite immigrants struggle in disadvantaged neighborhoods, often for generations. Wang (2008), examining the effects of individual and metropolitan-area characteristics on the earnings of U.S.-born whites, blacks, foreign-born Hispanics, and Asians, found that macroeconomic structure together with racial composition significantly influence the interracial and gender earning disparities among groups, impacting the immigrants' naturalization process.

Unlike both Lily and Alexa, Vikrant is from India and a part of "the migrant streams [that] have been reshaping the global landscape" (Kapur 2010, 2). The 1965 Immigration Act increased the number of highly skilled professionals and students who were looking to immigrate to the United States (53). This led to a significant growth in the Indian-born population in the United States, "from around 13,000 in 1960 to nearly one million by

2000, and 1.5 million by 2007" (53, citing 2007 American Community Survey, U.S. Census Bureau). In many ways, Vikrant was similar to many other immigrants of Indian origin: he was male, in his thirties, highly educated (he already had a graduate degree when he came to the United States), and from a (high-caste) Hindu background.[17] His profile in many ways was exemplary of the "segmented assimilation" argument, showing how his ethnicity (and background) could enable him to enter the middle or upper class that American Indian immigrants typically move into. Pew Research data attributes this success to a high level of education that enables Indian immigrants to often achieve higher and more rapid wealth accession than other immigrant groups.[18] Thus, Vikrant's ethnic identity, supported by his education, predisposes him to an entry into upper-middle-class American society. However, in contrast to many of his compatriots, Vikrant joined the armed forces, which meant that he did not obtain the expected median annual household income earned by his fellow Indian immigrants. His military career might prove lucrative, but it could also take longer to deliver on its promise.

Considering the paramount role that race and ethnicity play in civilian immigrant life, one can only wonder whether the armed forces are able to dissolve these factors by enabling soldiers to access social mobility based on their individual merit or whether the same segmented assimilation based on race and ethnicity is reproduced in military service. While little attention has been paid to foreign-born accession and mobility via military service, a large body of scholarship has focused on the American armed forces' experience in accommodating and empowering minority groups. Since World War II, the military has been a field of contested American citizenship—filled with recruits who challenged the common understanding of American citizenship, questioning and rearticulating American liberal and egalitarian values. Integrating minority groups into the U.S. military has been one of the nation's great challenges and—often—achievements. For example, Bristol and Stur argue that "one of the great ironies of American history since World War II is that the military, typically a conservative institution, has often been at the forefront of civil rights" (2017, 219).

Throughout American history, incorporation of groups, such as African Americans or women, into the armed forces has produced major changes in the organization's ideals and practices that have further impacted civilian life. For instance, to overcome recruitment shortages during World War II, African Americans were encouraged to enlist (Bristol and Stur 2017). After the war, pressure from black and liberal groups, coupled with an acknowl-edgment that African American soldiers were poorly used, led the Army to reexamine policies on racial segregation (Moskos 1970, 110). As a result, on July 26, 1948, President Truman issued Executive Order 9981, abolishing racial segregation in the U.S. military by mandating "equal treatment and opportunity for all persons in the armed forces without regard to race, color, religion or national origin."[19] This order did not immediately integrate the U.S. armed forces: desegregation of the military was not completed for several years, with all-black Army units persisting well into the Korean War. While the executive order started the process of military racial integration, it moved rather slowly amid much resistance from within the armed ser-vices, especially from the U.S. Army (W. Taylor 2016). After 1973,[20] African Americans assumed a greater presence in the military, reaching more than 17 percent in active duty and slightly over 15 percent in the reserve by 2007[21] and 17.2 percent in 2014.[22] This is typically attributed to the fact that the U.S. military is "perceived to be a more racially fair employer" (M. Segal et al. 2007), enabling recruits to achieve higher ranks, irrespective of their race (Hauser 1978). It could also be ascribed to the continuous decrease of welfare programs in civilian life, making military service the main form of access to life-supporting benefits (Mittelstadt 2015). However, in spite of this progress, discriminatory practices within the military against minorities persisted twenty years later (Dudziak 1988). Moreover, the large number of enlisted personnel of minority background does not directly translate into parity within military ranks.[23]

While recruitment and retention of African American military personnel continue, the Immigration Act of 1965 also resulted in recruitment activities being focused on incoming minority groups, especially second-generation immigrants, who were now seen as possible enlistees. Since 1973 there has been an increase in the number of "Hispanics of Mexican Origin" in the military forces (D. Segal and M. Segal 2005).[24] Whereas in 1975 the number of Latin Americans in the U.S. armed forces was 2 percent, the proportion climbed to 10 percent by 2001, and it is estimated it will reach 22 percent by the second decade of the new millennium. In spite of their increased presence since the late 1980s (reaching 13 percent in 2006), Latinas/os/x are still underrepresented when compared with overall U.S. demographics. However, when adjusted for those who qualify for military service on the basis of education, Latinas/os/x are actually slightly overrepresented. They are most likely to enlist in the Marine Corps and least likely to enlist in the

Air Force—unlike African Americans, who usually join the Army (Kelty, Kleykamp, and Segal 2010; Lowe, Hopps, and See 2006). Furthermore, Latinas/os/x are overrepresented in combat, as well as in nonadministrative or supply duties (Barreto and Leal 2007). The accession of Latinas/os/x into the military is similar to that of African Americans: there is a steady increase in the number of those serving, but a lag in their attaining higher ranks. In contrast to African Americans, who for the most part are already U.S. citizens at the time of their enlistment, some Latinas/os/x face the obstacle of their immigration status, lacking the documentation necessary to become a U.S. soldier.[25]

* * *

Race/ethnicity plays an important role in immigrants' assimilation in stratified civilian America (Zhou 1997a, 1997b; Kao and Tienda 1998). In this book, I explore how these factors operate similarly within the U.S. military. Lily, Alexa, and Vikrant were made aware of their race/ethnicity, both in the civilian and in military contexts. As we shall see later, when Alexa described the ruthless way her Army supervisor treated her, I asked her what she thought the reason was. She said bluntly, "I am not the right color!" and told me she was different from the supervisor, whom she called "white bread." In his civilian life, Vikrant seemed to be less aware of the impact of his ethnic origin and was taken by surprise when one of the young students he was tutoring referred to him as "dark." As stated earlier, Lily was not aware of her white privileges, and most of the time she took them for granted, but her ethnic accent made her painfully aware that she was a part of a minority. This made her feel different, and she perceived it as a marker of her inferiority and as an obstacle to her acquiring the civilian social and economic position of which she dreamed.

Gender, Military, and Immigration

Next to their ethnicity, the identity participants most often referred to, directly or indirectly, was their gender. Vikrant, being a cisgender/straight man, fits into the traditional gender profile of the immigrant and of the military recruit. Lily and Alexa, however, challenged gender stereotypes, in both the military and the immigration context. Like other pioneer military women (Biank and Thompson 2014; Hegar 2017; Germano and Kennedy 2018; Sullivan 2011; Stur 2011; Thorpe 2015; Weinstein and White 1997), they fitted the profile of immigrant women as primary breadwinners who settle in the new country by themselves and send money to the family back home, while (now) enlisting in the military.

Although women cross international borders at roughly the same rate as men,[26] a great deal of international migration scholarship has been based on the assumption that international migrants largely consist of male workers (DeLaet 1999). This assumption is often based on the idea that men are the breadwinners who immigrate to support their families. To tackle this preconception, it is important to examine "the interaction between patriarchy, racism, capitalism and the state in reinforcing gender stratification through the development process" (Cheng 1999, 41).

Historically, gender did affect a person's chances of becoming American. From the late 1800s onward, women's entry into the new country depended not only on satisfying a series of health and literacy criteria common to women and men, but also on their passing "a man test": women who arrived single at Ellis Island without the company of a man—husband or blood relative—were not allowed to leave the island and begin their new life in the mainland United States.[27] Single women were identified as possibly being connected to sex work: the Immigration Act of 1903, Section 3, stated that "the importation into the United States of women for the purposes of prostitution is hereby forbidden."[28] This act was challenged and changed in 1910 for singling out "women and girls" solely based on gender as possible criminals in the new land.[29]

Today, we see a steady increase in the number of women migrating to the United States,[30] but this numerical growth is not supported by adequate immigration legislation, which is primarily designed to control male migration. This blind spot in immigration policies is visible in the life of women migrants. For example, Cecilia Menjivar and Olivia Salcido show that while the incidence of domestic violence is not higher than in the native population, immigrant women go through more difficult situations because of "limited host-language skills, isolation from and contact with family and community, lack of access to dignified jobs, uncertain legal statuses, and experiences with authorities in their origin countries" (2002, 900). Menjivar and Salcido further argue that without the necessary immigration legislation, women do not have the same chance to assimilate into the new host country.[31]

Thus, in much of the traditional work on immigration, gender played a marginal role at best. Since gender has become a part of the conversation (starting in the early 1980s), it has been addressed as a question of "modernization" and empowerment through labor practices. Hence, immigrant women's assimilation is mainly discussed in relation to employment (Antecol 2000). In 1997 it was assumed that "immigrant wives will initially take dead-end jobs to finance their husbands' human capital investments and eventually drop out of the labour market or reduce their labour supply as their husbands' labour market outcomes improve" (Blau, Kahn, and Papps 2008, citing Baker and Benjamin 1997). However, just as with immigrant men, the number of immigrant women entering the labor force grew.[32] Studies conclude that the way gender is acknowledged and practiced in the immigrants' country of origin influences their employment behavior in the United States and impacts their assimilation (Blau 2015).[33]

The participants in this study, irrespective of their origins and gender, were eager to find employment and struggled to work in their specialized fields. Vikrant found work in education, but the salary he received was not sufficient for him to make ends meet and pay back his school loans. Lily and Alexa found it even more difficult to find professional jobs. While Vikrant used his master's degree and his temporary work status to find a professional job, the two women took *doméstica* jobs and to make ends meet worked as nannies, as well as in blue-collar jobs in the hospitality sector. Both took additional positions that paid their bills: Alexa worked now and then on a private boat for events, and Lily took a coat-check job in a restaurant for many years. For all three participants, the military represented the chance to obtain a professional form of employment that would ensure their livelihoods.

Although Vikrant's decision to enlist might be considered unusual because he was joining the armed forces of a country that is not his own, because the military is perceived as "the epitome of a male-dominated establishment" (Goldman 1973), his choice was not counterintuitive given his gender. For Lily and Alexa, however, the choice might seem more puzzling. Not only were they fighting for a foreign country, but they were also willingly joining in a predominantly masculine institution in which one might expect to find them in marginal roles.[34]

This assumption is in line with the expectation that women's presence within the military is related to a high risk of sexual violence.[35] Studies show that women "in traditionally female jobs were slightly less likely to leave the military" and that women's job turnover "occurs mostly within the jobs that have more than 25% and less than 90% females in the same labor force"

(Waite and Berryman 1986, 591). Women performing the "typically female" jobs (Stur 2011) tend to stay longer in those positions, which makes at least some jobs within the military desirable or at least acceptable.

While the integration of women within military ranks has been a topic that amounted to long-enduring controversy, after the Persian Gulf War women's opportunities for mobility within the U.S. military became a subject of heated public debate (Blacksmith 1992, 5). Even though women always worked in the U.S. military in different capacities, the limit on the number of women who were allowed to serve was not repealed until 1967 (5). During World War II, a large number of women served in the U.S. military, not as temporary workers but as continuing support-services members (Sherman 1990).

While this has been destabilized since March 2016, with women now being able to serve in combat, the structure of the military has not necessarily changed. Gender roles, practices, and expectations are often reinforced (Germano and Kennedy 2018). For example, Herbert says that because women in the military are simultaneously held accountable to be both women and "good" soldiers, they must strike a balance between displaying feminine and masculine traits. The difficult task of maintaining this sensitive balance leads to logical fallacies such as the "belief that men are somehow uniquely suited to serving in the nation's military." Thus, "the production of gender at the interactional level reinforces both ideological and institutional arrangements that place women at the margins of military participation" (1998, 122).

Furthermore, Herbert says, "as long as the military is viewed as the domain of men, women will be outsiders and their participation will be challenged, thus perpetuating a cycle of male dominance: the military is defined as male, a small proportion of women is challenged and penalized, the military remains ideologically and numerically male-dominated" (122). Similarly, Germano and Kennedy (2018) show while women are admitted to the armed forces, they are trained differently, which places them in an inferior situation. Military women often remain in marginal positions, unable to advance within the military hierarchy. The production and reproduction of traditional gender roles reflect how male privilege is present at different levels of military incorporation. For example, as early as in Reserve Officers' Training Corps (ROTC) training, "women must privilege traditionally feminine aspects of themselves in order to maintain a coherent sense of self. Through this process, these women ultimately reproduce traditional femininity and male privilege" (Silva 2008, 942).

Like other servicewomen in the contemporary U.S. military (Biank and Thompson 2014), Lily and Alexa faced various challenges, such as learning new responsibilities, managing the stresses of marital and family life, dealing with the issues of personal lives, and thriving to balance femininity standards with performance in the (male-dominated) work environment.

Through these feminist lenses, we can see how the military has an inherently masculine structure and that the marginal position it confers on women entering the armed forces is counteracted by voices predicting the "feminization" of the services. While advocates of expanding the role of women in the armed forces, including in combat, have been vocal for decades (Wilcox 1992), critics of "feminization" see the growth in the number of women serving in the military, as well as the policies created to accommodate them, as possibly detrimental to military effectiveness.

Contemporary immigrant women and men enlisting in the American armed forces have to enter these conversations and practices. While we know that change takes place slowly within large institutions such as the military, the fact that we are discussing these gender changes is a sign of transformation. When Vikrant, Lily, and Alexa enlisted, the military did not allow women in all positions in combat, but things altered while they were serving, and all three of them had to negotiate and practice their gendered "places" in the changing military. For Vikrant, his enlistment did not much challenge his gendered identity but rather—as he would say—amplified it. He liked physical exercise, and the military pushed him to get stronger; his masculine behavior was not diminished but enhanced by his enlistment. But Alexa and Lily had to negotiate their gender while serving. Alexa often told me, "In the Army you are either a whore or a lesbian. I am neither. That is why I have no friends. They do not know me." Lily maneuvered her gender as she did her race: she took it for granted and internalized the woman's place in the institution.

Through Lily's, Alexa's, and Vikrant's life stories, another role of the military emerges to the fore: the provider of services, such as housing, education, and health care. While American immigrants are expected to be independent, to create their paths and access services on their own in the new country, the three participants found it difficult and enlisted in the host country's military as a way to access welfare programs unavailable to them in the civilian realm. This finding is in line with Jennifer Mittelstadt's argument in *The Rise of the Military Welfare State* that because military service requires "frequent moves, family separations [and] personal risks" (2015,

65), those enlisted are considered to be different from civilians and thus are not subjected to free-market principles. As a result, the U.S. military took on the "Army family" image and provides its members access to social services, becoming an attractive career for first-generation Americans and working-class natives. While Mittelstadt argues that the U.S. military has drastically reduced its support programs since 1993, outsourcing housing, social work, counseling, and more to the private industry, these programs are still more generous than their civilian counterparts. Thus, we see that for Lily, Alexa, and Vikrant, military programs (while diminished) still offered better prospects than those available in civilian life.

Conclusion

While analytically distinct, gender, race/ethnicity, and class operate in tandem, intersecting, and thus creating the complex dynamics of power in which the participants of this study found themselves. These categories are fluid and connected markers that often surface in everyday experiences in the military and civilian life. In the following pages, I will tell Lily's, Alexa's, and Vikrant's stories and support them with descriptions of the roles their race/ethnicity, class, and gender played in the process of "becoming American" by way of military service. Specifically, in line with Laura L. Miller, in what follows I will explore how "individuals can simultaneously enjoy privilege and face disadvantage according to race, gender, age, occupation, and position within an organization" (1997, 32). As we become acquainted with Lily, Alexa, and Vikrant, we will explore how these markers helped or hampered them in their life journeys of becoming Americans.

CHAPTER 2

Lily

Who Is Lily?

Her talk is as sharp and quick as her smile—a smile that, along with her easygoing manner, garners friends and acquaintances. Lily gets along with people, and though she still has an accent, she uses it with a graceful charm, as she interacts with anyone who comes her way. Her story is the story of an immigrant woman who often uses the phrase "I like a challenge," but admits (sometimes in the same breath) that the military offers her a "safety blanket."

When I first met her in 2007, Lily was thirty-six years old, single, and living with a Romanian family in Queens, New York. Her olive skin, long brown hair, and dark eyes complemented her diminutive stature and her healthy, plump body, which was matched nicely by her casual attire. She had a business degree from Romania and was assiduously trying to make a career in the travel industry. She first came to America in the mid-1990s for the summer, and returned a few months afterward, this time to stay. Five years later, she became a permanent U.S. resident. She was sworn into the Air Force Reserve in October of the following year and began her service a few months later. While serving in the military, she took advantage of President George W. Bush's executive order[1] and became a U.S. citizen in just a few months. After she completed her original military contract, Lily obtained a master of science (MS) degree from a prestigious American university, using the GI Bill. As I write this, she has been a reservist in the Air Force for more than eight years.

Over the years, Lily was very generous with her time, meeting me for hours and inviting me to private events, and she became my friend. During an interview at a busy café in New York City's West Village, two years into the research, Lily looked straight into my eyes and confessed: "Everything you do is related. What you do now comes from things that you did in your childhood. If you look back, you can actually see this." Often, Lily revealed her views of life in intimate and informal settings when my recorder was switched off or when I was not directly asking her about her military experience.

Lily's entire life seems to be a challenge waiting to be undertaken—though at the same time, she longs for stability. This tension informs her entire story, and her desire for stability has often placed her in challenging situations. In some senses, Lily reminds me of the emblematic Hobbesian man who, in his search for peace, engages in many unsettling acts, including war itself. Lily's drive and tireless efforts to find "a safety blanket" are moving to witness, and she has so much energy that the world vibrates around her. Her life is divided between her reserve military service, an intense civilian job, her personal and love lives, and her many hobbies. Every time I met Lily, she told me about her numerous plans; she spoke quickly and often jumped from one topic to another. She was always "on the go" and often had to cancel our plans because unexpected circumstances arose that demanded her attention.

"I am never bored. Only when I close my eyes [that is, die] I will lie still; until then I will not relax. I do not know how some say that this weekend I just stayed at home and nothing happened. Oh God, please! Let it happen to me as well. It never does. I got tons of projects," she says rapidly, mingling Romanian and English words. "How many do I get done? 89.99999 percent. But there are 10 percent that do not get done. Those are the ones that I can't accomplish by myself. Other questions?"

A Glance into a Life: Lily

At the time of my writing, Lily has been in the United States for almost fourteen years. Her English is good, and she is what scholars call "a model immigrant": married and well educated, she serves the country, owns a home, and has a full-time job. In addition, her life seems to be following the classic path of "assimilation," a pattern in which the immigrant sheds an old identity and embraces the new identity of the host country. This process of transformation is not so streamlined as scholars would have us believe; in Lily's case, it has taken many forms over the years, and actually began a long time ago, when she was very young—back in communist Romania. In this process, her white skin gave her privileges she did not reflect upon, while her Romanian ethnicity acted as an unexpected obstacle to social and economic mobility. The military helped her gain access to the new country by offering her support to complete her higher education, and she performed her gender (mostly) to her advantage. But her path led to an incomplete and frustrating process in accessing social justice.

Lily optimistically thought that in the military she would benefit from nondiscriminatory treatment that would provide her better access to social resources. She often felt accepted in spite of being an immigrant, but her attitude changed when she applied for formal recognition and tried to become an officer. Her situation took a quick and devious turn when Lily was exposed to the fact that having a foreign background overruled individual skills and expertise, which also translated into limited social and economic mobility. Ultimately, in spite of Lily's assiduous efforts to become both an American and a soldier, the host country's system limited both her assimilation and her access.

From Home Country to the United States

Born in the mid-1970s in a small town in the south of Romania, Lily grew up under communism, but recalls little about it. "What about communism?" Lily replied with a question to my inquiry about her memories of the communist past. It was a cold winter evening, and we met in our regular coffee shop in the West Village, in New York City, where she confessed that she really liked the shop's European-influenced menu. As she bit into a crunchy Italian panini sandwich, she continued: "I was really young when it ended; I was not suffering. Of course, we remember the blackouts, [. . . and there was] no water. . . . We had to fill up the tub." Between bites, Lily laughed at the memory of the hard times she experienced in her youth: "I do not know. I remember the long lines to buy bread and one liter of cooking oil. And all the BS," she said, referring to the political propaganda that colored the news in communist Eastern Europe.

Lily told me that she was sixteen when the astonishing worldwide events of 1989 unfolded: the fall of the Berlin Wall, the protests in China's Tiananmen Square, and the emergence of glasnost and perestroika in the Soviet Union were signs that a "wind of change"[2] was blowing. These upheavals brought about drastic political and economic transformations in the Eastern European communist bloc, launching a wave of emigration from that part of the world toward Western Europe and the United States. Economic hardship, and the lack of any possible change on the horizon, forced many Romanians in the 1990s to look for better opportunities outside their own country. Lily—like hundreds of thousands of young people—had witnessed the fall of the regime and endured the seemingly never-ending transition to a brutal market economy. Now a university graduate, she found herself urgently weighing her options and looking for ways to leave the country in search of economic growth and stability. But the security that she hoped to achieve was not yet in sight.

In the first postcommunist decade, Romanians' options for going abroad were severely limited. Now that Eastern Europe was no longer communist, the policy of accepting immigrants in Western Europe and the United States changed, and new migrants were no longer welcome, neither by host countries nor by earlier immigrants.[3] New visa programs were unable to satisfy the large demand from people ready to leave their homes in search of a better life. The United States enacted strict immigration laws and practices at its overseas embassies: only the few who could prove "strong [economic] ties" to the host country were allowed to settle in the "nation of immigrants." These "ties" meant a well-paid job, an apartment, and money in the bank,[4] the very things Romanians lacked and were hungry for. While it was difficult for anyone to prove these ties, it was especially difficult for the youth of Romania. Like many, Lily's only chance of entering the United States was through a cultural program that allowed her to work in America for a few months.

In the 1990s, because the American economy was booming and many low-paid jobs were not filled, the United States permitted foreigners to work for minimum or less-than-minimum wage in high-demand industries, under the legal umbrella of "cultural exchange programs." These schemes became popular in all the impoverished postcommunist countries. Even if the programs were not officially described in these terms, the United States was effectively seeking a low-paid but highly skilled labor force to fill temporary jobs. Cultural exchange programs were sponsored by international organizations such as the YMCA, Work Experience, or Camp Counselor USA. The program's admission requirements were demanding: applicants had to be enrolled in a university course, be capable of and willing to do low-end jobs, hold good character references, possess experience in the field, and, on top of all that, have a decent command of English. Moreover, a candidate needed to obtain a J1 visa, which for Romanians came with strict restrictions, making it almost impossible to immigrate legally to the United States[5] at the end of the cultural exchange program.

"In America, I made money, $400 or $600, for all of the summer," Lily said when I asked about the pay that she received through the cultural exchange program. "It was bullshit," she continued bitterly, referring to the low payment she received for a summer of hard work. "In the first year, I worked as a kitchen aide. Of course, I spoke no English, I had to clean tables, but it was fine. I learned a lot, you know? So, the next year I went back. I was a counselor. They requested me to go back, and I worked five sessions with children with handicaps. They had physical and mental handicaps." Caught up in her memories, she went on nostalgically: "It was demanding, 'cause you know we had to do a lot, we had to change diapers, they could not wipe their faces, sometimes help them in the shower, pick them up. It was hard work. No American would do this job!"

In spite of her university training, Lily was assigned a low-end job and paid below the federal minimum wage. Nevertheless, her recollections of her first American experiences were quite positive: she acknowledged the linguistic barriers and internalized her position due to her inability to speak the language, while also accepting that the work she did, cleaning tables, was not done by Americans but was seen instead as a job fit for immigrants.

After their work in the camps, young Romanians, confronted with a choice between returning to their home country and staying "without papers" in the United States, often chose to overstay their visa. Placing their education back home on hold indefinitely, many became "undocumented" (or irregular) immigrants, working jobs that did not require their education or skills but enabled them to make enough money to live a better life than their fellow Romanians back home. Many needed to send money back to their struggling families. This arrangement might have been lucrative, but it denied them the possibility of making any claims to the state. Faced with the possibility that this temporary labor force might overstay its welcome, the United States restricted their immigration options and added the claim 21(e) (for Romanians and other Eastern Europeans) who applied for J1 visas.[6]

This meant that the bearer was subject to return to their home country, with no possibility of obtaining a working visa or permanent immigrant status for at least two years. This measure is intended to ensure that even if participants apply for jobs or marry American citizens, they cannot become legal immigrants and permanent residents.

Robert, another Romanian immigrant who joined the U.S. armed forces before he obtained his citizenship, recalled his journey to the United States. He was a university student in Bucharest and came as a participant in this cultural exchange program. He also worked washing dishes in the kitchen of a summer camp. While there, he received news that he had won the U.S. immigration visa lottery, which gave him the option to become a legal permanent resident in America. So he rushed home to Romania to receive it, only to find out that due to the fact that he had been in the United States with the cultural exchange program, he was no longer eligible for permanent immigrant status for at least two years.

"Why?" he recalled asking the embassy official. "Through this experience in the U.S., you have gained invaluable skills, which need to be put into practice in your home country," the counselor at the visa office told him, reciting the official description of the 212(e) claim.

"What skills? Washing dishes?" He was angry remembering the conversation. Robert decided to take matters into his own hands. He told me he wrote a letter directly to (then) President George W. Bush, and he succeeded in having the 212(e) condition removed and his immigrant status approved. When he returned to the United States, now as a permanent resident, he found that his "invaluable" skills were hardly employable, and he did not find a job for some time. Then he found out about the opportunity to enlist in the U.S. military, which would also recognize his Romanian education. Robert decided to apply for it. Later, he got his citizenship via military service and lives today as a civilian on the West Coast.

Like Robert, and other participants in the cultural exchange programs, Lily's first experience in America made her realize that she needed to accept the limited economic opportunities available to her. Her life in the United States, like that of many other immigrants, came with economic obligations abroad (Conway and Cohen 1998; Jones 1998). Her mother became terminally ill, her brother was in college, and her father lost his job, making Lily the main source of income for herself and for her family back home. Thus, in her twenties, Lily become her family's main breadwinner.

Lily's immigration experience, while unique, is not singular. Migration is typically seen as a predominantly male endeavor. This perception is related to the fact that migration and remittances data is often not disaggregated by gender (Orozco, Lowell, and Schneider 2006), which reinforces the myth of the immigrant male breadwinner. However, when gender is taken into account, the data disproves this assumption and shows migration to be a field of almost balanced gender parity. For example, according to the Pew Research Center, between 1975 and 2005 slightly more than half of migrants to the United States were women,[7] and slightly fewer (mean value of 49 percent) migrants worldwide were female.[8]

According to the International Organization for Migration, "At the global level female migrants send approximately the same amount of remittances as male migrants." Moreover, an IOM study from 2007 shows that, compared to their male counterparts, women send home a higher percentage of their earnings and also dispatch remittances more regularly and more often.[9] Lily was part of these global trends, being an independent migrant who engaged in a regular process of submitting remittances to her extended family back home.

While Lily was living in the United States, the memory of Romania and its poverty was fresh in her memory. She knew that if she were to return home, she would not be able to support everyone and make a life for herself. Therefore, she made a difficult choice, and for the next few years inhabited a legally gray area, working a succession of low-skilled jobs. Lily might not have come to America to stay, but as the years went by, she became motivated to transition to becoming an American citizen in order to access economic resources and improve her overall social position in the host country.

Two years into my research, Lily was comfortable in my presence. Her life was very busy, and we arranged our meetings to fit in around her schedule. Back then, she was working for a small travel company in Manhattan, and we met after work. One early hot summer evening, she came close to my apartment, and we went for a drink in a nearby German beer garden. She was wearing her casual work attire and, as always, was energetic and eager to talk about her personal life. There, with my recorder switched on, Lily spoke informally, telling me how she decided to stay in the United States: "I wanted to have a student visa, but it did not work out. I started to work with some lawyers. I said if it does not work out, I will go to Canada. I realized after a couple of years that it is better here in a civilized country rather than in Europe, or Romania . . .," she said, slowly sipping her beer. "Time passed by, and then I made friends. I was feeling more comfortable here. I still wanted to go to school. But I could not start anything. I did not know if I would remain. I had a horrible visa," she said, referring to the 212(e) stamp on her passport. "I was in a limbo. After three years, I got my work permit. I could work in my industry, and I started feeling better. I had more experience and more opportunities. It was not a choice for me—I never dreamed about coming to America!" she confessed in a firm voice, looking me straight in the eyes.

However, after she streamlined her immigration status, Lily did not find the economic or social stability she desired. With few or no employment rights, and excluded from state-sponsored social and economic programs, immigrants in the labor force face great uncertainties. They look for security in diverse ways. Lily was searching for a "safety blanket," and this led her to the U.S. military.

Her path is not so different from that of U.S.-born citizens from poor backgrounds who turned to a military service career when they found it difficult to access basic social services, such as decent health care, a higher-education degree, or stable employment (Mittelstadt 2015). The U.S. military came to fill in the gap arising from ever-shrinking state-sponsored welfare programs that ensure a minimum standard of living and enable social mobility. In return for serving in its forces, the military promised recruits a "safety blanket": access to housing, to the GI Bill, and to stable employment with health-care benefits.

Enlistment in the U.S. Military: "I did not know what to do with my life"

Lily's recollections of the earlier parts of her life were always descriptive, colorful, and detailed. She enjoyed talking about her past, often becoming emotional when she did so. During interviews she smiled and laughed, re-counting humorous incidents and choking up with tears as she remembered tragic events, such as the death of her mother. She was comfortable and happy to share as much as she could about her life, though it was sometimes rather difficult to focus on her nonlinear narrative, which consisted of in-terconnected stories from different parts of her life. It seemed almost as if she had been waiting for a long time for someone to listen to her and write her story—and she was happy to draw me into her world.

However, the entire atmosphere changed when I asked about her military life. Her long, interconnecting stories were quickly replaced by succinct answers, and her words became calculated. Rarely did she display any emotion in her tone; instead of telling stories, she now gave vague answers; instead of sharing memories, she gave abstract definitions and spoke cautiously, as if she were comparing her answers to a preexisting conceptual framework. What follows reflects this change: over hundreds of hours of interviews, in varied settings and answering differently framed questions, Lily constantly responded as if she had learned the official discourse of military service and knew only too well what she was expected to say. She was aware of the limits of (dis)obedience and was careful not to exceed them. Lily is intelligent and educated, familiar with how academic research is carried out and the requirement that it be transparent. I infer from this that she was aware that the military might be able to access the information she shared during interviews, and so, if anything she said could be construed as casting a negative light on the institution, she minimized it and, at times, even avoided certain topics. I also saw her word-perfect responses as an attempt to be in line with the U.S. military, as a performative practice meant to outline her likeness to the institution and its members.

This manner of speaking first appeared when I asked Lily: What made you join the military force? How did you become an Air Force reservist? Responding, she chose to adopt a pseudo–social science discourse and referred to motivations in general. When asked again, she finally said: "I had a broken heart." She looked straight at me and laughed nervously. "I really do not know. I did not know what to do with my life," trying to give some seriousness to her answer. "I wanted to do something different. I did not know what I was going into. I know people say I love this country so much I wanted to join so I can serve. It is true. But I think that this came after."[10]

Lily offered personal motives for deciding to enlist and did not reflect on any other motivations. However, even though she did not directly mention them, I found that she also based her decision on economic concerns and in this way was similar to American-born recruits who often consider being able to further their education and economic mobility as their main reasons for enlistment.[11] Lily's reasons did not surface in direct interviews but slowly during our social interactions. She always talked about the fact that for years she was the main financial supporter of her family, sending remittances on a regular basis. Thus, having a stable job, like the reserve military service, allowed her to send money regularly to her family back home. Lily's economic motivation to enlist was confirmed when I met her brother and father during their annual trip to the United States, when they corroborated and elaborated on her continuous financial support.

They shared with great pride the fact that soon after she obtained her citizenship, Lily applied for family-reunion immigration status to bring her brother and father to the United States. When asked why she was eager to become an American citizen, she replied, as if it were self-evident: "To apply for family reunification." She refers to the Family Reunification Act[12] that allows American citizens to apply for permanent residency for their children, spouses, parents, and siblings. Family reunification is one of the major (and controversial) avenues for new immigrants to come to the United States, and it is the source of more than 60 percent of U.S. immigrants.[13] Lily fully embraced it.

Serving in the armed forces is highly regarded as a demonstration of national allegiance and patriotism, but for Lily this was not an incentive to serve. She saw enlistment as a stable form of employment and a quick path toward naturalization, becoming a citizen, which would empower her to reinforce her ethnic ties with her family abroad and to expedite the immigration procedures for her brother and father. But this does not mean that Lily never developed patriotic feelings toward her new country.

Lily's Military Experience through Performative Practices

Love, loyalty, and a sense of national belonging were not Lily's main reasons for deciding to enlist in the U.S. military. Her blunt admission of the fact that these feelings "only came later" enabled me to see how, for her, solidarity, belonging, and loyalty developed over time, taking on overlapping forms and meanings. Speaking about them in interviews might be difficult, because these are feelings that develop slowly and are rarely reflected upon. Therefore, these forms of allegiance are better investigated through different means. In a similar way, through her work in Yemen, Lisa Wedeen (2008) discovered that citizens form national attachments through everyday activities such as chewing *qat* and engaging in public discussions. These activities, Wedeen argues, are performative practices[14] that enact and reproduce citizenry. Wedeen suggests that to understand the processes of meaning making, we need to observe participants' work habits, self-policing strategies, and leisure patterns and how they interact with their language and other symbolic systems. Wedeen names these "semiotic practices" and supports the importance of culture for understanding the creation of citizenship.

In the years I spent with Lily, I identified two types of frequent performative practices that constructed and enforced her loyalty and sense of belonging to the host country and the U.S. military. While in her daily life these practices were interrelated, here I present them as analytically distinct: recognizing and appropriating national symbols, such as the American flag, and performing in social networks, events, and training sessions organized by the military. While the performative character of these practices is more obvious in the latter case, symbolic identifications with the community via the flag are still subtly performative, establishing distinct behavioral patterns.

During interviews Lily asked me several times: "Are you trying to give a negative view of the military?" To this I replied each time that I was not interested in characterizing the military, but I wanted to learn about *her* experience in the military. However, the fact that she often brought this issue to the fore revealed that the military's image meant a lot to her and that she wanted to make sure that the institution would not be negatively portrayed. Her commitment to the military as an institution and the respect for her host country were also underscored when she reflected on being a soldier:

> Being in the military made me proud to be an American, much more than I would have been as a civilian. You know, to me maybe I am more like the sentimental person, but whenever they play the national anthem I just . . . it is a moment of emotion for me. That's when I realize I do something important, something that actually counts. . . . And this I came to realize, that what I do for the military is not just a job, it is not just getting up in the morning, putting the uniform on, and going and doing a job. Because in the end it comes down to that.

She stopped and then said pensively: "We all put on a uniform and we go and do what we are supposed to do. So, you know, it's not just running with a weapon, and shooting. This is not what we do!" Lily explained, responding to an imaginary debate. She then continued, with newfound contentment: "But, I think every time is like this: the military brings you a sense of belonging, belonging to an organization, to a nation, to a brave nation." When she enlisted, Lily was not a U.S. citizen, so she was not an official member of the "brave nation" whose flag she was saluting while pledging allegiance. But she was sworn into an institution that emphasizes its commitment to the unity of the American nation, and for her this was leveraged into membership in a larger national group. By becoming a member of an institution that serves the nation and defends its Constitution, and by pledging allegiance to a nation to which she did not yet belong, Lily learned to become American.

Responding to interview questions gave Lily a chance to reflect upon her life and her development over the previous years. She seemed to surprise herself with the discovery that she had become more patriotic since joining the military. And in doing so, she revealed that the sense of "belonging to a brave nation" was not formed during the times she spent in the United States as a civilian but was context based (Wedeen 2008), created through military practices.[15]

These symbolic practices, such as saluting the flag or singing the national anthem, made her feel close to a community that she would never meet, an "imagined community" (Anderson 1991).[16] By singing the national anthem in the military context, Lily imagined a whole community to which she belonged, a community of which she was an equal member, in spite of a reality filled with social, economic, and legal inequalities.

In this particular context, through these performative practices, Lily identified with the nation through the use of common symbols, which induced in her a feeling of being part of a(n imagined) group that she had not seen, but for which she was willing to sacrifice much of her life. Thus, both respect and identification with the country were made possible for Lily through symbols imbued with national value.[17] Singing the national anthem and wearing a military uniform are practices performed by soldiers as a part of their service and are constructed and reinforced through strict regulations that coordinate symbolism with precise use of the soldier's body, both in song and in appearance.

Thus, the national anthem is associated with a set of regular practices of the body, performed by others in the community, reinforcing a visible camaraderie and shared identity. What's more, singing the anthem creates a sense of participative equality—because enlisted soldiers as well as their supervisors, foreign and native-born recruits, have to sing together.[18] These precise military regulations create daily performative practices of allegiance and instill a certain behavior that spills over into civilian life, creating feelings of solidarity and simultaneous belonging to two groups: the military and the wider U.S. citizenry.

For Lily, a sense of belonging to the host nation was not the outcome of a series of personal achievements, but was built through ritualistic acts and the use of nationalist symbols. The military trained Lily to recognize them as emblematic of the group, of collective belonging, and she appropriated these performative acts as her own. In turn, this informal patriotic training socialized her and made her an integral part of the U.S. citizenry, which further translated into appreciation for her overall current situation, into assuming the belief in America is "the land of opportunity."

In my many conversations with other members of the military, they all pointed out that military branches differ greatly. Consequently, soldiers' experiences depend on their institutions and are quite diverse. With this in mind, I wondered if Lily's attachment was to the military in general or more specifically toward her "wing," the smaller unit of the Air Force.[19] To my surprise, she responded that she did not feel attachment to any particular branch but felt a connection to the military in general. When I inquired about this, Lily explained her military allegiance: "I got my citizenship while and through the military. So, to me, they are connected. So, of course I can be in the States and not be a part of the military, and this probably will happen when I retire. I think that can happen, but I can't separate them."[20]

Lily's reflection on how she felt about the two "imagined communities" with which she identified pointed out that, while she started from a position of being a disengaged patriot, through everyday military practices she came to feel more and more like a member of her host country. This became obvious in the way she responded when I asked her to describe what it meant for her to be a member of the military: "I think you feel a sort of attachment. It is very difficult to say. I think it is more at the emotional level. You know, you understand more about it, and it is a sense of pride: being a part of a nation. . . . After all, yes, there is a lot of uneasiness, but I think the military is able to keep the danger away somehow. Abroad. If they bring the troops back, then the danger will be here. They will come after us. The terrorists," Lily said with newfound conviction. "Yeah. As long as we keep the war *there*, we are safe *here*. You see, we are not afraid to go in the street. I think that people do not think of this. We take this for granted. Yeah, this is how it is supposed to be: peaceful, no incidents, no attacks. No bombs in the street. But this is not the reality: other countries' people are afraid to go in the street."[21]

Accordingly, through recognizing and appropriating national symbols and reiterating legitimizing narratives, Lily felt that she belonged to a community of people whom she had not met, but with whom she shared a common sense of righteousness and justice. She was now a part of an "us," different from a possible attacker, different from an extreme and symbolic "them."

* * *

Lily told me that before she joined the military, she lived in a Romanian neighborhood in Queens, New York, and had many Romanian friends. By contrast, once she enlisted, she developed relationships with other soldiers, mostly native born, which gradually developed and reinforced her naturalization process: "I think allegiance [toward America] came in time, when I started building a relationship with my coworkers, when I realized what the military is. I think it took me a while."

On military bases, soldiers live in closed spaces, secluded from civilians, with little means of communication; their training reinforces a "buddy" (that is, peer) dependency (Van Wormer 2012, 70–94, 136–43). These close relationships, which soldiers often have within the military, empowered (or maybe forced) Lily to develop social ties with other members of the host country, outside of her ethnic circle. "I *do* have friends because of the military," she told me when I asked about her military ties:

> I think they [the armed forces] build relationships. I do have close friends because of my military career. I meet them outside of the military. . . . One of the ladies I work with, she just invited me to a jewelry design party. So, you see, we do more than work together. She came to my wedding; she sent me a gift. I went to hers. I can count on her. She is a dear friend. And there is another guy, whom I went to school with. To technical training, and then it just happened that we are in the same unit. I visited him in the city. . . . He is like my big brother; if I want advice, I would ask him. Because he is a guy and he is an American. There are two things I can relate to: he is older than me and he was in the military, and he was born and raised here in the States. Whenever I have a question that is related to the [U.S.] culture, I say, "Hey Paul, what do you think about this? Is this something you guys do?" If I could choose a brother from the guys here, he would be the one. So, you know, the work relationship from the military turned into great friendship.

I never met these friends, nor have I heard Lily conversing on the phone with them, but Lily claimed that she felt close to them as a result of their sharing a military career. In contrast to when she first arrived in the new country, and she was alone, after a few years of service she came to rely on the extended social network she formed via the military, further adjusting her life to the host country.

These ties were reinforced through informal but organized military activities, such as the one Lily described when she reflected on being a part of the military: "I did a combat dining-in. It is usually a military function. A lot of units get together, and they usually eat." She explained that these events are usually organized in a big space where they park the airplanes and people have to wear old combat uniforms. Every unit or wing has its own table and a military superior who coordinates the ceremony. The event is a formal dinner, with celebrity guests giving motivational speeches, military rituals like "present arms," and the playing of the national anthem. All these greatly impressed Lily. "I really like it, because it was a great sense of belonging," she said excitedly.

The event was also a social night with "wings" reenacting combat activities as games. "They paint their faces like when you are in the field. . . . If there is friction between the units, they start throwing water, like a kids fight." Lily became enthusiastic as she told the story. "I said I will not paint my face; I thought it was silly. But the first sergeant got the paint from the supply room, and she was: 'Come on, I got this, do you want to paint your face? And I did it. And it was so cool! . . . You should have seen me! It was another unit that we did not get along with, and I was having these balloons filled with water and then you throw them, and they become like hand grenades. It was crazy." Lily ended her story with visible satisfaction.

Performative practices that induced Lily's feelings of group belonging were constructed through reenactment of war-zone action. These informal military activities enabled Lily to relate to a larger community and to understand her role in connection to the military and, implicitly, with the host country: "I consider them my colleagues because they have done something for my country; they made a difference," she said firmly, concluding her story. Then she talked about both social and training events[22] indistinguishably, which instilled the same sense of belonging, through community members' mutual interdependence. "The training exercises are the same thing, you kind of get absorbed by the team that you have around. And I like that I always, constantly, feel like I belong to a team, and if it is a game and maybe it is a day-to-day task that I have to do, I do not have to do it alone. In my civilian life, I do not have the same support of the team. This is what I like; this is why I decided to stay in the military. I like belonging to a team. Every time we have training exercises, I feel that there are people there to help me to push me through."

These informal military activities seek to train recruits, using games to build "a robust social networking infrastructure that enables homebound individuals to become a tight-knit brotherhood that circle[s] the globe" (Derby 2014, citing Zyda et al. 2005, 588).[23] Lily described them as social gatherings and made no mention of battlefields or war. When she told me this, she had not experienced deployment and had not applied these skills outside her military base, so for her these practices were social performances that brought her closer to her group and made her feel part of the military and the host country. And so, through repeated practice, Lily's understanding—and bodily comportment—changed, taking on the accepted and recognizable shape (J. Butler 1993, 1997; Wedeen 2008) of a national subject, which furthermore created and reinforced her naturalization into American citizenship. In her stories of naturalization via the military, Lily's personality resembles soft clay, molded in various shapes through regular performative practices to create a sense of belonging to the military and the national community. Her stories summoned the image of an abstract person who lacks any racial, ethnic, or gender characteristics and is willing to embrace a new military and national identity. This might be the idealized version of the story that Lily envisioned for herself and wanted to share. However, stories are created in contexts, not only through words but also through gestures and actions. And markers of Lily's identity became apparent in other situations. Following her line of argument, we can see how, in Lily's case, solidarity was generated through textual practices and social interactions, such as military training and socializing outside of the military space. "Belonging" was realized through a set of performative practices, that is, repetitive acts that she learned in time and to which she was subjected through social interactions (Wedeen 2008). Lily became an American soldier and developed her allegiance to her host country through daily performative acts that displayed her American nationalism.

Class: Military Service Is My "Safety Blanket"

The U.S. military, which has been an all-volunteer force for more than four decades, has come to be regarded as a form of qualified employment (Moskos 1966; Stillman 1969; J. S. Butler 1992; Teachman 2007).[24] Seeing military service as a path for upward social mobility (Mittelstadt 2015) creates two divergent goals for recruits. On the one hand, they dedicate their lives to the greater good; on the other, as the military has become more specialized, soldiers have had to prove themselves skillful employees, capable of performing set tasks.

This approach was strongly implemented in the 1970s, when the military embarked upon a program designed to attract diverse and skilled volunteer recruits, particularly into ground combat or onto warships. As neither lowering physical/mental standards nor seeking to include women among recruits had been sufficient to fill the ranks (Janowitz and Moskos 1979, 139), the U.S. military began to provide further enlistment incentives. This process did not start once the U.S. military began an all-volunteer force but began earlier, providing economic enticements and educational benefits through the Servicemen's Readjustment Act of 1944, known as the GI Bill, allowing recruits to transfer skills and experience,[25] transforming U.S. military service from a "calling" to a "professional employer" (Janowitz and Moskos 1979). Gradually, as Mittelstadt (2015) argues, the military came to offer welfare programs that the state was failing to provide for its citizens and as a result became a viable source of employment for immigrants and poor Americans.

Almost forty years later, the view of military service as a highly skilled job facilitating social mobility and delivering monetary rewards typically trumps the one of military service as a higher calling or duty.[26] For example, the U.S. Army's official recruitment websites, mirroring private companies' recruitment techniques, insist on the labor value of military service: "With so many jobs available in the Army, you might need some help finding the one that best fits your skills and career goals. You also may expand the results by creating a 'My GoArmy' account, which can show you more details about the jobs that 'Match Your Interests.'"[27] Considering that the U.S. Department of Defense was named the largest employer in the world by the World Economic Forum in 2015,[28] this description is hardly surprising.

Today the military is often seen as an employer and as a path for social mobility. Thus, it does not come as a revelation that "the all-volunteer force continues to see overrepresentation of the working and middle classes, with fewer incentives for upper-class participation" (Lutz 2008, 185). Lily, while a first-generation immigrant, shared class characteristics with native-born recruits. With a precarious job in hospitality/tourism, and a university degree not recognized by many employers, enlisting in the Air Force Reserve was for Lily a source of stable income and the only way to access social services:

Being in the military provides you with a series of services. Let's say, I get into a conflict, you know, the military has lawyers. So, in the military you can go and seek advice from military lawyers. Or medical care, how many companies do you know that they offer you so many benefits? They give you advice, they talk to you, they also have career advice. I think all of these are the reasons why the people join and stay in the military. Because they want to feel secure about what they do. . . . If things can get really bad, there is a system that will support me. It is a comfort. Especially for an immigrant.

Lily breathlessly explained all these forms of military support when I asked her about the benefits that she felt she now had as a result of her service.

Her firm statement, seemingly contradicted by the situation that many veterans face today regarding access to health care, further supports her view of military service as her "safety blanket." Her enlistment brought protection because she was now part of a state institution. When I asked her whether it seemed contradictory to think of military service as a safety blanket when, by its very nature, it might require the ultimate sacrifice, she replied with surprise: "[Military life] does not offer me insecurity. I have never thought of that. It does not. The proof is that I already did my first six years, and I already signed up for another six years."

Even though Lily's firm response did not match my thoughts on the issue, I had to accept that for her, military service was a profession, not a means of national sacrifice. It was clear that for her, security was mainly social and economic. She expressed her belief that the military trains her, constantly improving her and providing transferable skills that in turn positively impact her civilian career. By accurately performing these new practices, Lily hoped that in civilian life she would have better access to economic and social mobility, and these alone would ensure her "safety."

Overall, Lily's civilian social and economic mobility improved as a result of her military service. When she finished her first military contract, she was able to use the GI Bill to enroll in an MS program at a prestigious university. She completed it while working a civilian job, and serving in the Air Force Reserve, and then she was able to work in the field of her choice. As a result of assiduous work that went on without ceasing for years, Lily bought a house in the suburbs of New York City, where she moved with her husband. Yet in spite of her remarkable success, there are areas in which Lily felt that she could not break through, despite her hard work, military service, and willingness to conform.

When Ethnicity Meets Class

As we saw earlier, Lily was eager to describe her military experience as frictionless. Throughout our interviews, she painted a picture of the military as an egalitarian system in which she thrived, but when she was talking generally rather than responding to my questions, she reflected on her unequal place within her host country and within the military. In one of these self-reflective moments, she admitted that it was harder for her to accomplish certain military tasks because of linguistic barriers:

> Sometimes, I have moments when whatever I do, whatever I have to learn, is very overwhelming for me, because maybe, it was because I was a foreigner. Because I did not grow up here, it seemed harder than it was for my coworkers. You have to do some exercises, and you have to respond to commands very quickly. And when English is not your first language, and you're supertired, and it is superhot, and you are superaggravated, you do not respond to the commands as quickly as others around you. Think about it. Now you function under normal circumstances. You sleep; you eat. But when you are not sleeping for twenty-four–twenty-six hours, when you do not eat, when you are in a stressful environment, you do not react as easily or as normal as you would. But you see it in my character. I like challenges; it was hard, but I pressed on and I went on. So, it was okay. It was harder.

In terms of social mobility, language barriers signal structural hierarchies that produce systematic inequalities. Bourdieu argues that language is the fundamental part of cultural capital, which next to economic capital creates and reinforces an unequal distribution of resources.[29] This in turn creates systematic class inequalities. Bourdieu explains that not all languages are alike. While in France all people, including immigrants, speak French, not all forms of French are valued equally. Formal language is highly respected—along with everything that comes with it: the kind of linguistic skills acquired in educated families, where young people listen to their parents speaking, or gained through reading books. For Bourdieu, these are resources that transform into capital—and some people have more than others, meaning they can profit from this disparity. If all had the same quantity, if all spoke the local language perfectly, without an accent, this disparity would not have an effect. But because there are differences, it pays to speak well. Considering Bourdieu's view of language in constructing inequality, Lily's linguistic limitations, which created systematic obstacles for her mobility, become salient.

Lily's linguistic experiences show that while at the level of interactions with her peers and supervisors her diverse background was accepted, when it came to her performance her linguistic and ethnic circumstances were no longer invisible. Despite its claim that individual success will be celebrated and rewarded, the U.S. military shies away from offering programs that would help dismantle the implicit hierarchies that linguistic barriers create. Furthermore, language practices create, develop, and reinforce hierarchies and inequalities. Native-speaker soldiers are more successful in following orders and performing activities that require a quick response; ultimately, the soldiers who use language better are systematically preferred and promoted. Hence, while praising individual performance and by ignoring inherent linguistic hierarchies, the military maintains structural inequalities that empower recruits' performances, which could perpetuate inequality within its ranks.

Lily confessed that linguistic barriers had been a regular part of her military life since the early days of her military enlistment:

> When I went to "boot camp," it was a challenge for me. I thought maybe because I am . . . you know, trying to process double the information, because they make you do certain things, they make you march and do this [raises her arm] or that [lowers it], etc., and if I was an American, it would not have been hard to process everything. I had processed whatever they wanted me to do. . . . I felt frustrated because of it, [thinking] maybe I would fail this task. Sometimes they used words, and I was like: "God, what does it mean?" I never heard of them. I learned English recently, and there were expressions I have never heard. And then, I asked and they were explained to me, and then I realized it was not me, because I was a foreigner, but it was everyone. Because the whole idea with the training is that they put you in a stressful environment. They break you down to make you up again! They put you in strain, to see how you react.

Lily understood that she was at a disadvantage compared to her native-speaker peers. However, she did not engage critically with the situation, nor did she ask for extra help or demand that allowances be made for the fact that she was not a native speaker. Quite the contrary: she made an additional effort to fit into the structure of the system. For example, she told me that she asked her colleagues when she did not understand the meaning of a word. She continuously engaged in a double process: learning a new language and learning the necessary procedures of the military. Throughout her American journey, Lily has taken it upon herself to demonstrate that she can be as good as her American-born peers and has made an effort both to work and to speak English.

Lily's experience revealed the U.S. military's double approach. On the one hand, the institution designs and implements practices meant to develop loyalty, allegiance, and group unity through the cohesion of individual talents and capacities; on the other, it encourages the diversity necessary to succeed in war.[30] This approach ignores the (mundane) repercussions of ethnic identity, which could implicitly create obstacles in the way of immigrant soldiers' social mobility. Lacking specific (linguistic/cultural) support, Lily struggled to be considered equal to her native-speaker peers. She had been quite successful in obtaining access to resources, but—as we will later see in Alexa's story—this might not be the case for all immigrants. Moreover, the "hands-off" approach the military adopts toward its ethnic groups leads to the employing of immigrant recruits in generic and at times mediocre tasks, because it denies them the chance to put into practice their cultural, linguistic, and social skills.

Robert, the other military immigrant from Romania, told me he asked to go to Romania to serve as a translator for the American troops, but was denied his request in spite of having native language skills. Instead, he was stationed in Germany. Robert's situation echoes Lily's: if the military does not account for language differences beyond the level of recruitment technique or population survey, it may not get the most out of its personnel. Moreover, this would give rise to unintended consequences by perpetuating hierarchies and inequalities based on language skills, whereby soldiers of different ethnic backgrounds and first-generation immigrants would occupy the lower tiers.

The informal systematic construction of inequalities, as through language usage within the military, is hard to pin down and consequently to address, but at times such approaches are accompanied by overt and formal practices that reveal a systematic preference for one group over another. As stated earlier, Lily acknowledged that her ethnicity was not widely recognized within the military but stated that in her civilian life, her ethnic background was immediately visible. She consistently said that within the military, her ethnicity didn't deter her from trying anything, while when she was a civilian it played a negative role. As Lily's narrative of her life in the military had been continuously positive, I asked about the difficulties she encountered there. At first, she avoided the subject; only when I insisted, she said: "I had some disappointing moments; I had some things that did not come through for me. But like anything in life, you have to look at the positive side of it." The quietness of her voice and the way she looked away from me expressed her sadness. When she recounted her disappointments, she paid attention to every word she uttered; her recollection was void of value judgment, and I could sense her effort to sound neutral. She behaved as if there were more than two of us at the table, and under the gaze of this invisible third person Lily told a story that was short on details. She seemed to be submissive to the rules of the military environment and willing to show her compliance even when military representatives were not directly present.

This attitude was in line with the overall manner she displayed during formal interviews. She often seemed to mirror the military's agenda, controlling her emotions. But this time, she was willing to share: "Sometimes there is a lot of paperwork involved," she slowly continued. "Sometimes they take a long time. You put in an application for a position, and it is like in any other organization, it happens, you have to follow up a lot, a lot. No one tells you, yeah, here it is, fine, you can move forward with the application. It is a looong time," she exaggerated the word and then continued: "Sometimes changes happen, regulations happen, and they affect your career, they affect your life, and you have to follow up, so it is like in any other big organization. So . . . yeah, you get pissed off, and after a while you move on."

While this seemed to be an insignificant complaint, I sensed that it might be something more, something that affected Lily deeply, or something with which she was struggling. When the same line of reasoning and way of speaking on the subject reappeared a few months later, in another interview, I paid close attention: "Things are not that peachy all the time, but I understand, because it is a big organization, and things happen in life, and there is no ideal world, you get frustrated, you take a breath in, and you move on. That's all you can do in life. What are you going to do? Quit? I am not a quitter. . . . It happened, in one instance when I applied for commissioning, 'Deserving Airmen'."[31] Lily said it simply, as if it were an easy step. She was referring to becoming an officer, which was the next rank for her, but would also be a major accomplishment that completed her service as an "enlisted" member and placed her in a position of command. "I applied in January, and it took them a year to send me to school," she continued.

> Meanwhile, they lost the slot. I got to the board in January, I got approved, I got selected, and I was supposed to go to school, in a few

months, and that did not happen, and then in August I was ready with my packet [documents], and they told me that the rules changed and there was no slot for me. So, I had to wait for another slot. I waited. Meanwhile, the regulations changed, and instead of going to officer training for six weeks, I had to go for three months. And then, I could not finish it, and therefore I am not an officer today. So, you see, there are a lot of complications in life. Of course, I was extremely upset and frustrated, because I put a lot of work and effort to go to this program, and I was selected; I could have been an officer, you see. It was very frustrating for me that they could not complete the package, and then things changed.

She tried to recall the situation without regrets, and she found ways to remind me, and implicitly herself, that this was merely a logistical problem that had little to do with her military performance. Lily's account of the failure of the military to promote her to officer rank appeared both personal and fatalistic. She acknowledged these injustices as an inherent part of the bureaucratic system, but did not see them as acts of inequality[32] and injustice against certain groups.[33]

"Of course, I was upset; and it did change my life and my career," she said in a strong voice, referring to the Air Force's failure to complete the administrative procedure that would have ensured her becoming an officer.

Was it important to be an officer? Yes. Was it more important to be in the military? Yes. So, I went on. I did not like it, yes. Maybe it was someone's fault that they did not follow through, and they did not complete the application quickly, and I could get my commission and go to school? It took a long time because, you know, it takes a lot: it takes medical clearance, it involves clearance, it involves many things. So, the application moved slowly. . . . They did not know, and plus the regulations changed.

Lily repeated all of this in a firm tone, as she looked pensively toward the window of the café in which we were both sitting. She readily adopted the discourse that was expected of her, avoiding reflecting on her immigration status and the obstacles it posed to her military career, and she seemed to accept her situation fatalistically. Her application process to become an officer was clearly important to Lily, but it was one that stirred conflicting feelings. As this was a tender spot for her, she wanted to talk about it. As this was a complex process, with which she was obviously unfamiliar, and she did not know how to resolve it, she was understandably frustrated and often at a loss of words. And, as she was in an uncomfortable and precarious spot,

Lily did not want to come out firmly against the military as an institution in which she was currently enrolled and where she hoped to be promoted. Consequently, our communication on this topic was rocky. It took me years to understand why it was difficult for her to explain it. Only by the end of our collaboration was Lily able to articulate in strong words her view on the Air Force officer application process, as we will shortly see.

But for now, her attitude was swiftly changing, and she adopted an optimistic spin: "If I would have been an officer, if I would have gotten my commission, then I would have been deployed two, three times by now! So, I told you things happen for a reason," she smiled, looking me in the eyes. "Because if I would have been an officer, my career field involves a lot of deployment. And now in the career field I am currently in, I am not deployable. There are certain positions to be deployed. You need to have certain qualifications. Not everybody goes. Even me, if I would have gotten commission, I would have gone maybe a couple of times. Very dangerous ones. Because the commission would have involved a lot of deployment."

Lily's eagerness to portray her military experience in a positive light despite the obstacles she encountered was clear, and I did not push her further. However, a few months after our last conversation on this topic, I unexpectedly received an email from her telling a very different story. In a tone quite unlike any she had adopted up to that point, Lily wrote that she had (again) received a document turning her down for a program to become an officer and she now knew it was because she had a "foreign degree." In response to this, she wrote, "Hence, the idea that the U.S. military treats all immigrants equally and gives them the same right is a bluff!"

This email was unexpected because it was at odds with her main narrative, which insisted that her ethnic background was invisible within the military since the institution gave her a chance to shine by making the most of her individual skills. But in this email, she was pointing out the duplicity of the military. Whereas in daily practice the difference between foreigners and natives was invisible or at least insignificant (especially when foreigners were white or of European descent), the military betrayed a structural preference for natives. When it came to promotion, the military's formal, official way of showing appreciation for its staff, Lily's strangeness was visible. It was not possible for her to overcome this systemic distinction, and she felt rejected as a result of the foreignness of her background, now visible in her educational degrees.

If "everything you do is related," as Lily stated, then we can see how Lily's early experiences in communist Romania and of the postcommunist transition, combined with her desire to access social and economic mobility, led her to immigrate to the United States. In the new country, her immigration status meant she could not find relief from uncertainty and her access to economic and social goods was still limited. When she arrived in the United States, she entered the class system, and in spite of her efforts she could not easily access the middle-class life she desired. However, determined to succeed in her endeavor and to help her family back home, she looked for alternatives to the routes typically taken by immigrants, which are usually connected to ethnic communities. Unlike the majority of immigrants to the United States, Lily decided to enlist and to serve the country of her residence, not of her citizenship.

Lily proudly emphasized her identification with the military and with the Air Force. She earnestly tried her best to fit in, to assimilate. She followed instructions, dedicating time, energy, and commitment to the military to ensure her success. Her military experience was a part-time employment, which she enjoyed and in which others appreciated her work.

Her identification with the host country also came while serving in its military. In time, her allegiance was cemented through practices of naturalization such as saluting the flag, participating in social events organized by the military, and practicing training exercises. Symbolic membership in this community empowered Lily both to imagine and to experience belonging to the group. While her motives for joining the military were pragmatic (to get a better job and to improve her social status), her transformation process took on another dimension: it changed her identity.

The Battle with Ethnicity and Race: Being White While Being Romanian

Lily's description of her naturalization via the military creates the image of her identity being a blank canvas, on which the military was able to imprint its newly generated categories, identities, affiliations, and colors. But Lily's life and everyday dynamics relating to her ethnicity and race were much more complex and at times seemed to be contradictory.

As we have seen in the section of this analysis documenting her linguistic background, Lily came "already made" and entered the military as such.

For example, during our meetings and conversations, Lily self-identified as Romanian. She readily admitted that within the military, few people knew what it means to be Romanian: "Many times they do not even know where it is, and I leave it as that. I move on; that is it. They do not say it is a country of beggars," Lily added, referring to how Romanians are at times thought of as pariahs in western Europe. "It is a quick conversation: question and answer. Sometimes they ask, 'Where is Romania?' Generally, people do not know where it is." She laughed and added ironically, "Or people would say: 'They are gymnasts and Dracula!' Usually Dracula, and they ask: 'Is there such a thing like Transylvania?' And then I try to tell them, as I am a talker, 'Yeah, there is a part of Romania.' 'Oh, interesting,' [and] they move on; that is just conversation you have anywhere."[34]

She always said this with a smile on her face, accepting that her ethnic identity was mostly invisible to other military personnel. While her ethnic identity was largely unfamiliar, she did not believe that it had a negative effect on her military experience. She felt strongly that it was precisely this nonrecognition of her (collective) ethnic identity that enabled her to gain another type of (individual) recognition: as a member of the military. This attitude also showed that she belonged to a "nonproblematic" ethnicity. She was of European descent, and therefore she said that her background had little importance within the military. Nevertheless, as seen above, while people did not react negatively to her ethnicity, it was harder to accommodate her different background and promote her based on individual accomplishments within the military as an institution.

Her ethnic background being ignored or treated as a mere social entertainment within the military was seen by Lily as a blessing that she did not enjoy in her civilian life. She often said—as if determined to change my (assumed) position—that being foreign born did not create obstacles in her military career, but that in her civilian life her ethnic identity was differently perceived.

> "In my [military] career, I was put in charge of people, of a team of people," she often said with great pride in her voice. I have never got the chance to do this in my civilian career. 'Cause in my civilian career, I manage resources in a territory, not people. In the military, I had the opportunity to be in charge of a team. To be a leader! It did not matter: I was an airman, I did not even have a higher rank, and because I proved to be bright enough, I was put in charge. It did not make a difference that I was a girl, that I was Romanian. People saw that I was capable of

getting whatever I needed to do, and they put me in charge. And they
encouraged me, and they provided me with resources, and I did it.

She emphasized her last words, showing her determination to convince
me of the truth of her statements. "There was a difference," she admitted,
pensively referring now to her civilian experience. Then she lowered her
voice: "When I was in college, I had colleagues who were Americans, but
I never, ever developed a close relationship with them. But look, in the
military, I did. I did make great friendships," she said, without pausing to
take a breath. "When I was doing MA degree, I used to think they were
they [that is, Americans] and I was I. We went out a couple of times, but we
were not close enough to be friends. That was it. They were nice in class
and everything, but nothing else. We never built a relationship. You see, I
felt a little bit excluded," she concluded.

When directly asked to compare her relationships in the civilian and
military realms, Lily made clear that she preferred the latter. In the former,
she felt that her ethnic background did not allow her to be an equal member.
She found herself excluded due to something that she was unable to change:
her accent and her lack of mastery of the English language. Lily might not
have been resisting assimilation in the host country's system, but the system
was resisting her.

One evening as we were returning after a weekend on her Air Force base,
she confessed how hard it was for her to fit in despite her assiduous efforts.
She was driving her car, looking at the road ahead, and after a long pause she
suddenly started telling me, as if she had been longing to get it off her chest
for a long time, "It is hard for me. I work all week, and then I come here.
. . . I am not an American. I will always be a foreigner. It does not matter
how much I will try." "How come?" I asked. "Because I will always have an
accent, my English will never be flawless! So, they will always look at me like
a foreigner. And when I will go and apply for a job, they will always prefer
[a native-born] American. Even when I have equal or better qualifications
in terms of both education and experience. This is how it always is. This
is my experience. Of course, in civilian life!" she promptly added. "In the
military, life is different. They only have to check you off, and you are good
to go. It is a very organized system. Not the same in civilian life," Lily said
with sadness.

In her civilian life, Lily felt that her ethnic identity was misrecognized,[35]
or negatively recognized, hindering her chances of social mobility. But in

her military life, she experienced the lack of ethnic recognition as a positive, because it led to the destruction of ethnic hierarchies. Not having a relatable ethnicity worked to her advantage. The blind eye the military turned to her ethnic background made Lily feel that she could prove herself as an individual. As a result of this conscious dismissal, she felt that she achieved a different type of recognition: she was a soldier, and therefore she was no longer treated as a stranger and foreigner. Accepted as a member of the military, she felt that she should be able to transfer this achievement to her civilian life and become an equal member of the host country.[36]

Her experience is partially comparable to that of many African Americans in the 1950s, who through the desegregation of the military after World War II were able to access resources and social mobility within that institution that were unavailable to them in civilian life. On July 26, 1948, aiming to optimize the services of African Americans within the military, while also recognizing their service, President Truman issued an executive order abolishing racial segregation in the armed forces of the United States (Moskos 1970, 110).[37] As a result of desegregation, African Americans in military service had the opportunity (not necessarily speedily accomplished) to be promoted and to occupy higher positions within military hierarchies.[38] Lily's civilian life experience, while different from that of African Americans, did not give her access to social mobility, and she experienced this as being an effect of her ethnic origin. She insisted many times that while her ethnicity created obstacles in her civilian life, this effect was not visible (or obvious) within the military, and as a result she was able to access the same resources and positions the native-born recruits did. Nevertheless, though Lily celebrated her invisibility in military interactions using superlative terms, her analysis was an unreflective acceptance of her racial privilege as a white person.

Following Waters's argument, Rudrappa posits, "White people's experience with their own ethnicities—the ease with which they can slip in and out of being ethnic—creates a lack of understanding on their part regarding the experiences of those classified as non-White. Many cannot understand why Black or Latinos speak of discrimination" (2004, 161). Similarly, Lily is Romanian, therefore European and (mostly) considered white, and as a result she was not aware of the less obvious unspoken advantages that she has acquired as a result of her race and European ancestry, which allowed her great mobility within the military. This is because within contemporary American society, immigrants like Lily, of eastern and southern European descent, tend to be considered white or Caucasian. However, this was not always the case: in the nineteenth century, immigrants of European descent but of non-Anglo-Saxon background were treated as being above black and other racial groups, but not white (Roediger 2005). It took a long time and a number of policies, such as the New Deal, to incorporate eastern European and southern European immigrants within the group of whites, as well as to separate them from other racial groups (Roediger 2005). Thus, starting in the mid-twentieth century, groups such as the Polish, Italians, and Jews were acknowledged as white. Lily entered the military as white and therefore had privileges associated with whiteness, including the lack of awareness of one's race (Lipsitz 2006).

But Lily did not seem to be aware of her whiteness. Her attitude is in line with Peggy McIntosh's argument that "whites are carefully taught not to recognize white privilege, as males are taught not to recognize male privilege. . . . I have come to see white privilege as an invisible package of unearned assets, which I can count on cashing in each day, but about which I was 'meant' to remain oblivious" (2004, 188). Accordingly, Lily took her whiteness for granted within military interactions. This will become clearly visible when Lily's life story is paralleled with that of Alexa, a Latin American immigrant, whose military experience was very different.

Lily's experience, rather than contradicting Roediger's theory of becoming white, adds a new dimension to it—showing how her whiteness process is not complete. While she can interact in the military within the norms, when she works in her civilian job she is judged against the white norm, which she does not meet because she is a foreigner and has an accent. As a result, she is deemed inferior. Lily's experience shows that as an eastern European immigrant, she had to continuously negotiate whiteness and to prove her normativity. Furthermore, similar to African Americans who experienced (at least formal) economic and social mobility while enlisted but encountered a continuous racial divide and discrimination back in the civilian world, Lily's experience shows how precarious whiteness is for foreigners of eastern European descent and how easy it is for them to lose it.

Roediger's book *Working toward Whiteness* opens by quoting Diane Di Prima: "This pseudo 'white' identity . . . was not something that fell on us out of blue, but something that many Italian Americans grabbed at with both hands. Many felt that their culture, language, food, songs, music and identity was a small price to pay for entering the American mainstream. . . . They thought, as my parents probably did, that they could keep these good

Italian things in private and become 'white' in public" (Di Prima 1999, cited by Roediger 2005, 3).

Like Lily, the people in Di Prima's work experienced a similar intricate relationship with the host country. On the one hand, Lily entered the United States with an invisible racial identity that allowed her to move freely and establish her social position; on the other, her ethnic background was still a vivid part of her identity, something of which she, the people in the military, and those she met in the host country were aware. Hence, Lily experienced the intersectionality (Crenshaw et al. 1995; Crenshaw 2010) of her race and ethnicity. Lily was not just white; she struggled to come to terms with her "foreignness," with her being of a different ethnic background, and, like Di Prima's Italian parents, Lily hoped for a balance that would allow her to accommodate and accept both her whiteness and her "Romanianness."

Lily told me that she feels that her military experience changed her, and also proved her willingness to become an American soldier, to assimilate both into the military and into the new country. So, when I asked how all of these affected her national identity, she became confused. "What is national identity?" she asked. Without waiting for my answer, she continued: "I can't say that it makes me feel further from my culture. You know. They did not do that. I think that made me appreciate more being here in this country. I think there were opportunities for me."

Over time, I discovered that Lily's military life and identity are almost a secret in her civilian life. Only a few people know about her military career. She disclosed this information only on special occasions, to people who were close to her, or when she had no choice—for example, when a possible future employer directly asked her. Given how much Lily praised the benefits of her military service, this came as a surprise. In her civilian and private life, it was remarkable how smoothly Lily made the transition between telling me, first, that she felt close to the host country and proud of being an American soldier and, second, that she strongly identified as a Romanian: "I think Romanians are hardworking people. They do well everywhere they go. This has to do with nationality. I think they are bright. I think they really take [on] the opportunities. Whatever they are given. This is what I think about *our* [emphasis added] nation. I never think that they are stupid, lazy. I do not think so."

Her ethnic identification was a value judgment. Even though her description of the Romanian community was positive, the fact that she referred to it in a negative manner, speaking of what Romanians are not, points to how

Romanians are usually seen. At the beginning of the 1990s, Romanians were a part of a new wave of immigration and were assigned the characteristics of "typical" economic immigrants: lazy, criminal, and dirty. For example, in Spain, where 718,000 Romanians immigrants were registered, the EU Minorities and Discrimination Survey issued by the EU Agency for Fundamental Rights reported that on December 11, 2009, Romanian immigrants in Spain were identified among those "facing the most discrimination in the European Union." The survey concluded that "7 percent of Romanians living in Spain said they had been the victims of racially motivated crime in the past 12 months," but that "95 percent of the Romanians in Spain . . . have not reported discriminatory treatment to local authorities. The study also revealed that at least 56 percent of the Romanians living in Spanish cities were targets of discrimination acts."[39]

Lily was aware of these stereotypes and tried to distance herself from this view, acknowledging her ethnic background with pride. Besides having friends from her own ethnic background, she also participated in social events organized by a Romanian association that brings together young Romanian expatriates. On several occasions (approximately three to four times per year), I accompanied her to Romanian social events. Lily attends (irregularly nowadays) monthly social gatherings and meetings for the main holidays (Christmas, Easter, and New Year's Eve). She belonged to two diasporic social groups with online and face-to-face activity and was kept informed about the news in her home country and ethnic community.

When we met one evening after work, she asked me if I had seen the latest developments on one of the online forums. I replied that I had not recently read them. She continued: "It is fun. I read the emails. I am on the train, and I laugh out loud. People think I am crazy because I think some of them are just hilarious. One was Iliescu . . . oh my God, just too funny." A week later, she asked me again if I had heard the latest news from Romania. I confessed that I hadn't. "Adrian Păunescu died," she said in Romanian, in a sad voice, referring to a famous and controversial Romanian poet. "Did you know he had a lot of lovers, women, in his life? He had two wives and a lot of lovers. Two of them were like poets. And then, you know the singer Aldea Teodorovici from Russia?" She looked at my unresponsive face, and then she continued: "I do not remember the first name. She was in love with him. She sang for him with her husband, and then they both died in a tragic car accident. She died loving him and singing for him with her husband. I got a separate message from someone in Romania saying: *Iubirile lui Adrian*

Păunescu [Adrian Păunescu love affairs]. I was like: all right! I had no idea he was such a womanizer. He was popular. I know Cenaclul Flacăra.[40] You know, a cousin took me to Cenaclul Flacăra, and I remember 'til now singing those songs. It was such a big movement in Romania," she enthusiastically recalled.

She maintained a close connection to the Romanian community. She was aware of the latest events and often analyzed various developments. When she began thinking about marriage, Lily went on a Romanian online dating website, met a few Romanian bachelors living in the United States, and found her future husband. She had a bridal shower in the United States, organized by a good friend of hers, who was Romanian. I was invited to the party, and I was surprised to hear about it, because Romanians consider it bad luck to organize parties celebrating events set to happen in the future, such as weddings, births, and so on. But Lily threw a party and invited Romanians—mostly women—to the event. After the guests had gone, an elderly woman pulled Lily aside and began to instruct her in how to organize her wedding and how to find a Greek Orthodox priest. As I had never thought of Lily as a religious person, it struck me as odd when I found her deeply engaged in the conversation, asking details about traditional religious marriage rituals. The elderly Romanian woman detailed an (unfamiliar) archaic process, hardly performed even in Romania by women of Lily's age. These draconian rules included physical separation between future husband and wife for a number of days and fasting for more than a month. Observing these Romanian customs was a reinforcement of her ethnicity, and she did it with the same passion and care that she brought to her military incorporation and American naturalization.

Slipping in and out of identities enabled Lily to negotiate her ethnic identity, a process not so different from that of many other immigrants in the United States. Immigrant integration literature (Lyman 1972; Portes and Zhou 1993a; Rumbaut 1994; Karpathakis 1999) argues that the naturalization of immigrants is not a simple assimilation process but involves immigrants preserving their previously acquired identities and changing only partially. Lily did not put her ethnicity aside but reinforced it in her civilian private life. Thus, in spite of being part of an institution that asks for total allegiance, Lily played a double role: in the military, she conformed to the image of a model American soldier, while in her civilian and private life she engaged more fully with her ethnic identity, praising it and lamenting its lack of recognition in American society.

Lily was not an active member of the military but a reservist, which meant that she was on base one weekend per month. For the rest of the time, she lived in urban areas, where her incorporation into the larger military group was neither requested nor possible. If she had been on active duty or even deployed, as the other two participants in this research were, the space and time for privately negotiating ethnicity would have been drastically reduced.

Hence, while in military service, Lily was able to separately experience her whiteness and feel that because her military colleagues were ignorant of stereotypes regarding her Romanian ethnicity, she was able to create a good place for herself there. The invisibility of her race accompanied by the ignorance of her peers allowed Lily to be a model soldier, integrating well in the military and participating in various activities, and still hold on to her ethnic identity outside of the military, in her civilian and private life. Furthermore, Lily's ethnicity not only was slightly invisible in everyday interactions, but also did not clash with the vision of the U.S. military for its recruits, because the military and the Air Force recognize the need for diversity and argue that doing this creates a wider pool in which to find, use, and promote talent.[41]

Understanding that the military cannot be separated from the population of the country it serves, James A. Cody (chief master sergeant of the Air Force) declared: "The men and women serving in the U.S. Air Force are representative of the diversity of our nation. We value this diversity and it's one of our greatest strengths; our airmen come together to produce an incredible team that can accomplish any mission and overcome any challenge. The uniqueness of these Airmen and the ability to leverage this uniqueness over time will ensure we remain the world's greatest Air Force."[42]

While encouraging diversity, the military assesses the value of enlisted personnel on their performance in accomplishing set missions and not by using other criteria. This attitude suited Lily well, because she felt that her talent had been recognized in spite of, not because of, her being different. Her white race allowed her to be seen as "normal," and therefore be judged on her "individual" skills and performances. She hoped to restrict her ethnicity, which she felt prevented her from accessing social mobility in civilian life, to her private endeavors, and would not display it on her monthly military weekends. But tolerance of ethnic identities is not visible only in diversity statements; it is also pertinent in daily interactions with peers and supervisors. Tolerance (or intolerance) of diversity is part of the system of power that creates, re-creates, and reinforces hierarchies and inequalities through different acts, which in Lily's case also structured her life.

Gender: Lily's Everyday Performative Practices

Throughout the years we spent working together, Lily never mentioned anything relating to her gender or how it interacts with her life in the military. When I directly asked her, she shrugged her shoulders, asserted that there was nothing to say, and changed the subject. Given the predominance of males within the military, her lack of perception of gender dynamics made me curious, so I paid close attention to her gender negotiations in her civilian life.

While gender dynamics are complex and ever changing, we can say that in the late 1990s to early 2000s, Romania—Lily's (and my) country of origin—had relatively traditional gender dynamics, with males often assumed to be the main breadwinners, even if the recent five decades of communist rule had seen most working-age women in all labor sectors and created a tradition of both partners working outside the home. In addition, males are often perceived as the main immigrants, even though, as a UNICEF study from 2012 on migration profiles shows, Romanian women migrate in slightly higher numbers than their male counterparts.[43] Lily fitted into this larger migration trend, as she decided to migrate by herself, and in doing so she became her extended family's breadwinner. When she arrived in the United States, she found employment in domains allocated predominantly to females such as working in housekeeping, taking care of children with disabilities, becoming a nanny, and working as a coat checker in a restaurant.

However, Lily made a decision that not many immigrant females make when she enlisted in the armed forces.[44] In 2015 when Lily was serving in the Air Force Reserve, there was a ratio of four men to one woman for enlisted recruits.[45] However, though she chose a particularly masculine sector of employment, once in the military Lily sought a position in education and engaged in what would typically be seen as "traditional gender practices," allowing men to act on her behalf and naturally assuming a submissive position.

For centuries, eastern European countries have experienced the rule of centralized regimes, with powerful churches able to dictate gender roles and social dynamics for extended periods. However, these nations also experienced communist rule whose Marxist ideology promoted gender equality, at least in theory, aiming to include women in the communist project. As a result, new forms of gender practices emerged, imposing on women a "double burden." Under the paternalistic communist state, women faced both full-time state employment and many domestic responsibilities. In Romania these duties were accompanied by draconian reproduction laws, which made abortion illegal, and by systematic political marginalization (Einhorn 1993).[46]

After the collapse of communism, the transition to a neoliberal market economy was not any kinder to eastern European women, as the new "male democracies" pushed women's concerns further toward the margins, both by excluding them from political institutions and by denying them the freedom to move from one social level to another (Rueschemeyer 1994). As a result, women's situation in eastern Europe has been consistently precarious, and they have faced increasing disadvantages: not only the "double burden" but also the loss of employment and social benefits, inflation and declining incomes, and a rise in political corruption and crime—and all this while traditional roles were still observed.[47]

Moreover, as postcommunist societies underwent an often-turbulent transition, eastern European women were often blamed for upsetting tradition and degrading society by being "too emancipated" (Klimenkova 1994). Lily grew up under communism in the late 1970s and early 1980s and came of age in the postcommunist 1990s. She faced the demand to be successful socially and economically, as well as to conform to traditional gender roles, such as having a traditional family. And within this changing framework, Lily learned to navigate competing roles and dynamics. Like many other women in her situation, she sought to escape a perilous economic and social situation by emigrating to the "West." Due to geographical proximity and lower travel and social costs, most Romanian immigrants left for western Europe. Going to the United States required a visa, which has been extremely hard to obtain.[48] Lily enrolled in a cultural exchange program and obtained a temporary visa to come to America, where she joined other eastern European immigrants.[49]

Lily embarked on this transatlantic journey alone and did everything by herself. She applied for the program, was granted her visa, and traveled to America. However, while she defied the migration stereotype, when she arrived in the United States she found employment in gendered, female-dominated fields. Like many immigrant women, especially those missing necessary immigration documents, Lily started her life in the new country as a caregiver, employed as a *doméstica*, or domestic help. Many undocumented or irregular women immigrants rely on this field of employment to survive in the new country. Women receive low pay, most likely do not receive health-care benefits, and experience "acute financial hardships" with "little control over working conditions."[50] Furthermore, after working in *doméstica* jobs for some years, when she streamlined her immigration status, Lily found a hospitality job, working as a coat checker in a restaurant, where she received better pay, but was still unable to make much financial progress.[51] These traditionally gendered jobs enabled Lily to start her new life in the United States and kept her financially afloat, but they did not lead to anything more than that. Because she was able to survive by working these jobs, Lily did not reflect on her gender. However, once she confronted economic uncertainty, she lamented the traditional gender roles that make men the breadwinners. Her perilous situation became visible when she was fired from a newly acquired (civilian) job: "My God, when I was told I was letting you go, I trembled. I got home, I fell on the floor, and I started crying. I was so despaired: What am I to do now? My mother was not well, I knew that my parents couldn't send me money." Stopping only to catch her breath, Lily continued: "And I thought: Now what will I do? I have no brother, no father, no husband to take care of me. All my folks were back home, and they needed my support. And even if they did not, I need to care for myself. And I thought: What will I do now? How will I pay rent? I cried a lot, for two hours, until I had no more tears." Lily felt that she could not rely on her parents or extended family to help, as is typical for eastern Europeans, who in times of need reach out to their family (parents) for help (Robila 2004), and she felt the weight of anxiety over her survival on her shoulders.

*   *   *

Like many native-born Americans who enlist in the armed forces (Mittelstadt 2015), Lily acknowledged her fragile social and economic condition and hoped for a "safety blanket": secure employment with a decent salary and social benefits. By enlisting in the military, she joined a predominantly masculine institution, in which most generals are male, and where in 2018 only 5.8 percent of Air Force pilots were female (Higginbotham 2018), with a history of male dominance and of gender dynamics being omnipresent and visible. Considering Lily's ambivalence toward traditional gender roles and practices, I was interested to see how she was going to "naturalize" her gender identity within the military.

She did so in a manner similar to the way in which she handled her racial identity: she negotiated her gender, meaning that she was committed to respecting the status quo and avoiding any challenge to the existing hierarchy or gender practices, so she could fit in easily. Lily's Romanian upbringing made her familiar with what it means to "be a woman" and she is able to perform that role accordingly. As a result, whenever she was required to assume a submissive position, she did not rebel, but accepted the situation as normal. For example, when I asked her how difficult it was for her to perform military exercises, she recalled with pride: "It is not easy. You had to walk for hours with very heavy equipment. For hours! But the guys in the team would come and help me. You see," she looked me straight in the eyes, "I am treated nicely. They came and took my equipment and helped me. That is how it is!"

Lily appreciated the assumption by the men in her unit that it would be too hard for her, a woman, to fulfill her duties. Her positive recollection is close to the criticism that conservatives make when they argue against the integration of women within the military forces on the grounds that it amounts to a lowering of physical standards.[52] By gladly accepting the gentlemanly behavior of her male peers, Lily also accepted being the "weaker" gender, the one that needs further accommodation, and in doing so performed her assumed "inferiority."

In the time we spent together, I saw Lily's interactions while serving. One day while visiting the base, at lunchtime, she suggested we eat at the "chow." I agreed, and we walked in. It was filled with people in fatigues lining up with gray trays in their hands in front of the food counters.

"There is a salad bar, there is an omelet bar, and regular food," Lily instructed me. "So, pick what you want to have." She moved quickly, and she stood in front of the egg station. She saw my confused look and yelled in Romanian: "Well, just pick one station! You want salad, right?" She raised her hand up high and pointed toward her left.

I listened to her and mixed a small salad. Holding my salad, I walked toward her, and I saw that she had some trouble getting her food. As she would recount later, she asked for eggs, sunny-side up. The cook was willing to make them, but another soldier in fatigues, one of the dining-hall supervisors, told her they no longer served eggs cooked that way. After Lily tried to convince them to serve her, a different cook asked for her order and made her the forbidden eggs. When the supervisor saw the food, he asked for the plate back. "So, I handed them back to the cook," she told me, "and he flipped them on the other side for another, what, twenty seconds? and gave them back to me. So, they were still how I wanted them! The cook was trying to help me, but this guy [the dining-hall supervisor] was trying to give me a hard time," she said with contempt. As I listened to her story, I asked for fish and a piece of bread. Lily looked at my plate, took the salad, and placed it on her tray, so I would not have to pay for it. Holding our trays, we got to the counter, where she showed the cashier her identification. He swiped her card and let her pass. Then the cashier looked at me. I pointed to Lily, and the cashier became confused.

The dining-hall supervisor who just argued with Lily about her eggs soon came and asked if I was military personnel. I replied that I was not. "Sorry, you can't have the food; it is only for the people on base." He turned to Lily and scolded her: "You should know." She protested, but the cafeteria supervisor firmly said that I needed to leave the food at the counter. Lily was visibly upset. I tried to appease her by saying that I was not hungry. She took her food and quietly sat down at the table. I could tell that she was still thinking about it. Suddenly, she raised her head and said: "I will go to get a container for this salad, and you will eat it out." Before I could stop her, she stood up and quickly went back into the food area. I took another look around the dining hall. The place looked like a regular cafeteria, such as many private companies have. The difference was that almost everyone was dressed in uniforms/fatigues, and their hair was either short or pulled back. Most of the people were in their midthirties to midforties.[53] They all talked in low voices, looking at their plates while eating. The noise level in the dining hall was medium level, like an airport waiting area.

Lily came back upset. "The guy did not want to give me a container. Can you believe it?!" I told her that I did not mind, that it was not a big thing. She remained upset. "He saw us, and he knew I will take it for you. But it is my food! Why would I not be allowed to take it?"

A tall African American man crossed the dining hall and came straight toward us. After she introduced us, Lily started commenting in anger: "He did not let me get a container. I wanted to get the salad out for her," she explained in anger.

"That ain't right," the man replied, standing in front of us, holding some food containers in his hands. Lily repeated the whole story. When she was done, without saying a word, the man set his food on our table and went back in the buffet area. Lily ate quietly, and then she raised her eyes toward me: "Now wait! He'll solve the issue for us!" and she laughed. Indeed, the man came back with a container filled with a mixed salad.

"Now you have to take this salad out, as the guy would be looking at us," Lily instructed the man, after she gave him a smile and thanked him.

Then she told the story one more time. She was all worked up because of the incident. The guy sat down next to me and tried to calm Lily. She could not be stopped, so she continued talking about it. I told her that it was no use getting upset over it, because I was not hungry anyway.

"I feel bad, and I need to eat, and you will only look at me?" To this I replied that it did not bother me, but she wouldn't let it go. She said, "It is a matter of principle! How can he talk to me like this?! And he has one less stripe than me! He needs to stand up when he talks to me. I have more stripes than him. What is this, a democracy or what?" Lily said all this in one breath. I broke into a small smile, wondering what democracy had to do with one's stripes, but said nothing.

After she finished eating, the three of us walked out of the dining hall. The man carried the salad out of the building, and then he handed it to me. I thanked him, and we said good-bye. Lily told me that we needed to walk to the library. I watched her walk, closely following her steps. She was dressed in her fatigues, with a new hat on. Her boots covered the bottom part of her pants, and her jacket was closed to the last button. She cut the path by walking on the nicely trimmed grass. I smiled, thinking of her performative practices of resistance[54] and of Edmund Burke's theory that no matter how well one designs city parks, people will still find their own path and walk on the grass.

This incident showed that faced with what she perceived as an unjust act, Lily did not try to address it through military protocol. Rather, Lily looked for ways to address it, finding glitches in the power system (in this case, asking one of her colleagues to legitimately request the food), and used her gender to empower a man to act on her behalf. Lily displayed similar traditional gender practices throughout this research. As seen above, when I asked her who her friends were within the military, she mentioned a male colleague who was like her "big brother," to whom she turned when she did not understand an English phrase or needed someone to explain military regulations. While she breaks gender stereotypes left and right, when she has to get things done, Lily has no problem using gender dynamics as tools and slips into the traditional feminine subordinate role, using traditional gender dynamics to her advantage.

While serving as a reservist, Lily displayed a similar sinuous relationship with traditional gender roles and performances in her civilian life. When she was almost forty years of age, she married a rather traditional Romanian man. She had one wedding in the suburbs of New York City and a traditional ceremony in Romania. While her wedding age was not typical of Romanian women, the ways in which she decided to go about it satisfied conservative criteria. However, once married, Lily did not meet the expectations of her husband. Being busy with her career and her military job, Lily did not iron his shirts or make him lunch, much to his chagrin, and Lily confessed this was a continuous source of tension and bickering in their new family.

While Lily challenged many traditional gender roles, her performances rarely (and never openly) defied the existing gender hierarchies, especially those within the military. As a result, she was able to navigate the host country's gendered system. On the one hand, her enlistment and relatively successful career in the military indicate the liberal aspects of the institution; on the other, the fact that, once enlisted, Lily often engaged in conservative practices, which made her a gender/feminist pioneer no more, reflects further the diverse and divergent gendered dynamics at work in the U.S. military today. For example, she did not seek to go into combat or to have a job typically assigned to male Air Force recruits. Instead, she chose to work in education within the Air Force, re-creating the gender dynamics of power with which she was familiar.[55] However, her smooth maneuvers and the subtle movement between her acceptance and reinforcement of the patriarchal system and her gender-resistant practices, both in civilian and in military life, empowered Lily to negotiate a place for herself in the Air Force and in America.

Conclusion: "The Show Must Go On!"

While working on the manuscript, I heard from Lily once more via email. She wrote from Canada, where she was on a civilian business trip: "The story of my life goes on. But nothing fascinating." As I write this, Lily has reached her forties and is still a reservist in the Air Force with an E4 rank. She has not yet fulfilled her wish to become an officer. However, she does work for a larger travel company, which satisfies her longing to travel, to be independent, and to advance her career—"nothing fascinating" by Hollywood standards, but a fitting development in her life story.

Her story is one of success and failure—but one that reflects the position of her intersectionality. She obtained her American citizenship, which enabled her to apply for family reunification, and therefore permanent residency for her father and brother. She used the GI Bill to further her education and obtain an MS degree, which in turn enabled her to pursue a career in the field of her dreams, as she is now a business development executive. These decisions and commitments also enabled Lily consistently to help her family financially.

While she faced limitations (at times unacknowledged) like other women who enlist in the military (Biank and Thompson 2014; Dietrich 2018; Hegar 2017; Germano and Kennedy 2018),[56] Lily also needed to negotiate her ethnicity within an institution that claimed to be meritocratic and—in this context—ethnically blind. She was eager to assimilate into the military, praising it highly and avoiding making any criticism of her overall experience. However, her commitment was not so unwavering. On base, under the military's (real or imagined) eyes, Lily engaged in performances of assimilation: tearing up when she sang the national anthem and eagerly participating in all military activities. She found the military to be a place in which she could prove herself and be rewarded on the basis of her individual achievements, and she was proud of how much she accomplished. She attributed her success to her individual skills and practices and did not acknowledge that—in spite of being a foreigner—she was also white and of European descent, which allowed her to enter the host country's system in a position of privilege. But, in spite of her willingness and efforts to assimilate, and despite the military's official commitment to diversity, Lily encountered a thick glass ceiling when she attempted to advance within the institution. Her ethnic background and her foreign educational degree denied her the chance to become an officer, and in doing so the military compromised her social and economic mobility. In spite of it all, Lily made peace with this. As she said in her most recent email to me: "The show must go on!"

CHAPTER 3

Alexa

Who Is Alexa?

I spoke to Alexa by phone on an early June day in 2011, when she had just returned from a doctor's appointment in Washington, DC. During our conversation, it struck me that Alexa was incredibly brave—nothing in our discussion betrayed her concern or fear about the precarious situation she was in. She simply related it as a matter of fact: "They told me I have to go for surgery. It could be a complicated one, but they will try to do the simple one, they told me." She continued: "They will cut me open, and if they see something they will go in deeper, and they will take it [a cyst] out. So, when I do this [procedure] I will also freeze the eggs. I need to go to an infertility clinic."

Speaking in a low voice, Alexa told me that she needed to undergo a complex medical intervention on her reproductive organs, and this surgery, she had been informed, could affect her ability to ever have children. Over the previous year, she had been talking a great deal about having a baby. Knowing how much she wanted children, I could imagine how hard it must have been for her to accept the possibility of not having offspring of her own. But at the moment we were talking, none of these struggles and emotions surfaced. Instead, she was focused on resolving the issue at hand. She decided to speak with the doctors, to inform the fertility clinic about the results of the surgery, and to find a treatment that her medical insurance would cover. She was firm and seemed to have a thorough understanding of the laborious medical and administrative process she was about to undertake. She knew her options and her rights and was determined to make the best of them.

A Glance into a Life: Alexa

This was just one of the many instances that revealed Alexa's tenacious character. Over my years of knowing her, I could see how Alexa defied many of the stereotypes about immigrants: Alexa is your everyday girl, who generally fitted in and felt comfortable within the first few minutes with everyone who crossed her path. She often found a common topic of conversation and engaged people from all walks of life.

Alexa is of medium height, with dark, gleaming eyes. Her wavy, dark hazel hair is pulled tightly back when in a military environment, but becomes unruly and falls over her shoulders in civilian life. She has olive skin, is amiable, has a soft accent, and dresses in an unassuming manner—but behind her pleasant and flamboyant surface, a deeper inner being could be uncovered. Life had not been smooth for Alexa, yet in spite of this—or maybe even because of this—she is an eternal optimist. Her optimism runs so deep that she does not even acknowledge it. It has become her way of being.

While Alexa came to the United States by herself, most of her migration decisions were made with her family in mind. She worked for many years as a *doméstica*, a job that ensured a regular cash flow, which she used to support her family back in South America. When she (finally) decided to become a U.S. citizen, she did so to make it easier for her to bring her sister into the country. Then, to support her younger sister, she decided to set up home away from her military base but to continue her Army job, so she could meet their living expenses. In doing so, Alexa worked hard to be included in the new country and be recognized as an equal, to access social and economic mobility, and to go to school—which she understood as her chance to have a career. Enlisting in the military made it possible for her to see forms of injustice more clearly and articulate her disagreement with them. It also made her aware of her ethnicity and of the power of her military identity. She was successful in helping her family, bringing her sister to the United States and caring for her here. But in spite of her unstinting efforts, she fell short in her attempt to be recognized as an equal and as a South American. Moreover, as I write this, she was not able to achieve her dream of continuing her university studies.

When her health started failing her—shortly after her enlistment—Alexa tried to address it by using the Army medical support but was finally honorably discharged. While she dealt with unfulfilled military promises, Alexa was not derailed from her struggle to find employment. She persevered in addressing her health issues and seeking ways to empower herself and her family.

Leaving in the Home Country: Dreams of a Better Life and Remittances

I first met Alexa in the summer of 2000, when I was working for an international company, in charge of a "cultural exchange" program in the United States. She and her boyfriend arrived at JFK Airport on a hot summer's evening, and I picked them up and took them to the company's site. At the time, she told me that while in the United States, they would be working in New Jersey for the entire summer. They were both from South America,[1] but had arrived in New York from the Czech Republic, where they had been exchange students for the previous few years. After this first brief encounter, Alexa and I kept in touch. Her life in the United States followed a different path from mine, but we always managed to stay in contact. I know her intimately and am familiar with many of her wishes, from years of affectionate and devoted friendship.

When in 2009 Alexa decided to enlist in the U.S. Army, I was one of the few people privy to her decision. She is a rather private person, so I felt privileged to be one of the close friends with whom she shared the news. After she enlisted, we discussed her decision: I asked her if she would agree to be a participant in my study and whether she would allow me to tell her life story. She consented, and our relationship took a turn that led me to see her differently, to know her better, and to open up the possibility of sharing her story with people who would otherwise never hear it. Since that day, our many long encounters, social and professional, were documented and archived. Because of our long friendship, at times Alexa only implied what she wanted to say, referring to well-known conversations we had previously had. Because we were intimate friends, she felt comfortable calling and sharing all the details of her personal life with me. Hence, Alexa's life story relies both on her narrative and on my own memories of her life.

Often in my conversations with Alexa, a certain sadness arose, when she was talking about her life in the United States. Every time I was abroad and talked to her on the phone, she would say in a soft voice: "Ohh . . . you are in Europe. . . . Bring me something! Something to remember Europe by." Her sadness was not due to extraneous hardships. It came rather from a feeling of being trapped. While she was well aware that she was living in the United States by her own choice, she couldn't help dreaming of seeing, living in, and exploring other places. First her immigration status and then her military job limited her mobility, and this often made her blue.

After she nostalgically recalled her previous European trips, during an informal discussion, Alexa confessed, "Here, what did I do here? I went five times to Las Vegas. Because it was cheap. . . . There was nothing else to do. Where else to go here?" she stopped, pensive, before continuing: "Freedom. The country of freedom does not give me freedom at all. Because I used to travel a lot before that. A lot! And I went to different countries."

Originally from South America, Alexa lived the first part of her life in a country considered one of the smallest and poorest on the continent that was recovering from military dictatorship. Alexa has always been reticent to recognize this country as her main homeland. Her complicated personal and family history leads to her having roots in at least two South American countries. Hence, Alexa preferred to identify as a South American rather than a member of a national community. Respecting her preference, I will refer to her identity this way and make minimal references to national history, instead focusing on the shared history of South America.[2]

When Alexa left in the mid-1990s, her home country's economy was still recovering from a dictatorial regime. While there has been relative growth, Alexa's family depended heavily on the remittances she sent from the United States. One late evening, in her small apartment near her military base in upstate New York, Alexa, her sister, and I were looking at the map of South America on the Internet. They showed me the capital of the country: "We live here. Well, not really here. Well, we actually live here." Alexa zoomed in the Google map and showed me a neighboring town. "It is like a suburb of the capital."

This was a single occasion on which Alexa decided, of her own will, to talk about the country in which she grew up. Typically, what she readily and happily remembers from her past is her life after she left, when she began to travel extensively: "South America: Argentina, Brazil, Chile, Uruguay, Bolivia, and Ecuador. Europe: France, Belgium, Spain, Switzerland, Czech Republic, Germany, Slovakia, England," she used to tell me with pride.

Alexa's love of traveling began when she was a child dancing in a folklore group from her native country. This early experience opened many doors for her, and as the years passed Alexa wanted to explore more. When she finished high school, she left South America for the Czech Republic. Here, supported by a small scholarship, she studied for a few years. Coming from the Americas, Alexa did not have it easy in eastern Europe: "I knew only five words: *babika, learna, benize leba* [bread], and . . . *maminka*—mother—that is it," she remembered, laughing. "I had to [learn Czech]. On the first day they say, my name is blah, blah. All in Czech. We will do mathematics, everything in Czech. And you are like a . . . a . . ." She mimicked a confused face.

Alexa told me this story on an early August afternoon, when I was visiting her for a week. That day I told her that I wanted to know everything about her past, in her own words, however she remembered it. I turned on the recorder and left it in the living room, and the conversation that followed went on for more than four hours. During this time, we had lunch and lounged on her spacious couches. Over the course of those four hours, I interrupted Alexa only a few times, and when I did it was only to clarify certain points. The advantage of this nonintrusive form of interview was discovering what was dear to Alexa, what she considered important. She was comfortable with the process, and I could also further my understanding about how these early memories affected her military experience in the United States.

For Alexa, as for Lily, the decision to come to the United States was financially motivated. At the time, she was living in the Czech Republic. "My ex, once again he was jealous and envious and told me [that] I should never come here. 'Cause America is not for me. He always said that." To prove him wrong, Alexa went to the American embassy and obtained a tourist visa. But while this enabled her to enter the country, it also limited her legal employment options. As a result, she turned to the informal sector and (like Lily) got a *doméstica* job: "I had my first job as a nanny, and it was $450 per week, without even speaking [English] properly!" Alexa proudly said.

At the end of her first few months in the United States, Alexa went back to the Czech Republic, where with the money she had earned during the summer she applied to and paid for the exchange program through which I met her. Thus, she obtained an American work permit, which allowed her to be legally employed for a few months. She arrived back in the United States with her (then) boyfriend in the summer of the year 2000. "Got a very good job as a couple. He was a driver and was supposed to work with the dogs, and to drive him or her [that is, the employers] to the supermarket. And I was inside of the house, cleaning and cooking. Aha. Seven thousand dollars a couple!! That was the best money!"

Alexa was always open about her past and often shared the fact that she came to the United States to get a job and to find the means of supporting her family back in South America. She was not much concerned about political freedom or other cultural and political ideals. Although in 2000 she had the right to work anywhere in the country, she chose to work again in the *doméstica* field because it was the most lucrative job she could find: it enabled her to save money, buy necessities, and send remittances to her family. Over the years, this choice of employment shaped Alexa's expectations of the social and economic positions in the new country. During her first ten years in the United States, she immersed herself in an economic system that brought immediate financial gains, but supplied no benefits and made it hard to plan for a long-term career.

Throughout her years as a live-in nanny, Alexa's experience mirrored that of other women who come to the United States in search of a livelihood. Similar stories were captured by Pierrette Hondagneu-Sotelo in her work *Doméstica* (2001), in which she described the experiences of primarily Mexican and Central American immigrant women in Los Angeles, exploring how live-in nannies and housekeepers typically work long hours and are available around the clock for inadequate pay. In spite of difficult working conditions, immigrants laboring as *domésticas*—often in a precarious legal position—rarely voice complaints or change jobs. Employers often do not recognize domestic labor, and workers lack the legal assistance and education to organize and demand further rights.

Even though the circumstances of Alexa's life were not identical to those of the women described in Hondagneu-Sotelo's book, her experience as a live-in nanny was similar. We often discussed her long working hours, lack of agency over her life, and the fact that she received minimum pay for long hours of work. More than once, Alexa had to cancel her plans at the last minute, telling me—almost crying—that her employer needed her to babysit or drive the children around. She was often unhappy about it and told me she could not take it any longer, but she never refused to go along with their demands. The last family she worked for as a nanny, the Buicks, promised her many times that they would support her by giving her evenings off if she wanted to go back to school to finish her university degree. Whenever they promised this, Alexa would research schools (mainly community colleges) in the area, meet with advisers, and plan her coming semester. But every time she was ready to commit, something would come up, and she would give up her plans. When her dreams were crushed, she was always disappointed but still willing to "enroll next semester."

When sadness overcame her, I would ask, why not leave this family and try something else? She admitted that she would have done this but that she could not find anything else. Alexa understood that working as a nanny was going to be the same no matter what family she was with. But she also knew that this type of employment supplied her with a much-needed flow of cash, which she often sent to her family back home. These financial commitments greatly influenced her life choices. The need to send money back home, mostly to help her family start a small private business, limited her career alternatives and kept her working as a live-in nanny for several years. She was not able to save the money she earned, get a place of her own, or go to college because the money, always tight, went to the people she had left behind.

Her situation was not very different from that of many other first-generation immigrants, men and women, who often are the main providers for relatives in their home country. Much of the literature on remittances and immigration focuses on how money influences the economic, social, and political processes of the receiving countries. Such studies either support or argue against the value of remittances for destination communities (Conway and Cohen 1998; Ghosh 2006; Jones 1998; Keely and Tran 1989; Orozco 2002). However, less well studied is how remittances also impact the immigrants, those doing the sending, who initiate the process.

"Yeah . . . and not everybody knew that," Alexa told me. "When I went home last time, they told me that I am very selfish, that I have never helped them. Maybe it was miscommunication. They [other family members] never told them it was from me. I almost took all the receipts in my hand and slapped the person who said that," she said as she looked away, becoming upset for a few seconds.

Alexa's life choices and day-to-day behavior were driven by her family's expectation that while in the United States she would support them financially. And this meant she could only pursue jobs that produced maximum cash flow and minimum expenditure. As a live-in nanny, Alexa was not paying for food, housing, or a car, but had access to all of these. This experience created a type of self-acceptance of her socioeconomic position in American society. Once, at a time when I myself was struggling financially, she offered to recommend me as a babysitter to the family she worked for. The mother of the child wanted to meet me beforehand. Alexa's employer was a blonde white woman in her midforties who had married into a wealthy and prestigious northeastern American family. At the "interview," I told her that I could work during the summer before beginning my PhD in the fall. To this she looked at me with surprise: "You've been admitted?!" Realizing the faux pas she committed, she quickly added, "I mean, you have been admitted and everything?" Her knee-jerk reaction reflected not so much on my position (we had just met), but more on Alexa and the image her employer had of her. Clearly, the employer-mother did not expect her nanny, or any other nanny, to pursue higher education or to have friends who had this kind of education.

The attitude of Alexa's employer, and the place she assigned her nanny in the social hierarchy, rubbed off on Alexa. I told her about the incident when she was driving me in her employer's car back to the train station. To this Alexa anxiously replied in Spanish: "You should not have said that. They do not like that. Now, she will probably not ask you to come again," she said nervously. After she finished scowling at me, she immediately checked the ceiling of the car with her right hand for hidden microphones. She did not find any, but she was right. After this incident, I was never asked to babysit for the family.

In spite of her employer's expectations, acquiring a higher education was something that Alexa had always wanted. However, her social, economic, and legal position in the United States, in particular her long-standing gray legal immigration status, prevented her from realizing her dream of social mobility. The segmented assimilation theory (Portes and Zhou 1993b) describes her life rather well: Alexa arrived in the United States with limited education and unstable immigration status, and she did not easily enter or access the middle class. She was, rather, relegated to the margins of society, to a lower-class position, from which upward mobility was difficult. Alexa was a valuable part of the American economic and social system, providing child care and domestic work for low pay and no benefits, but it was hard for her to access anything else. She accepted the status quo and maintained a steady plan for overcoming those limits.

Listening to her often telling me about the happy days before she came to the United States and reflecting upon her early American experience,

I wondered how she had envisioned her "American dream." Why had she decided to come to the United States? During interviews it became clear that living in the United States was seen as a temporary stepping-stone that enabled her to cope with her financial hardships: "Yeah. That was the only reason [financial]! I did not want to stay here. I wanted to go to Europe. I still want to go to Europe. I will live in Europe. Oh yeah! This is just . . . [for] a couple of years of my life. That's the reason why I worked hard." She paused and her voice softened, becoming slightly sad. "So I will forget. . . . That is the reason I go to Las Vegas; I need to go somewhere."

In spite of the sadness that now and then overcomes her, Alexa decided to remain in the United States, and, considering her feelings, the decision to stay and to apply for permanent residency was somewhat surprising. When I asked her about her motivation in applying for a green card, she promptly replied, as if it were self-evident: "To bring my family here." She said this while looking away pensively, seemingly overwhelmed by her thoughts and emotions. "For my family. My sister got married and my brother will get married, and I think they do not want to come here. My other sister never wanted to come here. There is another sister, who I say I will never bring her here! 'Cause she will make a hole in my pocket," she said, laughing. "And there is the young one who I promised I will bring her here. But so far, I couldn't. And that bugs me."

Alexa was never interested in having strong ties with the South American immigrant community, as immigration scholarship (Buchanan 1979; Laguerre 1984) would lead us to expect. Her immigration status and efforts to better her economic condition were both motivated and mediated by specific ties with her family/community back home. Her decision to remain in the country, even her enlistment in the U.S. military, was driven by the desire to support her family financially and to live up to her promise to bring her sister to the United States. Her entire attitude remained focused on helping her family. She wanted neither to become a member of her immigrant ethnic community nor to become a U.S. citizen.

Enlistment in the U.S. Military: Alexa Becomes a Soldier

If living in the United States was only a temporary stopgap, why did Alexa decide to enlist in the Army? After approximately seven years of work as a nanny, she obtained her permanent residency permit, that is, her green card.

This came with a work permit that allowed her to be employed wherever she wished, which opened up new avenues for social mobility and better overall adjustment in the host society. However, despite her better social position and newly improved immigration status, Alexa did not advance her economic situation. Quite the contrary. Leaving her live-in nanny job would mean that she lost the cash income she had enjoyed for years. She was ostensibly free to work in various fields, but—like other immigrants—she found she could not enter the labor market like the native-born Americans (Hjerm 2005). "I got the green card. [But] I was four months without a job. I used all my savings. It was hard to find a job; it was the time of the recession." I recall her telling me this during earlier phone conversations as well, right before she decided to join the armed forces. Never before had Alexa been worried about her finances, but now she was visibly concerned about her future. "I found [some] jobs. But they wanted to pay me five or eight dollars. I never worked for less than fifteen to twenty dollars per hour. So, I did not want to do it for five dollars."

Lacking employment opportunities that would offer her good benefits, Alexa looked at the possibility of enlisting in the armed forces, which seemed to offer her a good life overall. "The Army pays my school and health and dentist insurance. I do not pay anything. And that is important because insurance is expensive. So, I am covered. I do not have to worry about food. They pay for my food. I do not have to worry about where I live. They pay me where to live. I do not worry about transportation. They pay for it as well," she said a few months into her enlistment.

In many ways, Alexa's job in the military was similar to her job as a nanny. In both jobs, someone else supported her daily expenses, and she felt that as long as she could work, she would be protected. Both the employer family and the military provided food, housing, and transportation, while they determined Alexa's schedule. The difference was that in the military, the schedule was developed according to a systematic plan. In her previous domestic jobs, daily activities could be highly variable, in an arbitrary way, based on last-minute caprices or needs.

Being used to having little agency over her personal life, Alexa looked at the military simply as an employment opportunity. Her decision to enlist was not motivated by her desire to become an American or by political or cultural ideals. She viewed enlistment in a pragmatic way, as a strategy for social and economic mobility. A few months into her service, when we were on her base, she seemed to be very proud of her job and kept telling me that once her health improved, she would work on an airplane. Her eyes sparkled as she said she would learn about the engine and perhaps even how to fly it. She was optimistic and hopeful of the new military career that awaited her.[3] Her aspirations did not contradict the U.S. Army's recruiting strategies. On its recruitment website, the U.S. military advertises the importance of its values and praises the high moral quality of its recruits, yet it also accepts that some people join military service as a form of (highly) specialized employment that offers social and economic mobility as well as a "safety blanket," as Lily called it. Similar to Lily, Alexa's approach adhered closely to the latter.

Both of Alexa's employment choices in the United States reflected her need, like Lily and Vikrant, to access help in providing for herself in the new country. When she did not find this support in state programs, she looked at employment opportunities that would offer it. While, as Mittelstadt (2015) argues, the U.S. military had been cutting its welfare programs for its recruits and their families in the first decade of the new millennium, moving toward a rapid privatization, it still provided more services than other forms of employment for which Alexa—a first-generation immigrant—was eligible.

Alexa saw her military service as the key to obtaining her college degree and securing options for further class mobility. Like Lily and the women in Jill Sullivan's book *Band of Sisters: U.S. Women's Military Bands during World War II*, Alexa enlisted in the military also in the hope of achieving "exciting prospects" (2011, 1) in life. Thus, her passion for life was coupled by her need for economic stability. She had already spent almost a decade as a civilian in the United States and was acutely aware of her economic limitations. To overcome them, she opted for a life of military service. "In the Army, it is easier [to attain a college degree]," she said, referring back to her dream of a higher education. "Because I do not have to pay. Outside, I tried. I got good money being a babysitter, but I did not have time to study. I never had time!"

In her answers and through her actions, Alexa revealed her understanding of the socioeconomic dynamics in her host country, revealing how money alone did not ensure her social mobility. She knew that in addition to accessing finances, she needed the social-legal status that would permit her enrollment in a school and logistical support, that is, an accommodating schedule. And while in her civilian life she did not have access to these, the military—at least in theory—makes all of it possible. So, like many other women trying to find a way to pay for higher education, Alexa enlisted in the

U.S. military.[4] Echoing the claims made by Mittelstadt (2015), "soldier girls" like Alexa and Lily turn to the military to access social support programs. Furthermore, just like Lily, Alexa joined the armed forces in search of social and financial stability, as a way to move beyond the precarious economics of her way of life and to support her family abroad.

Just like Lily, Alexa found once she had enlisted, the structure of the organization was to her liking. She received specialized training, which she eagerly embraced,[5] and proudly told me about it. She enjoyed wearing the uniform in civilian settings and reported that her new look won respect and recognition.

She shared with me that soon after she enlisted, she paid a surprise visit to the Buicks, the family for whom she had worked as a nanny for years. She went dressed in her military uniform and rang the bell. When the father of the family opened the door, he was shocked to see her as a U.S. military person. She told me this, laughing out loud. I asked her why she went there. She replied that she wanted them to see her as a soldier, to know that she could make something of her life. The new military identity gave her the recognition she craved, which she felt she could not access while working as a nanny. Furthermore, in Alexa's case, military life directly affected her private/personal life. Her military beginnings were filled with optimism, as it was through the military that she met her husband (who was also a soldier) and started a new life: "The Army gets my life complete. I have a job, I will go to school, I have family, and I have a doggie. That is the good part," she told me one afternoon while sipping tea on the couch in the apartment she had recently rented on the base. But after that, she went silent for a few moments, then slowly continued: "That is the only good part."

Alexa's Military Experience through Performative Practices

After Alexa enlisted in the U.S. armed forces, often when we were in public she acted as if she were under surveillance. Shortly after she joined the armed services, she visited me in New York City. As we were walking in the streets of my neighborhood one evening, Alexa told me that she could be seen at all times. I did not understand what she was referring to, so she cautiously pointed to the camera in a neighborhood bodega. The store was obviously not connected with the U.S. Army, but this local monitoring made Alexa aware that her behavior was recorded and, if needed, could become traceable and visible. While we were walking the street, as we had done countless times before, Alexa was newly aware of the possibility of military surveillance, and her behavior was modified to align with what was expected by this powerful institution.

As time went by, and she became more comfortable with being in the U.S. Army, Alexa also became critical of it, but her criticism was carefully constructed. It was always done in a civilian setting, with only civilians whom she trusted like her sister and myself, away from the military's "eye of power." The same themes surfaced in most of our conversations and encounters, as exemplified in the vignette below, which describes an event that occurred late one evening while I was visiting her in her apartment off-base, almost three years into her service, in March 2012. Alexa was preparing dinner, which she had proudly announced would be a typical South American meal, and as she laid out the ingredients and named them one by one—eggs, milk, cheese, butter, *maiz* [corn powder]—I asked her: "Tell me, what is your typical day like?"

"I wake up at four o'clock in the morning," she said. "I take a shower, go back to bed if I am tired, then I get dressed, I go, drive for twenty minutes, [enter the base], sleep in the parking lot for one hour, and go to formation." Her choice to leave so early, and wait/sleep in her car, seemed illogical, so I asked her why didn't she go later. "Because the gates are packed and I will be late for formation, I get a counseling statement. I do not go late anywhere!" I acknowledged that this was true, and I encouraged her to proceed with her story. "There are only four lanes [for the two adjacent military bases], and everyone tries to get there at six o'clock in the morning. Aviation has two hundred people. And they all have cars, so it is like two hundred cars. And they all try to get in at the same time. They start early, but formation is 6:45 a.m. So, you have to be there to get a parking place. There is no parking, you know that already," referring to the time I had spent at the base previously, "and now is a lot worse. Pretty bad."

Alexa said this in a slightly sarcastic tone, which revealed her slight frustration with the delays that regularly occur. And she went on to tell me: "I go in my PT-exercise uniform. . . . Now, I do not exercise [because of the medical condition], so I walk. But even that hurts now . . . it hurts to walk." She moved slowly, turning up the cooker's gas flame and placing a large pan on the stove. "And after that, you get one hour and fifteen minutes to get changed. And then you go with the other uniforms." She described a well-regulated schedule, but one in which she did not fit well, due to her physical limitations. This ritualized daily routine, to which Alexa was conforming, was not accommodating her physical limitations, so she felt that she was relegated to the margins of her group. As a result, she was not eager to spend time with her peers more than was required, like sharing meals. "I live in an outpost; I do not eat there anymore. Please cut this in little squares," she directed me, showing me how to prepare the cheese we needed for the meal. "Just a little less. Just make tiny!" After showing me the proper way to chop up the cheese and approving my technique, she continued. "I eat in the car. I do not want to see them. Anybody. It is considered my free time! Then after 1:00 p.m. . . . you go back to work and sit! There are no planes. *No hay aviones! Se están hacienda preparaciones, inspecciones* [They are doing preparations, inspections]." She stirred the pot, and said in disappointment, looking at the pan, "I sit in the office and deal with the sergeants. Because they kick you out of the room every five seconds. 'Everybody out!' so we are like standing out and coming back. They need time to talk about ourselves."

While Alexa appreciated the order and organization of the military, she was frustrated by the fact that she could not perform, and as a result she was increasingly unhappy with how her days went by. "[I sit] in the hallway. Yep!" she laughed ironically. "We wait until they are done. The Army is a sit-and-wait! *Sienta te y espera. Esto es por que en Army hay gente que no tiene cabeza. Ahora me di cuenta* [Sit and wait for orders. This is why the Army is for the people with no brains. Only now I realized]. Just for lazy people—*gente aburrida que no tiene iniciativa. Que sienta . . . Se levanta Ok, y se vaya* [bored people, who do not have any initiative. . . . They sit, they stand up, and they go]." She kept on stirring the food and then added: "*Y nada, my vida es aburridisima* [And nothing more, my life is very boring.]"

Her frustration with her daily job was related to her expectation that she would be more engaged. She compared her life now to the specialized training she had undertaken right after basic training: "We did a lot of exercises. Normal exercises for me. *Pero para los otros es tan dificil. Esta llorando: me quiero ir para mi casaaaaaaaa.* [But for the others, they were difficult. They cried: I want to go hooooooome]." She mimicked a loud child. "*No sabia hacer ejercicios, no sabia correr . . . no podía dormir en la cama. Que quiere su colchón que tiene en su casa, quiere su ortopedico . . . que quiere su* 'blow-dryer.' *Estas chicas estan asi: que quiero mi secador, que quiero mi planchita . . .* Hahahaha [They did not know how to exercise, they did not know how to run . . . they could not sleep in the room. They need their mattress, which is orthopedic . . .

they want the blow-dryer. These girls are like this: I want my blow-dryer, my hot plate]."

Trying to get a better understanding of her sarcastic account of her peers' comments, I continued the conversation in Spanish, asking her why it was not so difficult for her. She promptly answered, referring to her immigrant experience: "*Por que yo me mudo siempre, yo no tengo mi cosas aqui . . . entonces es fácil adaptarse cuando uno no tiene nada! Uno no se adapta cuando tiene todo su comodidades. Por que quiere su cama, que quiere su planchita, su perfume, su mesa, su platillo. Y el Army te saca todo. Nada te deja!* [Because I am always moving, and I do not have my things here . . . so, it is easy to adapt when one has nothing! One cannot adapt when she has all the commodities. Because then they want their bed, their hot plate, their perfume, their shoes. And the Army takes it all from you. They leave you with nothing!]" She turned to her sister: "*Te acuerdas cuando tiempo?* [Do you recall how much time?]," she asked, referring to the food. She looked at the recipe. "*Aceite, sevilla; le pongo en procesador, queso, ya esta . . .* [oil, onion; I put them in the food processor, cheese, here we go]. *Cristina, necesitamos pan. En la 'mitad* [Cristina, we need bread. Cut it in the middle]."

After she briskly told me how to cut the bread, she continued: "*A mi me gustaba* [boot camp] *por que conoci la mentalidad Norte Americana*: [I liked boot camp because I got to know the North American mentality]. 'I think I can, I think I can, but I cannot!'" she mimicked ironically. In response to my puzzled look, Alexa continued: "*Asi mismo; asi dice: yo puedo, yo puedo, y despues dicen; ya no puedo!* [Exactly like this; they say: I can, I can, and then they say: I cannot!]." Alexa's frank, bitter, and piercing accounts of her military experience were completely unexpected, but much appreciated. While Lily and Vikrant were eager to conform to the (imagined) expectations of the military, Alexa was ready to share her disappointment with her daily life in the Army.

I finished cutting the cheese, and Alexa showed me the vegetables I had to cut. I jokingly lamented: "*Oh, que mucho trabajo me das* [How much work you give me]." "*Si!*" She promptly responded. She kept organizing the kitchen, checking on the dish. "*Me hace boot camp a mi* [She puts me in boot camp]." I turned to her sister. Alexa laughed. "*Si, cada vez cuando dices una mala palabra en Espanol, haces un push-up!* [Yes, every time you say an incorrect word in Spanish, you do a push-up!]" We laughed and set the table. The food was done. Alexa pulled it out of the oven, and the strong smell of baked food filled the house. She placed it on the counter, cut out generous pieces, and placed them on our plates. We took the hot food to the table and started eating it at once, before it had cooled. We ended up burning our mouths—and smiled about this mishap. Then, when at last I had had my fill of this delicious cornbread baked with butter and cheese, I asked her to give me more of her views on the North American way of thinking, as she had learned about it while in the U.S. military.

"I am on top of the world. They think like that. And then another thing that I have learned: I do what I want. Everyone said that. Sergeants. You do what they tell you. Why, Sergeant? I do what I want! You do that. *Es todo . . . yo! Yo! Yo! Tu no tienes celebro. Tu haces que yo te digo!* [This is all . . . me! Me! Me! You do not have any brains. You do what I tell you!]". While eating she continued, "I knew that they were selfish—this is what I knew! *Tu quieres este pan entonces?* [Do you then want this kind of bread?]." She briskly changed the subject and handed me toast. Alexa was clearly disenchanted by her military experience and was trying to make sense of it. In the years she spent in service, she learned about the U.S. military culture and its practice, and while she had a pessimistic take on her experience, she praised the U.S. Army's high standards: "Discipline. I really liked the discipline. *Uno se despierto temprano, hace que necesita hacer. Uno hace guardias—a mi me gusta hacer 'guardias.' Si, me gusto!* [You need to wake up in the morning. You do whatever needs to be done—you make 'guards.' I liked doing them!]." She stood up and told her sister and me to clean the table. Soon after we retired for the evening.

As we were getting ready for bed, I thought about her military experience and about the way she put it into words. I often heard her voicing the same criticism to her husband, who was serving in another unit down south. On these occasions, she expressed the same criticism, as a response to particular situations she or he had faced that day. Alexa's criticism, or "gossiping" as Scott (1985) would characterize it, was stern about the people she was currently working with and the relationships that she was part of, but was accompanied by great respect for the values of the military and for her continuous integration. She was caught between competing aspects of the Army: the side she respected and valued, which represented how she thought the Army should be running, and the other side, the one she disapproved of—the way she experienced the Army. She experienced two sides of the U.S. military: an organized system, with highly trained individuals, and a faulty, bureaucratic system in which certain people, like Alexa, could quickly spiral downward.

Alexa's frustration at the way the military operated (and the way it treated her) prompted her to find ways of bending its rigid system to accommodate her needs. In this way, through performative practices of resistance, she found a place for herself. At the same time, she also disrupted the overall order of the system. While in status and practice she became an American soldier, her identity was not complete. She needed to continue in order to gain acceptance in the institution and the host country, by performing her new identity.

Class: Moving Downward

Alexa's life changed a great deal after she enlisted. Her life as a soldier gave her clear advantages, such as medical insurance and public recognition as a member of the host society when wearing the military uniform. However, she was not well off—and had been in a better financial situation in her years as a nanny. Using herself as an example, she told me many times that I should also get a live-in nanny job in Connecticut, leaving behind my poverty-stricken graduate student life in New York City. She was always able to make a decent living and to help her family back home. Yet after enlisting, these things drastically changed.

Before the evening described above, I had not seen Alexa in almost a year. In the spring of 2012, I traveled to her base and visited her new home. After a seven-hour bus ride, there she was, waiting for me at the bus station like many times before. I was happy to see her and to meet her sister, who had just arrived from South America. Alexa drove me straight to the house, and, as I had arrived in the evening the small town's streets were almost empty. The houses were low to the ground, old, and poorly maintained, with discolored paint on their external walls. We passed a Laundromat, a Dollar Store, a sign directing us toward Walmart, and a Chinese restaurant.

Later on, Alexa confirmed what I had presumed from the landscape: the town was impoverished, and although the military—whose base was located on outskirts of the town—supported local businesses, it was not well regarded by the locals: "They said that the military brought a lot of drinking and fights in bars. . . . They don't like that, and they do not like the military." When we arrived in front of her house, I got out while she parked her car, and I took a close look at the building. It was old and small, with two floors, and it seemed to be slightly falling down on one side. Alexa told me that together with her sister, she lived upstairs. After she parked, we went around the house to Alexa's entrance. We climbed the old, creaky wooden stairs and opened a loose door. Inside the house, we entered a dark hallway, where Alexa and her sister left their coats and shoes. I took off my jacket and my boots and climbed the wobbly and groaning stairs to the other parts of the apartment.

It was clean, neatly arranged, and simply decorated, with basic furniture. The living room, where I was staying, had a pullout couch. "I got it from Goodwill," Alexa said proudly. "Can you believe it? A hundred bucks. It is good and comfortable." The room had a small window with a broken white plastic shade. In the other room, where she slept with her sister, there was a large inflatable bed, a set of drawers with a TV on top, and in one corner many small plastic toys and memorabilia, such as hats for the St. Patrick's Day parade. The third room was empty and used for storage.

I recalled the previous homes in which Alexa had lived as a nanny. True, she had not had her own place, but those houses were mansions, with large entrances and many rooms overlooking swimming pools or gardens, with designer solid-wood furniture, fluffy scented towels, and expensive soaps in their many bathrooms. Now, Alexa lived on her own, and her lifestyle had changed.

In spite of this dramatic downturn in her lifestyle and in her "economic *bonheur*," Alexa seemed content: "Army life is easy for me. You see how I live. Very modestly. I do not need much. When you are an immigrant, you are used to that. You move many times, and you only have a few things. But for Americans, [this] is difficult: 'I need my blow-dryer; I need my convenience,'" she said, mimicking the high-pitched voice in which her colleagues complained.

All of Alexa's choices made it obvious she had a modest lifestyle. As she was putting dinner together, she opened up the cupboard to take out the ingredients she needed, and I saw the interior. There was a perfectly organized line of canned food: corn, condensed milk, peas, pears in heavy syrup, and so on. I was puzzled, so I asked her: Why do you have all of this?

"You can get them for free," she said with excitement. "You go and you tell them how many people are in your family, and they give you this for free. Look!" She opened another cupboard, which was filled with cans. "Also, they give you cereals, and even Starbucks coffee." She bent down and opened a third cupboard, pulling out bottles of the expensive ready-made coffee. "Everything you need. You can do it, too, in NYC!" she promptly advised me.

Alexa was highly resourceful in finding ways to save money. Every expense was carefully weighed up, so she could make ends meet. Now that her sister had arrived in the country, she needed to provide for her as well. Alexa's sister was ten years younger, had a degree in design, and came at her older sister's insistence. She was on a tourist visa, had limited English skills, and therefore could not find employment in a town with a small Latino/a/x population. This situation made her entirely dependent on Alexa's financial and social resources. While making ends meet is not a problem only for immigrant soldiers, Alexa's case was special, different from the ones faced by American-born recruits: she had a dependent sister who, with a tourist visa, had no means at all of supporting herself. Alexa needed to provide for her, and the military's assistance fell short.

Further evidence of Alexa being forced to live modestly struck me during her visit to New York City later that year. At lunchtime, together with her sister, we were strolling in the area of the Port Authority bus station in Midtown Manhattan when, in a crowded area behind the station, Alexa noticed people congregating in front of a building and asked me what was inside. I told her it was a soup kitchen and explained that people can go there and eat for free. She smiled and turned to her sister, translating what I just said into Spanish. They were both happy to hear this. "So, that is good to know. Next time we come to NYC, we can come here and eat." I was surprised, but she did not notice and continued: "And I will let everyone else from the base know. So, when they come to NYC, they can eat here, too."

"Why?" I barely articulated my astonishment.

"Because they do not have money, Cristina!" she said, speaking emphatically, as if it was self-evident.

During my visit to her upstate home, we drove toward her Army base. The drive that took about thirty minutes started in the little sleepy town where Alexa lived and took us farther into the countryside. The houses were built low to the ground and made of vinyl siding. The cold spring day, with clouds hanging in the sky and a sharp wind blowing, made the place look desolate and deserted. The trees were still, empty, and gray, but the green of the grass had started to appear, hinting at the promise of new beginnings in spring.

We passed by more small towns, and I looked at the houses. As if she were reading my mind, Alexa told me: "They are trailer houses. You can take the house with you, and then you come and you put it there. It is around $900 per month." I was surprised, and I asked how military families can afford them. "I do not know," Alexa replied. "They do. And they have to pay for everything else: electricity, water. They do not have it [a power line], but they have an *enchufe* [a plug]." The poverty of the region was striking and heartbreaking. Even more puzzling was that it seemed to be inhabited by so many military personnel. The presence of the military was easy to spot because of the American flags hanging from the roofs of the homes or the five-point stars signifying membership in the Army, as Alexa explained.

As we saw earlier, Lily enthusiastically embraced the military practices she performed: saluting the flag, singing the national anthem, and so on. They helped her achieve membership in the group of her choice and in the American mainstream. Like Lily, Alexa took pride in identifying with the military. Yet, in contrast to Lily, Alexa had to make difficult economic decisions in order to survive in the new military environment. To provide for her sister, she had to move to a modest neighborhood and search for alternative ways to find daily food. In this way, Alexa became a member of an impoverished social group in the host country, marking a downward economic assimilation. As Portes and Zhou (1993a), Portes (2007), and Rumbaut (1994b) have shown, American society is both diverse and segmented. Some immigrants may follow the traditional model and assimilate into the white middle class or attain upward mobility within a tightly knit immigrant community ("straight-line"). Others, like Alexa, follow a less prosperous path and assimilate into the underclass ("downward assimilation"). Portes and Zhou (1993) further argued that the group into which the new immigrants settle plays a crucial role in their development in the host country.

In contrast to the other two participants in this study, who both had (at least) BA degrees upon enlisting in the U.S. military, Alexa had (at best) only "some college,"[6] and this makes her similar to many of her military peers. In 2011, 88 percent of Army enlisted personnel had a high school diploma or GED, and only 5 percent had a BA degree.[7] Entering military service offered Alexa a salary comparable to that of the U.S.-born recruits, but at the same time it curtailed her economic improvement. As an enlisted soldier, Alexa took a pay cut from being a live-in nanny, representing "downward" economic assimilation.[8]

It was a counterintuitive finding to discover that Alexa had a precarious economic situation after she enlisted, because joining the military is considered to be a way of enhancing economic and social mobility. This brings into view how interrelated economic mobility and social mobility are. Specifically, Alexa had to support her family abroad and her dependent sister within the United States, and while the U.S. military recognizes and supports family members such as spouses and children, even if only partially, it does not recognize soldiers' additional economic ties (or debts), and thus fails to offer assistance programs for military personnel who might be facing an excessive social and economic burden.[9]

The Battle with Ethnicity and Race: "Maybe I am not the right color!"

Before she came to the United States, Alexa lived as a student in Europe, where she was exposed to the homogenous population of the Czech Republic, where people found it easy to see that she was ethnically different. To fit in, she tried to be like the host group and to appear white (even ultra-white) and Czech. During one of the long interviews at her home on the base, she happily remembered her time as a student in Czech Republic and told me the following story:

> When I went to the city, they said: "Are you from Brno?"[10] "Yes, I am," I said. I used to hang out with skinheads. I was the only female international student at that university. . . . And you know how it is in Europe. I lost my color. And I picked up the way they talk. One time, we went to the Christmas shop on the street and I was like: "My god! Skinheads!" And then my friend, who was with me, said: "Come on, meet my friends." "You are friends with skinheads?! And you bring me to meet with them? Are you nuts?" "Do not worry, you are Czech already. You talk funny, they will not notice you are not a Czech." So, I talked to them.

Alexa took pride in being considered "one of us," even by this racist and exclusionary group, and she understood the moment as a personal success. Because Alexa came from South America, her understanding of "assimilation" and "whiteness" is rooted in the historical legacy of this continent, but her view of her race was a more fluid, complex understanding than the one she inherited (Padrón 2015).[11] South American history is closely linked with the history of colonization and the emergence of a large mestizo population, and in many South American societies, resemblance to European ancestors often results in a privileged social position.[12]

Aware that beauty and social, political, and economic power are rooted in a history of white domination, Alexa struggled to be identified as white. Thus, during the years she worked as a nanny in Connecticut, she changed her physical appearance to resemble her employers. She cut her hair medium-short, wore it straight with highlights that made her look almost blonde, and wore clothes bought from the neighborhood malls. By making these changes in her physical appearance, Alexa tried to overcome her social status and become integrated into the dominant group. Her behavior was not unlike the actions of other immigrants of color, whose "constant reminders of their outsiders' status pressures . . . non-White immigrants to assimilate into a dominant cultural norm and even try to pass as European 'ethnics' in public spaces" (Rudrappa 2004, 23).

When in Europe, Alexa engaged in a similar performative practice, trying to speak the local language well and even to appear physically similar. She was proud to be seen as Czech. But after eight years in the United States and the years of military service, did Alexa consider herself an American? Did she aim to be like the others in the host country?

When she was not yet a citizen, but was already serving in the U.S. military, I asked Alexa if she was an American. She looked me straight in the eyes and clearly stated: "I am American. Remember that. I am very good at defending that I am American, too." She immediately reflected on her narrative: "I was just born in South America. But I am an American." I quietly accepted that I had made a mistake by overgeneralizing and reformulated my question to reflect both my interest and Alexa's critique. To this she answered: "What about being North American? I cannot think about it; I am not North American."

As seen in the previous section, Lily often made it clear how strongly she felt about being a member of the host country and how emotional she became when she practiced performative acts of assimilation, like seeing the American flag, but Alexa's attitude was different. Often, she made a point of distancing herself from the image of the United States. Since citizenship status is the most visible sign of one's belonging to a nation, I asked Alexa several times if she would become a U.S. citizen. Considering that via the military she was able to do so quickly and easily, I assumed that she would eagerly embrace it. Surprisingly, Alexa was uncomfortable at the prospect of being an U.S. citizen. She did finally decide to become a U.S. citizen, in 2012, but in previous years, whenever I asked her why she had reservations, she replied along these lines:

> There is too much trouble with the United States. People hate them. Having that passport is putting my head on the target. Everywhere.

You do not know that, but I traveled with a lot of people, they *hate the United States* [her emphasis]. At the airport in Frankfurt how they treat them, and how they talk about them . . . Of course, that is not because they are nice, that is because they are arrogant. Nobody likes them, and the whole situation with the war thing. They are going to a war where nobody invites them. Iran, Iraq, they have been at war for years. They have been at war since Christ. They go and try to do stuff. I do not know why.

Alexa's attitude contradicted both her willingness to resemble those who often employed her and her enlisting in the country's military service: if people "hate the United States," then becoming physically similar, or a soldier, equals becoming an American symbol and implicitly makes her a target. But stationed on her base in New York, away from those who "hate the United States," Alexa was unaware of these contradictions. For her, being a member of the U.S. military and being a U.S. citizen were different. Alexa was willing to become like the military, as an institution, but she refused to become like the larger national U.S. community.

Despite her reluctance to be naturalized, she admitted that she might one day have to become a U.S. citizen. Like many other immigrants, Alexa was not motivated by the desire to become a member of the host country (Lyman 1972; Portes and Zhou 1993b; Rumbaut 1994a; and Karpathakis 1999). She was driven by the need to help her family back home. She understood that having U.S. citizenship would enable her to bring her sister to the United States and help her immigrate legally, and finally, in September 2012, Alexa became a U.S. citizen.

Alexa's questioning of the viability of U.S. citizenship revealed a distancing from the country in which she had been living for more than a decade and under whose flag she served. It also outlined her unwillingness to be simply "assimilated." Alexa always described (North) Americans as different from her, as people with whom she had minimal ties and understanding.

> [Now] I am becoming one of them. Two-face. Because I am saying: Oh, okay. And behind them I am talking. Oh yeah! That is what America teach me! Scream like crazy [she said in a high voice], and then [in a soft voice], "Hi, how are you?" This is what I have learned from the Richies.[13] . . . They are like that! They are creepy. They scream at you. They do not take care of the kids. I used to be a nanny. I took care for twenty-four hours of people who aren't my own flesh and blood. They do not care about their families. They care about their car, furniture, and dogs.[14]

Her life in the United States made Alexa aware of the ways in which she was changed by living there. She considered knowing how Americans behave to be an important part of "playing the game" and made conscious and continuous efforts to separate herself from them and tried to avoid cultural transformation. When people in her social circle said that she exaggerated, arguing that Americans don't all behave in the same way, Alexa responded firmly: "For me, all the people (that is, Americans) that I know scream like crazy. They threaten you with just their looks, because they are so mad, and then two hours after: 'Hi, I love you,'" she mimicked them in a soft voice. "No wonder they have HHD, or ADD, or whatever. All the ADDs they have. And that is another thing that I am very upset about. A lot of people have attention deficit disorder. What is that? We do not have that. 'Oh my God! I have to take my pills. Oh my God! I have to take my pills!'" She imitated the gesture of looking for something in her pockets. "I am like: 'What?' 'I can't concentrate, Alexa.' For Rob," she said, referring to the child whose nanny she was for five years, "that was his excuse: 'I can't do my homework. I have to take my pills. I can't concentrate, Alexa.' 'Just relax—go and wash your face,' I said. 'I can't concentrate.'" She imitated the voice of a distressed young child. "'You do not know how it is in my head.' 'Yeah. In your head! Aha! Try to concentrate without your pills. That is bad for your body.' 'No, you have no idea.' And he was jumping, all excited. All sugar. I am always amazed by that. You can see that in the Army, too. Those are the people who kill somebody else."

Even after a couple of years of military service, Alexa's view of (North) Americans was still shaped by her experience as a live-in nanny and as a result was mostly negative, leading her to resist assimilation into the new culture. This choice was clear in her speech, in the passion that she put in emphasizing the distance between herself and (North) Americans, but also in the friends she made. Before her military service, many of Alexa's friends were international nannies and au pairs who came with one-year contracts and worked for families in the Northeast. After their contracts expired, many returned to their home countries and continued their careers, but Alexa stayed and was thus faced with a rapid turnover of people in her life. Now that she was in the military, she argued that she had no friends. She typically identified the Army personnel as Americans or at least as non-Europeans, and therefore she said she couldn't trust them. Moreover, their proximity led neither to her feeling closer to (North) Americans nor to an overwhelming desire to become like them. She cherished and cultivated her contact with the civilian world and the few people she knew outside the military. In stark contrast to Lily, who often talked about her good relationships with fellow American soldiers, Alexa chose a different path and reinforced her extra-military and non–(North) American ties.

Alexa's identity (not unlike any others) is complex, and she navigates it with care to access both recognition and economic/social mobility. She strongly identified as a South American, and in spite of enlisting as an active-duty soldier in the U.S. Army, she distanced herself from self-identifying (at least in private) as an American soldier. She was not against the military per se. She appreciated the structure and order that the institution imposed, but the link between the military and the host country (which was so obvious to Lily) was not so evident to Alexa. She was preoccupied with maintaining her South American ties, bringing her sister to the United States, and providing for her family back home.

As her family ties were strong, I asked if she had formed close relation-ships with members of her ethnic community within the military. Alexa told me that her sergeant was Puerto Rican and that at times he spoke Spanish to her: "When he wants to be nice to me . . . he talks to me in Spanish in a nicer way. Then [when he speaks English] he wants to blend with the rest of the military." Furthermore, this identification of her ethnicity as "Latina" or "Hispanic" incited Alexa's fury:

> I am not Latin American! I speak a Latin Language. But I am not a Latin American. This is a misconception. It is a derivation of the Latin language. I do not know [what it means to be Latin American] because I am not. I do not know. They qualify everybody who speaks Spanish as Latin American. But we are not. . . . I am from South America. If you want to put me in a group! But I am not a Latin American. That is why I keep on fighting with everybody: "I am not a Latin American!" Everybody tells me [that I am Latin American]. In the Army as well. Everywhere: "You are from Latin America." No! I am not!"

She said this in a raised voice, her eyes focused, explanations tumbling from her lips, making abundantly clear how strongly she felt about this misrecog-nition, and in doing so bringing to light the limits of the "Latino/a/x" and "Hispanic" categories.

Demographics and statistics have their inherent benefits, but using general labels also highlights the arbitrariness and overgeneralizing nature of this approach.[15] The Office of Management and Budget Directive 15 specifies whites, blacks, Hispanics, Native Americans, Asians, and Pacific Islanders as racial and ethnic categories for the purposes of enforcing civil rights legislation; however, the OMB admits that this is in fact an arbitrary classification scheme, which may owe its high level of recognition to Directive 15 itself.[16]

According to Pew Research Center surveys, even though the terms "Hispanic" or "Latino" have been widely used by federal agencies to categorize Americans who trace their roots to Spanish-speaking countries, the labels are not embraced by the group to which they have been affixed. More than half of surveyed individuals said that they identify themselves most often with their family's country or place of origin, using such terms as "Mexican," "Cuban," "Puerto Rican," "Salvadoran," or "Dominican"; another 21 percent say, just like Alexa, that they use the term "American" most often to describe themselves, while only about one-quarter of Hispanic adults say that they most often identify themselves as "Hispanic" or "Latino."[17] Thus, like other immigrants who trace their roots back to South America, Alexa did not identify as a Latin American.

Alexa's forthright reaction when identified as a "Latin American" further highlighted the shortcomings of this term. The category is too large to encompass the differences that exist among subgroups. Her argument was rooted in her belief that she had little in common with people coming from Central American countries. Even though in the Army most people labeled her Latina (or Hispanic), she vehemently argued against this identification.

One of the groups most visible in the U.S. military is the Puerto Ricans. Because they have U.S. citizenship already, they can easily enlist in the armed forces.[18] Alexa compared herself to them to spell out the ways she was different: "[Puerto Ricans] try really hard to fit in the society. Me not. They have one advantage: they learn more English than me. In South America, you do not really learn English. In Puerto Rico, you kinda have to. So, instead of talking the proper way, they come here and they talk bad English. To fit in. Like they talk in New York. I see from my sergeant," she continued explaining the difference. "He tries to fit in the Army. He is Puerto Rican. He talks, he has more accent than I do, but he plays with my accent. And I told him a couple of times: 'Sergeant, why do you try to mock me with my accent? You have more of an accent than I do,'" Alexa recalled in good humor.

The other large group in which Alexa was usually placed was Mexicans. In reaction, she struggled to establish a different profile for South Americans as "better immigrants":

If you want to get into this point, there are a lot of differences. We do not speak the same way; we do not look alike. We do not come here in the same way. [Mexicans come] by water, illegal way. Crossing the river. The wet cross—or whatever they call this. The majority get settled in Texas or Arizona, and from there they go. I do not know. I kinda defend them. 'Cause it is hard to get here, and no one treats them well. They do not get paid well. And that is also different. I came and I did not speak so well [English], and I got a good job: $450 [per week]. Lucy, she is Mexican, her first job here was $200 for a week. Because they [Mexicans] do not really push to learn more. They do not try to learn. I am always like that. If I go to a country, I try to speak the language, so I can see and I can have my own rights. I will not be like, "Yes, I will do that." On the other hand, she has been here for twenty-five years, and she speaks funny.

Then she continued: "'Cause she worked with me and . . . when she started she was like h, h, h . . . 'What is she saying?'" Alexa started reproducing the dialogue. "'Can you please tell her,'" she said, mimicking the girl. "'Why don't you tell her?' 'You say it more easily, Alexa.'"

Alexa's attitude toward other "Latino" or "Hispanic" groups was a mixture of compassion and discrimination. In one breath, she accepted the superior English skills of Puerto Ricans and challenged their capacity to use "proper" or formal English. On the one hand, she was sympathetic toward Mexican immigrants' hard lives. On the other, she accused all Mexicans of lacking the drive to better themselves and learn the language of the host country. Her comments exposed Alexa's confusion regarding different migrants' modes of entering the United States, but also reflected her refusal to become like other Latin American migrants. By highlighting the differences between herself and her Mexican and Puerto Rican colleagues and friends, she intended to position herself on a better social level, and she tried to maintain the distinction. To ensure this (assumed) privileged position in the hierarchy, when others referred to her as a "Hispanic" or called her "Latina," she called them out and held her ground, insisting she was "South American." In this way, Alexa engaged in claims of identity recognition. She asked for her identity to be recognized beyond clichés and demanded to be treated equally, that is, not to be mocked by her supervisors. But in spite of her efforts to redress the lack of equality and to claim her own identity, the process escaped her control. Her physical appearance, as well as her accent, always made her battle difficult to win. For Alexa, as for many immigrants, "despite the existence of multiple origins and identities, others often react to only a set of these identities, quite often the aspects of identity that are most visible and are situationally and culturally salient" (Sanchez-Hucles and Davis 2010, 171). Similarly, even if Alexa self-identified as South American, of (white) European descent, she was typically regarded as Latina and an (illegal) immigrant by her peers and by her supervisors, a generalized identification that, for Alexa, ignores her diverse (and European) background.[19]

The self is dialogical (C. Taylor 1994), rooted in culture and a specific community. Hence, if the self is always constructed in relation to others, not recognizing, or misrecognizing, a person's identity deeply affects their core individual existence and fundamental rights as a citizen. As Alexa's identity was not "monological" (C. Taylor 1994), it never depended only on her own self-image but always also depended on how others understood her; when they misrecognized Alexa's identity, her ability to be an equal member of the society was profoundly affected. To restore this precarious balance, she undertook a series of acts through which the others would more easily recognize her as an equal member.

Her story echoes Amaya's concerns regarding Latinos/as serving in the U.S. military. He says that the U.S. military is "presented to the American people as a 'volunteer' Army," which is "often constructed as a liberal institution that *uniformly* distributes the civic responsibility to protect the United States and constructs heroism along the lines of volunteerism" (2007, 4). However, this ideal—he argues—comes at odds with the status the Latinos/as have in the United States, "whose social and cultural marginalization had been manifested in laws that limited citizenship rights in the Southwest during the 19th century" (5).[20]

In contrast to Lily, who was (mostly) identified as white/European, Alexa was often seen as part of the larger Latin American group, and she felt that this surfaced in everyday interactions, impacting her military life and performance. During a phone conversation, she described an incident that had taken place earlier that day. Her sergeant yelled at her and shamed her in front of a whole group, even though Alexa felt that she had done everything "by the book." She further reflected upon the situation: "I am not the right color, [and] I do not want to be one of them," and she bitterly expressed annoyance with what she perceived as unfair treatment, from someone whom she described as "white as bread." As she was recalling her day, she grew sad. She sounded overwhelmed by a feeling of helplessness. She typically did not have this attitude, and the fact that she straightforwardly expressed her feelings showed how deeply she was affected by the situation. This was in fact also the first time she reflected on her skin color.

Alexa never talked about her skin color as an abstract topic of conversation, but as a lived everyday experience. One afternoon, as she was telling me about her African American sergeant, she also reflected on her own race: "And I am . . . in a minority. I am not white and not black. I am in between. 'In between' is a minority. Others see me like that as well." While not learning about racial differences and dynamics in the United States from textbooks, Alexa understood that the term "minority" refers to her. For her, the people who were the least represented were a small number compared to the rest, and therefore a minority. While seemingly unaware of the political usage of the term, Alexa intuitively used "minority" politically, to denote her subaltern position within the U.S. Army. She understood her identity by comparing it to that of others. While she recognized and saw herself as being a part of a larger American, South American, and at times European community, for her peers and supervisors she was a Latina or a Hispanic woman. Their reaction and their view of Alexa partially constructed her identity and made her wonder if she was "the wrong color" and thus a subject of marginalization.

One evening two years into her military service, as we were walking and browsing through the items on the shelves of the Dollar Store in her upstate town, Alexa was sharing with me details about her daily military experience and her interaction with her colleagues. She spoke in Spanish, in a low voice, and began by telling me that while she was at her base, she did not do anything all day long. I asked her about the people with whom she worked, and she raised her right hand in despair and told me that she did not get along with them. "Sometimes, they look at me and say, 'Alexa, *migra, migra!*'" *La migra* is a term used among undocumented urban immigrants meaning "Run! The immigration police are coming!" Since Alexa was clearly not an undocumented immigrant, because she could not have enlisted in the military if she were, the comment seemed misplaced, so I looked at her in surprise. "Yes," Alexa confirmed. "They just want to make a joke, to make fun," she said in English, dismissing their intentions with a gesture.

Alexa took this comment lightly. But it brought to the surface the gap that exists in the American military system between natives and foreigners. It illustrates that no matter how much Alexa tried to identify as a South American, or a person "of the world," she was still thought of as a Hispanic, as possibly an "illegal immigrant," and treated accordingly. This "joke" further underscored the importance of the way in which members of the host country/group identify and act on immigrants' identity.

Alexa began to recognize and be critical of the way she was seen and treated in the United States only when she had become part of the military after being in the country for many years. This is perhaps not surprising. In her civilian life, Alexa occupied a marginal position and accepted it, never arguing against it, because throughout these years, lacking stable legal immigration status, she had limited (if any) claims for recognition. But now, as a U.S. Army soldier, she was eager to voice her views and state her demands for justice. Her claims for recognition create a strikingly different pattern of behavior from the way she acted in her premilitary life. Over the years, whenever we were in social situations where people asked the classic question "What do you do for a living?" Alexa had a hard time admitting that she was a live-in nanny. Instead, she avoided answering and quickly shifted to other topics or engaged in semantic gymnastics saying she was a "caregiver"—a term she heard one of her nanny friends using. Her attitude always made me sad, because I realized that, in spite of all the economic benefits her job brought her, she was uncomfortable with her social position. After her military enlistment, the situation changed drastically. Different from her identifications in private, every time we were in a social gathering, she asked with confidence if there were any "military discounts" and, without bragging, stated that she was a member of the U.S. military. Through her military service, Alexa learned the host country's system and was able to articulate it, asking for social and economic access. Thus, through her military service, Alexa was able to understand herself as a possible equal member, and when her position was challenged or not recognized, she learned to interpret it as an act of injustice and to fight in order to obtain parity.

While not entirely absorbing her American and military identities, or allowing herself to be absorbed by them, Alexa still felt that being identified as a soldier facilitated her adjustment into the host society. For example, she acknowledged that people looked at her differently when she was in uniform. Some praised her courage, while others asked her to quit, but overall, she felt that the uniform made her visible in the eyes of the community at large, and she found these changes empowering. The military uniform has the power to superimpose one identity over others. Identification within the civilian realm with the military uniform endorsed and highlighted Alexa's American soldier identity and placed her immigrant identity in the background. When wearing it, she felt she was on equal footing in the host country.

Overall, Alexa had an ambivalent relationship to her racial and ethnic identity—but so did her host country. She had been determined to be recognized as South American and as an American soldier, and therefore to be treated as an equal member of the host country. In contrast to Lily, who accepted the "ignorance" of others as a way to claim her equal spot, Alexa struggled to combat stereotypes and achieve ethnic recognition. But she was confronted by a system unwilling to accommodate her. As we have seen, identity is dialogical. Thus, no matter how hard Alexa tried to fit in, the host country still found ways to recognize that she was different.

Gender: Alexa as a Female Body within the Military

Typically, literature focused on women in the military (Weinstein and White 1997) looks at gender, gender identity, performance, and social/economic advancement. The story of Alexa brings to view a different but interdependent aspect: the female body and its treatment within a highly organized and masculine institution. War and military training are inscribed in the body, in the form of (educated) muscle memory, which creates a "bodily *habitus*" (MacLeish 2013). To perform as a soldier, one needs to embody this, because any bodily limitations could lead to lack of success as a soldier and thus failure to integrate. Alexa's daily military practices, ready and willing to serve her country, were drastically curtailed by her health condition. In the summer of 2011, she was preparing for a surgery that was covered by the Army medical insurance. This was done in a time when more than 48.6 million people were uninsured in the United States, so having access to decent medical care at an affordable cost was almost a luxury.[21] Alexa knew this firsthand from having lived and worked in the United States for more than a decade, when she had to cover out of pocket the medical costs she incurred. Now that she was a member of the U.S. military, she felt that her situation had changed and that she had achieved (at least partial) social protection.

After approximately one year of military service, in spite of her robust constitution, Alexa's health rapidly deteriorated and she required regular medical care. While her unit was preparing to be deployed, she was taken to Washington, DC, where she was hospitalized—and the military ensured that she received the treatment she desperately needed. Both for her and for the U.S. military, her health was an overriding priority. Her deployment with her unit to war zones was of secondary concern. However, in spite of this care, over the next few months, while she was still under medical supervision, Alexa's health condition worsened. After each intervention, she went back to her new base and started work shortly after. At times, she called me in pain. Her voice was weak and she mainly listened, as talking required too much energy. She constantly felt the need to lie or sit down, but this was not always possible due to her work assignments. Her new medical condition brought to light the challenge Alexa encountered in the military: on the one hand, as a soldier, she was required to perform the assigned tasks relevant to her position; on the other, she had an "Army physical profile" ("Army profile," for short), which detailed her particular condition and outlined her physical limitations. For Alexa, the two assessments often contradict one another, yet not following either one continuously led to "breaking profile," as according to her job description she was required to perform certain tasks prohibited by her doctors and outlined in her "Army profile."[22]

Alexa was often frustrated and acknowledged this issue when she shared with me the absurdity of the situation. Due to her precarious medical condition, she was not deployed to Afghanistan when the rest of her unit left, which meant that she was separated from her group and placed in a new one. This change put her at odds with the members of her new unit, who, according to Alexa, never fully believed that this was the true reason for her not being deployed and instead suspected her of looking for a reason not to join her unit. As a result, she always felt like a stranger. In the following year, when her original unit returned, she rejoined them, only to feel even further alienated. New developments had taken place and new bonds had been formed, and Alexa was not part of them. She made consistent efforts to keep up with her peers, but her body was failing her. Early in 2012, she told me over the phone that she was feeling really sick and preparing to "leave the Army."

When I saw her in March 2012, I was surprised. While she still had a good-humored and optimistic nature, she tired easily and often needed to crash on the bed. Contrary to her usual demeanor, she was silent for long periods of time. When asked "What's the matter?" she would softly reply, "*Me duele* [It hurts]," gently touching the lower right part of her abdomen. I tried to find out more about her medical condition and see if I could be of any help, and she told me that she was taking a lot of pills that had many side effects and that she didn't know what would happen to her. She was still undergoing medical tests and was being kept under routine observation. Even though she never raised her voice, I could see the frustration in her eyes.[23]

Early one afternoon, while I was at her home in upstate New York, Alexa called and said that she would be leaving the base early that day and coming back into town for a medical appointment. Thirty minutes later, dressed in her uniform and with her hair tied back in a perfect bun, she came, picked up her sister and me, and drove us to the clinic. We entered a low office building. The room was filled with people of all ages waiting and filling out forms. There was a young couple with a crying infant son, and some older people with dark glasses, waiting in silence. The room was well equipped, with many chairs carefully arranged in rows. It was crowded and had the same poverty-stricken atmosphere as the rest of the town.

As we were waiting, I finally got a chance to ask her what the checkup was for. She answered that it was an eye exam. One of the side effects of the medication she was taking exposed her to the risk of gaining a lot of weight and gradually losing her eyesight. She had received hormone and cortisone treatment and over the past few months had gained almost twenty pounds. These developments had severe repercussions on her military performance.

The military in general, the U.S. military in particular, has a constant and detailed preoccupation with the body of the soldier. The institution understands that to have qualified troops who can perform at an optimal standard, it is crucial to maintain their physical health, and for this reason, bodily measurements and performance levels are meticulously recorded.[24] Thus, the military creates comprehensive manuals and gives specific instructions on how to identify, categorize, and address physical ailments. Alexa's diagnosis led to her obtaining a note on her "profile"[25] that set limitations to her duties. As maintaining proper weight is also supervised and regulated by the military,[26] Alexa was in danger of "breaking her fitness profile" by gaining weight.

Given the military's concern with each soldier's physical condition, Alexa's change in body mass was bound to attract her supervisor's attention. Sure enough, she was told that she was too big and that she needed to lose weight. But, she explained, another side effect of the medication was that her bones and muscles were atrophying and she could no longer exercise and lose the excess weight. Yet the sergeant did not seem to show any leniency: "You need to lose weight! Your uniform is too tight for you now!" Alexa quoted her supervisor's statement as we were waiting for the doctor to see her.

I looked at Alexa. Her uniform was definitely tight. The material of her pants was stretched across her upper thighs. She looked down and told me she had trouble buttoning them. As she confessed this, she was visibly upset.

It was obvious that she did not like being as big as she was now, but she felt that there was nothing that she could do to change it. "I asked them to let me go to the pool. It would be good for me, and I can exercise and lose pounds. But they do not let me. One day I took my sister and we went. Yes, I was not allowed to do it . . . but I did it." Interestingly, when Alexa broke military rules by going to the pool without permission, it could be seen as an act of resistance, but it was in fact an attempt to engage in a performative act of assimilation into the wider military organization by losing weight and conforming to the institution's strict bodily standards.

A member of the medical staff called her name, and she went in, only to come back in ten minutes. "They told me that I have 25 percent chances to get glaucoma in the next five years . . . And this is the side effect of the medication I got. This is the Army. First, they give you medication, then you have to deal with the side effects. Before I entered the Army, my eyes were fine. Now . . . I also have these eye and back problems." Before we stepped out of the building, she looked at the time. It was 4:15 p.m. "I'll call the sergeant to see if he needs me back." We sat waiting for the sergeant's answer. There was none. Alexa patiently dialed again and tried to reach her unit colleagues. Still no reply. After fifteen minutes, finally, one of her other colleagues answered: the unit had just completed formation, and now all the soldiers were free for the rest of the day. Alexa still did not get a response from the sergeant. She looked at her sister and me. "Let's go home! They are done." We left the clinic and went home, where her sister prepared traditional South American food.

As we were eating, I reflected upon what had just happened. As Alexa was "away from the eye of power" (Scott 1985), unseen by the military and in the presence only of her sister and me, she vented her frustration with the situation at the base. When it came to returning to the base to do her job, she did not bluntly reject it, but she "dragged her feet" (Scott 1985); she took the maximum time possible to perform the task until she reached the time limit for returning, and therefore there was no way she could be expected to go back to the base. She succeeded in getting her way, while she was seemingly obeying the rules.

Having medical insurance and receiving the medical care she needed while being integrated into a large system was a great achievement in Alexa's life. However, due to her medical problems, she felt that she was pushed to one side and was not fulfilling her promise in her career. When asked what she did at work, she always said, "I get there and I sit. Most of the time. Yes.

I am not allowed to do much, so I sit." She would rather have worked on a plane, or even volunteered at the library, but because her physical profile did not specifically mention any of this, she had to sit and wait. The medical insurance provided by the Army helped her a great deal, but it was not enough. Alexa's complicated health situation needed further attention and support, neither of which seemed to be available, pointing out the limits of an overstretched and underresourced military care-delivery system (MacLeish 2013).

Alexa: Gender Identity and Military Life

Just like Lily, Alexa rarely directly addressed her gender. She reflected neither on her gender nor on the gendered dynamics she entered. Once I asked her about gender in the military, to which she briefly answered, "Do not get me started," and changed the subject. Just as in Lily's case, my understanding of Alexa's gender came primarily from the dynamics I witnessed.

Even though she did not openly acknowledge it, Alexa entered the gender dynamics of the host country even before she decided to immigrate. When she applied to come to the United States, she found a family in which she could work and took a *doméstica* position serving as a nanny, employment mostly allocated to women. Like many other Latin (South and Central) American immigrants, she started working almost immediately upon landing in the country (Eggerth et al. 2012).[27] Blau, Kahn, and Papps argue that when immigrants come from countries "that have a more traditional division of labor by gender in terms of female labor force participation and fertility rates than the United States," in the host society they will reproduce the gendered dynamics of their home country (2011, 12).[28] Also, according to Ramos, "The gendered division of labour in Latin and Central America is expressed through the concentration of women's reproductive work in the home and gender-specific paid roles and positions, which systematically produce salary differences to the detriment of women" (2012, 399).[29] Within the framework of this scholarship, Alexa would be expected to engage in gender-specific employment, such as *doméstica* work. Research often places the immigrants' source countries at the center, assigning them responsibility for perpetuating gendered hierarchies of power, but this argument does not interrogate whether these hierarchies and divisions of labor would be reproduced if the receiving country did not operate along the same lines. With an ever-shrinking welfare system that has limited programs for child care and education, and in which two-career households are the norm, hiring "domestic servants to accomplish childcare work" (Tronto 2002) is not uncommon. Expected to deliver a "labor of love" (Lerner 2013) and not provide work for fair compensation, *doméstica* employees are mostly women, who are expected to perform in line with the receiving country's gender stereotypes.

Alexa worked as a nanny for several years. Even though the families for whom she worked did not always take care of her or treat her with the respect that an employee deserves, Alexa never challenged them. She readily accepted that work as a live-in nanny was the best she could do, considering her precarious immigration status. Her last job as a nanny lasted a few years and was with the wealthy family in Connecticut I mentioned earlier, the Buicks. The family had a young son, and they ran a family business in New York City, and while she was hired as "help," Alexa did not miss any opportunities to be involved in their work. She hoped that they would notice her and eventually hire her for the company and not for the "house." A few times, she told me that she was doing some "design" project for them, hopeful that this was her big break. But she was never offered any other position. While she was ready to change her "patterns of socialization and organization" (Jones-Correa 1998), she remained a nanny. A year after she left her employment "of love" (Lerner 2013), she went back to see them, dressed in her military uniform, as described above. "You should have seen his face," Alexa said with a laugh, referring to her former employer who opened the door when she rang the bell, only to find Alexa dressed as a soldier. His surprise was not different from many others, because in spite of the growing number of Latinas in the military,[30] immigrant Latinas are not yet part of the symbolic face of the American armed forces.

For Alexa, gender—like her racial/ethnic identity—was not just a box she checked when she enlisted, but a lived experience. And in her case, it was a vivid one. She did not go so far as to claim that "the military controls women and polices gender lines" (Weinstein and White 1997, xviii), and she did not refute or challenge her gender identification, but she complained about how women were seen in the military, referring to her relationships with the other soldiers in her unit. She bluntly stated that in the Army, you have to be a "whore" or a "bitch."[31] She was neither,[32] she said, and this put her at odds with the other soldiers. When I asked her what that meant, she explained that many girls enjoy the attention of the male soldiers and engage in sexual activity quite freely, and this was so common that male recruits learned to expect sex from their female colleagues. Women who would not engage in multiple sexual experiences were thought to be lesbians and expected to adhere to another form of gender identity and dynamics, Alexa further explained.

Alexa had a conservative, rather religious, upbringing, with strict rules about how to behave in her private life. In the decade of our friendship, I saw her dating only one man, and otherwise she mentioned only the ex-boyfriend with whom she first arrived in the United States and one other man whom she was talking to back in Europe. Considering her restrained behavior, it came as a surprise to me when, a few weeks into her initial military training, she called to tell me that she was engaged and that she would be coming to visit me with her fiancé in New York City.

While Alexa's behavior was unexpected on a personal level, in terms of gender dynamics in the military this development should not have come as a surprise. According to Lundquist and Smith, the military is "a surprisingly 'family-friendly' institution" (2005, 1), with a preference for personnel to enter into monogamous relations regulated by the state and, furthermore, by the military. For example, the military exerts power over the recruits' sexuality via control over their living conditions. Unmarried military personnel share rent-free barracks, and if they decide to live off-base, they need to pay their own rent. But married service members, or those with families (that is, children), live off-base with the support of a monthly housing and food allowances. Moreover, married soldiers receive both "higher moving allowances and a family separation allowance" (2).[33] Housing incentives, coupled with economic benefits for families, encourage single recruits to find partners and marry while in the service. While visible in her life (as she lives off-base), Alexa did not mention either of these benefits, but she described her relationship as a complicated love story.

Compared with most of the other native Army soldiers, who typically are between twenty and twenty-four years of age,[34] Alexa was more than ten years older and single at the time of her enlistment. It was during basic training, as she waited in line for food, that her eyes caught those of a young, tall, slim, dark-haired man. His name was Ben, "Benny" to his friends, and he was from a state in the South, had a strong accent, liked guns, and was a newly enlisted soldier, only nineteen years old. When their eyes met, their cultural, linguistic, and age differences melted away, Alexa recalled.[35]

They began to steal moments in one another's company, away from the Army's omnipresent eyes, meeting at the corners of the base and helped by their recently made friends, who facilitated their brief escapades. Just weeks after they met, they decided to get married. They told no one, did the paperwork themselves, took a few hours off, and made their relationship official in the town near their training base. I had never seen her speaking with so much passion about someone. Her eyes lit up, she had a faint smile on her face, and she would look away dreamily, lost in the remembrance of the initial moments of their love.[36]

But due to their military engagements, Alexa and Benny did not have a chance to spend much time together once they were married. Their love story hit the buffers when they were separated right after "basic," with Benny's new base in the Deep South and Alexa's a long way to the north. These months were hard on both of them, yet Alexa spoke with her husband daily and advised him on many aspects of his life. I heard her on the phone with him and was surprised to notice that there was something extremely familiar about her tone. It was firm but kind, giving practical advice and critically engaging with invisible third parties. I stopped and thought about it: Why was it so familiar? Then it dawned on me: it was the same voice Alexa used when speaking to her sister and explaining the American way of life and when talking to the children in her care. Her tone of voice brought back many memories, but also suggested to me that Alexa's ways of being were transferring from one part of her life to another.

A few months into their new marriage, Alexa and Benny grew apart. Alexa tried hard to have them moved to the same base, but all her efforts failed. Yet, in spite of her many unsuccessful attempts, Alexa kept asking for her transfer. This put her at further odds with her unit, whose members thought she was seeking a transfer in order to avoid an imminent deployment. She confessed that her urgent requests for transfer threw a dark shadow on her intentions and her willingness to commit to the Army. This grew even stronger when she received the diagnosis and was declared incapable of deploying, which her unit members saw as suspicious. Several times she told me she felt helpless in a large institution that did not seem to understand or care for her. I asked if she reached out to counselors or other officials who might have helped. She threw her hands up in the air in disbelief and rolled her eyes. She confessed that she had made several attempts, but they were lost through a lack of organization or an unwillingness to help.

Then she added that she reached out to a priest in Benny's unit to act as a counselor and help them with the overwhelming logistical and personal situation. This confession came to me as a surprise. In all the years of our friendship, I had never heard of Alexa going to church for any social or spiritual reasons, but now—in a time of need and searching for a solution—she was reverting to what was familiar from her Catholic background. I listened with interest when she told me that she had seen an interdenominational priest who wanted to meet Benny as well, but that he refused. In any case, she reasoned, the priest was not even Christian: "He was married!" she provokingly told me. "And?" I asked her. She turned her face and looked me straight in the eyes. "How can that be? How can you marry and be a priest?" she asked rhetorically, revealing her mistrust of any man of the cloth who was not a Catholic.[37] This attempt to resolve her marital issues with the support of the Army proved to be futile as well. A few months later, her husband was discharged from the military, and Alexa saw her relationship breaking to pieces. When the situation got to a crisis point and she had no other means of saving her marriage, she took the matters into her own hands. Alexa put her sister in a car and drove south to find her husband and bring him to her home. They lived for several months in a small apartment that they shared with Alexa's younger sister.

Lily and Alexa thus acted in a strikingly similar manner. Although their principal interests were different—Lily wanted to become an officer, and Alexa wanted to be reunited with her husband—both reached out to the military, followed its rules, and filed reams of paperwork. They patiently waited for the outcome. When no word came back to them, they followed up and sought out alternatives. But in both cases, the files were delayed and eventually lost, time passed, and the issues fell apart. Lily reached the age limit for commissioning, and Alexa's husband was discharged. Lily and Alexa tried to carve a path for themselves inside the institution, but in a Kafkaesque manner the institution's slow-moving power structures frustrated and overwhelmed them.

Their defeat begs the question of the role their gender played in the outcome. As we have seen in Lily's chapter, the military is typically thought to be a male institution, modeled on masculine values. Its inherent propensity toward violence, together with its competitiveness and reverence for physical, mental, and technological strength, has created an institution that favors men and male participation. Both Alexa and Lily had difficulty in asserting their views and in accomplishing their goals. Alexa's unsuccessful bid to transfer to another unit might have failed in this way. The officers charged with deciding such claims, faced with her unit's deployment and cuts in training quality and budgets, might have judged the family life[38] of enlisted personnel to be of negligible importance and therefore decided that her request should be quietly dismissed or pushed to one side as not worthy of the attention of the military hierarchy.

* * *

Even though they described their military experiences in great detail, neither Alexa nor Lily talked about their experiences as women in the U.S. military. Of course, being a woman in the Army or Air Force Reserve impacted their experience greatly, but they never discussed it openly. When observing Lily's daily performative practices, I observed her subtle flirting with her male peers to get things done easily, like having her male colleagues get food when she was denied. Also, as we have seen, Alexa—while sensitive to the mechanisms of ethnic and racial discrimination—never expressed overt concern over gender dynamics. Even if this issue was not directly addressed, being a woman placed Alexa in delicate situations: her female body defeated her career plans in the Army and placed her in medical care, took her out of deployment, and often limited her mobility. While Alexa was a pioneer in joining the American military as a first-generation immigrant of South American descent, she was similar to many other immigrant women who challenge gendered dynamics and enter male-dominated fields (Morales and Saucedo 2015).[39]

While in the United States Alexa first found employment in the female-dominated field of *doméstica* work, she subsequently enlisted in a more masculine field. In contrast to Lily, whose experience of being a woman in the armed forces was mostly a positive one or one she accepted with ease, Alexa's gender identity (accompanied by her class identity and ethnicity/race) gave her the opportunity to mainstream her position and get married. Lily found ways to avoid deployment by engaging in more "feminine" fields like education. Alexa was eager to pursue everything the military had to offer, even hoping to be a pilot or an airplane engineer, but was prevented from realizing these opportunities.

Conclusion: Return to Civilian Life

At the end of August 2012, due to her worsening medical condition, Alexa received an honorable discharge from the military. In late October of the same year, she became a U.S. citizen. On becoming a civilian, she set to work to improve her economic standing and was still dreaming of obtaining an

American university degree. One day before her naturalization ceremony, Alexa stopped by my apartment. She was exhausted from walking around the city, doing interviews, and filling out paperwork, so she crashed on my bed. I asked her about a job she was applying for, and she told me it was to be a security guard and that she would be paid twenty dollars an hour. "It is good," she assured me, adding, "So, I am waiting to see my schedule, and maybe then I can take some college classes. I tried to transfer credits, but they did not want to do it." She lowered her eyes and said in a soft voice: "[The] military failed me on that."

In March 2014, Alexa was an Army veteran. She had been looking for employment for months but was unable to find anything, while still supporting her sister, who lived with her and her husband in an apartment near New York City. For more than a year, I had seen her quite often, after her doctor's appointments. She no longer had to undergo surgery, but she needed a lot of medication and several times ended up in the emergency room. Even though her veteran health insurance was far from perfect, in the midst of so much uncertainty, she was quite relieved that she was covered.

Alexa wanted to be recognized simply as a member of the military or, more precisely, what she imagined the military to be. She was not willing to give in and accept overswiping ethnic identifications. She was proud to wear her military uniform in her civilian life; she used the health services provided by the military and, whenever given the chance, asserted that she was serving in the armed forces. Even when she experienced difficult situations, she kept mentioning the image of the U.S. military she held dear: the perfect institution. Moreover, even though she often engaged critically with her service branch or with her unit, and with the host country, she never criticized the U.S. military as an institution. Nevertheless, when she tried to become a full member of the host country and achieve social mobility and a better education, she realized that the military's support might not be as effective as she had imagined. Her admission that "the military failed me on that" sounds like an overwhelming defeat. Just like Lily, she did not engage in further criticism but accepted the status quo—even though it was far from perfect.

Dealing with a serious health issue, her characteristic and unbridled optimism shone through as Alexa still struggled every day to fulfill the military's promise. From the position in which the intersection of her gender, race/ethnicity, and class placed her, Alexa had limited access to social justice. Thus, health care, education, and access to economic resources were still not in her immediate reach. Alexa learned a lot about the new system and tried to make the best of it. Her life journey sheds light on the process of "naturalization" via the military and indirectly underlines the strengths and the weaknesses of this powerful American institution. In spite of the U.S. military's promise of equality and its focus on individual capabilities, Alexa's visible race/ethnicity, gender, and class impacted her transition from being an immigrant to being a soldier, a veteran, and an American.

The divergent points in the stories of Lily and Alexa reveal the different ways in which immigrant soldiers access membership in the host country. Both are stories of success and failure. Lily was able to use the GI Bill to obtain an American master's degree, further her career, and join the middle class. While she was not able to pursue a higher military career and become an officer, her story was marked by military recognition and economic accession. Alexa was successful in attaining recognition of her identity outside of the military, but she struggled for recognition within the institution. While in her civilian life people related to her through military symbols such as the uniform, which made her ethnic identity recede, in the Army she still faced misrecognition of her identity, which revealed the tensions still present regarding ethnicity.

In Lily's experience, ethnic differences, which create a certain social hierarchy in civilian life, were (mostly) obliterated in the military. Simultaneously, within the military environment, she accessed different parts of a career that she found inaccessible in her civilian life because she was not an American (in spite of her citizenship status) and because she had an accent. For Alexa, enlisting in the military led to a dramatic downturn in her personal economic circumstances, and she engaged in performative practices of assimilation in the lower economic (North) American class. While her gender did not seem to impact her military enlistment, it became an obstacle when she could no longer perform her solider duties.

Alexa's path from being a foreigner to a soldier to an American was marked by her ambivalence toward becoming like the other members of the host country, and she often rejected any resemblance between herself and them. Her eagerness to succeed socially, academically, and economically was driven by her aim to improve her life and the lives of her immediate family. Even though many of these dreams remained unfulfilled, through her numerous and diverse practices, Alexa succeeded in carving out a place for herself in the host country while also aiding her family.

Finally, Alexa's story shows that neither money nor social status is enough on its own to access the benefits of society. A combination of both (and more) is needed. Alexa was aware of this and put it bluntly: "I am just part of the group that wants to get something from the military. The one which wants to take advantage of the military," she laughed. "A lot of people want to go study, and for that they want to go to the military, just for the length of the study. That is it."

CHAPTER 4

Vikrant

Who Is Vikrant?

I first met Vikrant on a windy fall day in 2009. We had arranged to meet in Manhattan, where he was visiting friends and putting the finishing touches to the paperwork he needed for his military enlistment. As I approached the busy intersection at Forty-Second Street and Eighth Avenue, I saw him from far away: an Indian man with dark hair and dark eyes, of slim build and medium height, wearing a blue sports jacket (two sizes too big) and an army backpack. I introduced myself and asked him what he wanted to do that day. He told me that he would like to see Ground Zero, which at the time, eight years after 9/11, was still under construction and was a vibrant tourist attraction. We took the blue subway line and headed downtown, and as we emerged from the underground we were surrounded by a crowd of tourists and commuters. Vikrant immediately took out his small camera and, holding it high above people's heads, snapped several photos. We walked slowly around, he read the inscriptions on the memorial plaques, and then we left. Later that day, he had to take a bus back to Washington, DC, where he was living at the time. Before he left, we sat in a small coffee shop at the New York Times building and talked for some time. He seemed a shy man, comfortable speaking only when he was talking about familiar things.

Throughout our research relationship, which continued for years on the phone and online, he displayed the same personality: cheerful but slightly timid—though, once he was at ease with the person he was talking to, he would engage in long monologues, happy to describe his daily life. I came to know him because a few months prior to our meeting in New York City, an article in the newspaper reported on the Army's swearing-in ceremony for a group of recruits consisting entirely of immigrants. The event took place in the middle of Times Square, in the presence of both a general from the Pentagon and the colonel who initiated the program that allowed Vikrant and other immigrants to join the Army. Upon reading the article, I contacted the author, who was generous with his time and put me in touch with one of the immigrant soldiers who had participated in that ceremony. Shortly afterward, I contacted Vikrant by phone. We also connected on social media, and for the next couple of months, we spoke regularly. Although I had not yet met him in person, our long conversations enabled me to get to know Vikrant rather well. He often spoke of his desire to become an Army man, about how hard he worked to integrate himself in this way, and the bureaucratic challenges he encountered. As time went by, when he started his "boot camp" and later when his specialized military training began, our conversations grew less frequent. Less than a year after we first met, he deployed to Iraq, where he was stationed for almost a year. During that time, we had little direct contact, but I was able to follow him and stay connected on social media.

These connections took place when social media was still considered an unusual form of academic work, and taking this road for analysis was considered hazardous research. However, this risky road allowed me to enter the "field" and the "front lines" together with Vikrant. Since, this method has been mainstreamed. For example, it was used to analyze new media habits, soldiers' attitudes, and their behaviors of troops on the ground, while in deployment in Iraq and Afghanistan (Silvestri 2015).[1]

Like many Indians of his generation (Gadekar, Krishnatray, and Gaur, 2012), Vikrant was a prolific poster on social media, so I was able to keep up with his life. I decided to reproduce the entries verbatim, even when his style and grammar were questionable, which might create some difficulties in reading the text. His passion for online communication started back in India, years before he joined the U.S. military, and he continued to participate in online forums after he moved to the United States. He often posted his own opinions and thoughts, shared pictures, commented on other people's views, and tried to widen his social circle and group of acquaintances. Vikrant's deployment interrupted our communication by telephone, but these social forums nevertheless allowed me to "see" him and tell his life story in his own voice, by putting together thousands of threads he created over time.

A Glance into a Life: Vikrant

In the following pages, I will present how Vikrant's life changed upon his enlistment in the U.S. armed forces. Joining the military meant achieving the integration he had been working for and which he had not been able to attain as a civilian. In a short period, he went through several dramatic changes: he reshaped his body, altered the way he spoke and wrote, changed his social circle, and rearticulated his political views. In contrast to Alexa and Lily, he found it quite easy to establish himself within the predominantly masculine institution of the U.S. military, and he was content with it. But as in Lily's and Alexa's cases, his ethnicity and race made him stand out. In spite of his willingness to immerse himself in the ways of his new country, his race/ethnicity kept him at a distance from his fellow recruits within the military community. Another thing that made Vikrant different from the majority of enlisted recruits was that he had several graduate degrees at the time of his enlistment as an E4 soldier, including one from an American Ivy League institution. Given his education, it would be expected to find him in a superior economic bracket. But at the time he enlisted, Vikrant had not yet advanced to an elevated economic and social level. His financial standing was closer to that of his American-born fellow enlistees than that of typical Indian immigrants to the United States.

Leaving in the Home Country: The Journey to the Ivy League

As in the case of the other two participants, Lily and Alexa, Vikrant's life story started in a land far from where he currently serves and pledges allegiance. When we met, Vikrant was forty years old. He came from Jaipur, in the state of Rajasthan, northern India, and was born a Hindu of a high Brahmin caste. While his parents were separated, and he spent most of his childhood years with his mother and siblings, Vikrant mentioned his father a great deal, referring specifically to how his father's high level of education and career in the Indian military served as a model for his life.

Vikrant told me during early interviews that he was not close to his relatives back in India, even proudly saying that this set him apart from typical Indian immigrants who "tend to be more connected to 'home'" (Chakravorty, Kapur, and Singh 2016, xiii). He had not returned to India since first arriving in the United States and—unlike most Indian immigrants—did not make regular contact with his family back home. Nevertheless, even though he emphasized the weakness of his connection to his family and friends,[2] he was proud of his past and shared it with the world via social media. On social media he posted old pictures of his family, including his grandmother, father, mother, and siblings. The picture of his grandmother was taken by a professional photographer, probably on a set. It showed her in profile, dressed in the white sari usually worn by older widow women, with her white hair flowing over her shoulders, partially covered by a white shawl. She was sitting cross-legged, wearing large dark-framed glasses, and looking slightly to one side. Her old, frail body resonated with dignity and calm. Next was a black-and-white picture of his young parents: Vikrant's mom wore a decorated sari, with hair pulled back and a *bindi*, a red dot in the middle of the forehead; his father stood next to her, taller and slim, wearing a light shirt and dark pants. He looked strikingly like Vikrant. An old black-and-white picture, much deteriorated due to the passage of time, showed Vikrant at three years old, a beautiful young boy sitting and smiling while looking away from the camera. His clothes, a striped shirt and a pair of dark pants, made him look like a small adult. He was sitting cross-legged on the floor, with bare feet, next to his young sister, who was flipping through a coloring book. The next picture Vikrant decided to share was one of a teenager, Vikrant's brother, wearing his hair relatively short, with a light shirt unbuttoned at the top, looking straight at the camera as if posing for an ID. These pictures provided a glimpse into Vikrant's past, of a family to whom he was no longer close. Another set of pictures showed Vikrant in college and as a young adult. He grew tall and slim and was wearing his dark hair in an irregular cut, always with a thin mustache covering his upper lip. He made these online posts, with pictures and captions, many years after arriving in the United States. They show his pride in his Indian past and exhibit a certain nostalgia for those days.

The India that Vikrant represented in these images and his posts was an India of fairy tales. The mountains he hiked were high and cold; crossing them required a certain amount of determination. But for young Vikrant and his friends, these trips were moments of adventure, perseverance, and joy. One of the albums on his social media page compiled old and faded pictures showing Vikrant and two other men on a hiking trip—the color pictures were discolored, taken with an old film camera. The three boys were in their twenties, slim, with dark short hair, and the pictures followed them as they hiked the trails in the highest mountains, unveiling a beautiful setting. One image showed a large valley richly covered in abundant vegetation, a gorgeous display of sunlight, and Vikrant, shirtless, lying in a bed of grass. Another showed Vikrant and his friends inside a house with an old, humble interior. "There is no light. Ever. See lamp," Vikrant explained in his comments referring to the lack of electricity. There were five beds jammed close to the walls, covered with old blankets of different colors. Vikrant was in an oversize jacket, wearing a large and slightly ill-fitting woolen hat; he was sitting on a bed covered by an old blanket at the end of a room holding an oil lamp in his hand. Hunched over, next to one of his friends and shyly looking up to the camera, Vikrant seemed to have sprung from antiquity for his appearance—slim figure, prominent cheekbones, dark mustache, and oversize clothes. In his extensive blog posts, Vikrant wrote with care and pride of those times. All these references pointed to the strong connection Vikrant still felt with his past, his country of origin, and its people.

During our interviews, Vikrant recalled being a young man and going to school. He proudly said that, while in India, he received a good and affordable education and excelled in all subjects, and he mentioned that his early academic successes, along with his father's example, propelled him to pursue higher education. After finishing high school, Vikrant went straight to college and in 1994 obtained a BS in economics from a prestigious university in Delhi; then he completed an MBA degree from the Hindu Institute of Management. His educational background enabled him to continue his studies and also return home and teach at his father's school. For four years, he "worked in diverse capacities, including teaching English and practical science to various classes and handling educational administration" (Vikrant's PhD application).

As we will see in more detail later, while Vikrant was beginning his career in education in India, he was simultaneously exploring options for work or study outside of India. He went to Internet cafés, patiently looking for options to continue his studies abroad, and soon after, like many other Indian immigrants from a high caste and with at least a medium level of wealth, embarked on life abroad as a student at a prestigious university. Indians' immigration to the United States has been well documented in studies of the diaspora (Kapur 2010; Chakravorty, Kapur, and Singh 2016; Rangaswamy 2000), racial discrimination (Gonzales 2020), gender (S. D. Dasgupta 1998), and integration (Bacon 1996; Chandrasekhar 1984; Fenton 1988; Jensen 1988; Kamath 1976; LaBrack 1988). In addition to the standard differentiation within immigrant groups—such as first versus later generations, male versus female, educated against uneducated—Indian immigrants also divide along other lines: according to place of origin, language, religion, or caste.[3] Placing Vikrant on the Indian immigrant map is only a small drop in the vast pool of knowledge of a rich and diverse community.[4]

Enlistment in the U.S. Military: Struggling to Become an American

Vikrant's coming to America was part of a large[5] Indian migration movement that took place after 1965,[6] and is considered the third wave of Indian migration[7] to have spread across U.S. territory.[8] In addition to earning advanced degrees in the United States[9] and striving to obtain lucrative jobs,[10] Indian immigrants tend to place a strong emphasis on social network connections, within and beyond their ethnic community (Poros 2004; Bott 2013; S. Dasgupta 1992; Bhattacharya 2011). According to Helweg and Helweg, Indian immigrants "realize that to get ahead they must seek help from a mentor as they actively cultivate relationships with people of power and authority. They realize that they have to excel individually, but they also know that to get anywhere they have to be noticed by those in power" (1991, 152). Vikrant worked on his social connections and became friendly with another Indian immigrant, who helped him obtain his U.S. visa and later on became something of a mentor. Similarly, when Vikrant ran into problems with his paperwork after enlisting in the military, he reached out to the commander who had initiated the enlistment program—he had met her briefly at the enlistment ceremony. She intervened on his behalf and helped Vikrant resolve his immigration status.

Vikrant is "both typical and atypical [of his] racial, ethnically and religious group" (Joshi 2006, 12),[11] and in his efforts to remain in the United States, he not only attempted to shape a career for himself, but also made a careful study of the legal system, as is evidenced from a number of his online posts. He found ways to get ahead without breaking any rules. Like many other members of his immigrant community, he acquired an American educational qualification and tried to obtain a job. In contrast to most Indians who relocated to the United States between 1995 and 2015 as a part of the so-called IT Generation with "specialized skills in . . . information technology" (Chakravorty, Kapur, and Singh 2016, xii), Vikrant held his main degree in education, and so he could not access the entrepreneurial networks of the Indian diaspora. Finding a job in his field proved to be harder than he first envisioned.

After completing his American graduate studies, Vikrant had to make the difficult decision that international students always face: Should he return to his home country or remain in the new country? After receiving their degree, international students in the United States have the option of staying and working legally for a period of twelve months under the Optional Practical Training (OPT) provision.[12] This is granted to facilitate international students' work within their field of study and to enable them to gain experience before returning to their home country. In reality, the period is typically used by international students and American employers to start the hiring process and possibly to apply for an extended right to work (a work visa, typically H1B) when the OPT expires. Vikrant took this opportunity and started working for a tutoring company. This employment paid him a salary barely above minimum wage. When his OPT provision expired, Vikrant expressed his desire to stay in the United States, and the company applied for an H1B work visa[13] on his behalf. Obtaining a U.S. work visa may seem a straightforward way to immigrate legally to the United States, but in reality the process is filled with economic and legal obstacles. This is a disquieting time for applicants. The application process is an expensive and lengthy endeavor for an employer, because it typically requires the support of a legal firm well versed in proving that the candidate meets the exigent requirements outlined by the U.S. government with respect to that specific job. And if all of this is not enough to put people off, after obtaining the U.S. government's approval the applicant has to apply for a physical work visa, which is issued only outside of the United States at U.S. embassies and consulates. Whether you succeed in getting this visa stamped in your passport can be random, a mere game of chance, because a visa officer can still reject an application even if it has already been approved.

For Vikrant, obtaining his H1B visa was a strenuous and stressful process, which he documented thoroughly on social media, where he wrote about every step of the application procedure and deliberated about which solution was suitable for him. He discussed it with other Indian immigrants in online forums and conducted extensive online research. When he finally got his documents in order, he made an appointment at the U.S. consulate in Toronto, Canada, to obtain his H1B visa.[14] Vikrant detailed his experience, which brought different aspects of his situation into view. It demonstrated how thoughtful he was in understanding and complying with the host-country immigration system, detailed how precarious his situation was and how likely it was that he would lose his right to legally reenter the country and remain and work there, and showed that, once he obtained his visa, Vikrant was eager to be seen as a successful member of his immigrant community, able to advise immigrant novices who might be undergoing a similar process.

Throughout this process, Vikrant fought an uphill battle to control everything in his power. He was aware of the consequences of a possible visa rejection and committed to leaving nothing to chance. He prepared for the interview at the embassy by gathering together every legal document he imagined could be needed and took great care as to how he presented himself by trying to improve his physical appearance. In his blog, Vikrant started by describing his wardrobe: "I ironed my only full-sleeved white checked (Raymonds Rs 300) shirt I had brought and the black pants," he said, describing the clothes he bought at a chain store selling men's clothing back in India. "I was told by my host and her mother [that is, the family that hosted him in Canada before the visa interview] that the all American tie (with stars and stripes—I bought it in DC—3 for $10) was too inappropriate and recommended I wear a gray patterned one. . . . I decided to wear an inner warm vest under the shirt—and a windcheater on top," he continued. His desire to present himself as a part of the host country and attuned to its culture made him want to wear the most obvious symbol of the nation—the U.S. flag—on his body in the form of a Stars and Stripes tie. His anxiety about succeeding in the interview blinded him to the fact that this might be seen as an unnecessary performance act that could provoke the suspicions of U.S. Department of State officials.

Anxiety about the visa procedure touched every fiber of his being. His worries hounded him in his sleep, filling his nights with vibrant nightmares.

> I could not sleep nearly all night (my cellphone was set for 3 alarms—at 6:30 a.m., 6:45 a.m., and 7:00 a.m.) so did not need more than one alarm and kept waking up all night. (Even had a nightmare where a calf in

someplace near Jaipur is biting my arm—and stopping me from racing
on to some school in some village near there. The previous night I had
a dream that somehow I am at Jaipur School and talking to a student's
parent—of 2005 batch—and suddenly I look at my watch and lo! it is
already 8:40 a.m.—and then I remember I have to rush for the visa interview—the US consulate building at vancouver appears [in a dreamy way]
to be located in downtown Jaipur—in my mind. So I rush outside—how
will I get there. Oh!! then I see my red, chrome and black bullet enfield
parked under the tree in front of my house. Does it still work after my
two year stay in the US? So confusing—all mixed up—across time and
space. That was the end of [that] terrifying dream of last night. (blog)

The fretful fear that he might not be able to return to the United States
was reflected in the incoherence of his dreams and his storytelling and
made his perilous situation all too visible. Vikrant's entire life was unfolding
in front of his eyes, and he was aware that he had only a minimal role in
controlling it. Once inside the U.S. embassy, he tried his best to cope with
the unnerving situation. He set out to take in every piece of information by
studying the people working in the embassy and the office building—and
the procedures involved. Finally, he met the visa officer. Vikrant transcribed
this interview verbatim and posted it on his blog. During the interview, he
complied with all of the officer's requests; he showed respect, even obedience, understanding the power of the man standing before him. His attitude
was in fact analogous to that of many others seeking American visas. The
modus operandi of embassies' agents of power is often overwhelming for the
applicants. The construction of these official U.S. government settings—the
uniforms, the weapons, the security, the physical structure of the institution,
and the impersonal language—establishes and maintains a clearly unequal
balance of power. This visible, palpable power structure creates the feeling
that anything, any abrupt gesture or thought, could set off a disturbance
and lead to drastic repercussions.

Like Vikrant, many people attempting to come to the United States
have nightmares, wake up early, check their documents twice, and go to the
embassy much sooner than necessary. In Romania the line in front of the
embassy used to form at midnight. People lined up and slept on the cold
pavement, just to get the chance to interview for a visa.

This instance described in detail illuminates the effect of the power networks that connect embassies, consulates, and border facilities. Such institutions divide the world starkly in two: one half (the immigrants or visitors)

asking for admission and the other granting or denying entry. During encounters with officials, foreigners do not describe themselves in a positive manner. Instead, they have to make sure they have dispelled any suspicion about potentially criminal acts—for example, that they stayed in the host territory for longer than they were permitted or tried to find unauthorized employment. There is also the matter of the visa officer's authority.

Vikrant understood these power dynamics and knew that he had to counter any possible concerns as to his intentions. When the officer asked him: "So where will you be working now?" he replied, "At Washington, DC. Potomac." When the officer followed up by asking: "Do you mean Washington state?" Vikrant interpreted this question as "a trap" (as he described it in his blog) and promptly responded: "I mean Washington, DC—Potomac in Maryland, actually." It might well be that the U.S. officer's question was genuine; nevertheless, Vikrant's belief in the "traps"—imagined or real—compelled him to perform specific acts aimed at proving his obedience.

He successfully avoided the "traps" set by the immigration system, and his work visa was approved. What is particularly remarkable about this situation is that Vikrant was able to access the legal immigration system without the aid of a lawyer. His in-depth research and his online network involving members of the Indian diaspora gave him a good understanding of American immigration legislation and enabled him to be well prepared, which ensured his success. After he completed the interview, Vikrant focused his efforts on detailing the process on social media forums in order to help other Indian immigrants applying for this type of visa, and this is where I found his story told in detail. After he received his H1B visa, Vikrant returned to the United States and started working in an educational nonprofit organization, a job he seemed to enjoy, although it paid him only fifteen dollars an hour. The pictures from this time showed an apparently rather shy and isolated Vikrant, eager to pose with his colleagues in the office even though they appeared restrained around him. His blogs did not comment about his social life or about the friends he was making. The image of Vikrant at this time is of someone eager to assimilate to his new environment, whose keenness to engage is met by others with a degree of reticence. He was similar to Lily and Alexa in that throughout his premilitary life, in spite of his efforts to be recognized as a full member of the host country and make a stable life while assimilating both socially and economically, he could not make ends meet and was still seen as "the other."

Vikrant often tried to distance himself from his immigrant ethnic community, which proved a tricky process. During our interviews, he described himself as being out of the ordinary as an Indian immigrant, in that he did not enter the host country to study engineering or computers—he was obviously an "outlier." He accepted that his unusual educational background was not shared by many Indian immigrants to the United States and emphasized that his interest was in teaching and learning rather than the more lucrative fields—such as IT or business—preferred by his compatriots. For Vikrant, this choice was emblematic of his unique character, which he linked with his decision to enlist in the U.S. military, another choice rarely made by first-generation Indian immigrants.[15]

During our talks, Vikrant proudly told me that he was not choosing a field of employment typical of immigrants or of Indians in the United States when he decided to enlist in the military.[16] Even though Vikrant often mentioned that "tradition and family" inspired his enlistment, military service was not his first choice. Like Alexa and Lily, his aim was to get a legal job, but in contrast to them, he had to find a way to stay in the United States that enabled him both to make a living and to pay back his student loans.

He mentioned these reasons during our many conversations and also shared them in various online posts: "I applied for jobs in the U.S.: in Hawaii, Alaska. . . . I applied [even] for jobs in Africa. In 2005, I graduated and I applied. I did not get any of these jobs." His willingness to look far and wide in order to find employment was matched by his desire to explore the world: "I want to travel. I do not want to be seen as a guy who gets a job, makes money. I do not want *to be seen as a stereotype*," Vikrant told me in June 2009, just a couple of months after he was sworn in. His decision to enlist in the U.S. military, like that of Lily and Alexa, was not motivated by civil or political ideals or by an appetite for adventure, as many supporters of military enlistment argue.[17] His choice was fueled by many seemingly divergent reasons. First, as mentioned above, he sought to strengthen his ties with his family abroad; second, just like Alexa and Lily, Vikrant saw military service as a viable source of employment. Just like Alexa, he did not mention this reason directly, but it was revealed when he talked about his failed search for civilian employment. When his hope of succeeding in making a life in the United States drastically diminished, enlisting in the Army offered him both a job and American citizenship, thus opening up (or at least promising to open up) his economic and social opportunities. Thus, in line with Mittelstadt's (2015) argument that contemporary military service supplements free-market employment opportunities, Vikrant turned to the Army as a means of obtaining a job, when he could not find a viable employment option in civilian life. He was hopeful that in the military he would gain stable employment and the possibility of a career and travel abroad. Furthermore, Vikrant's decision to enlist was further motivated by his desire to become an American. He wanted to cement his legal belonging to the host country by obtaining U.S. citizenship.

During our first telephone interviews, Vikrant was enthusiastic about this new development in his life, and he was always full of energy and happy to tell me about his most recent accomplishments. Soon after he enlisted, he embarked upon the process of changing his legal status—he used his work visa status to enlist in the MAVNI program and to apply directly for citizenship, bypassing the "permanent residency" requirements. "Naturalization" in the civilian realm entails becoming a permanent resident alien (that is, a green-card holder) for at least five years prior to being eligible to apply for naturalization as an American citizen. However, through the MAVNI program, recruits are able to go from nonresident alien status directly to U.S. citizenship within as little as three months. While Lily and Alexa were already permanent residents when they enlisted in the armed forces, Vikrant was officially on a nonimmigrant (H1B) visa that required him to leave the country at the end of his employment. From a legal perspective he was "an alien," "a foreigner," but one who could serve in the military and defend the nation. The military offered him a quick path to U.S. citizenship, but during this process Vikrant was confronted with a rigid bureaucratic system.

To apply for U.S. citizenship, Vikrant had to pass a background check and be fingerprinted at his local immigration office, so he went to a local office in Washington, DC. But his application was denied. During a phone conversation, he explained to me that the staff were not familiar with the MAVNI program and recent changes in immigration rules issued by the Pentagon, and therefore they were not able to accommodate him. Vikrant was not frustrated by this turn of events. Instead, he was amused and proud, because he understood that his position was unusual and that very few people were becoming U.S. citizens via military service. Faced with this administrative obstacle, he was resourceful. He contacted the colonel who had created the MAVNI program, whom he had met earlier, and with her help he was able to apply for a change of status with no further difficulties.

Vikrant understood that by enlisting in the U.S. military, he could access a quick path to American citizenship and a U.S. passport. In contrast to Alexa, who believed that traveling on a U.S. passport represented a possible threat to her security, Vikrant saw U.S. travel documents as a guarantee to free entry in many countries. "You can get a post in Italy, Germany, or Japan, wherever the Army is," Vikrant excitedly told me during a phone interview, imagining his deployment in the European countries that have U.S. military bases. "The people in the Army, they can get to wherever they like. I do not want to be here [that is, on U.S. territory] for four years. Now I am stuck here because I have a visa. So, even if I stay in a small town, I get an [American] passport and I get mobility," he told me during a phone interview in 2009. For most Indian nationals, traveling abroad is a complicated endeavor. Like citizens of the Central African Republic, Chad, and Timor Leste, as of 2009 they had a visa-free entry in only 37 countries. By contrast, U.S. citizens enjoy visa-free entry to 155 countries, more than a fourfold difference (Naujoks 2012b). Vikrant's love of travel echoed that of Alexa and Lily. All three hoped to further their exploration of the world via military service. However, though shortly after enlisting he envisioned going to western Europe and completing his boot-camp training there, like many of his peers, he was in fact deployed to the front line in Iraq.

Vikrant was one of the first immigrants to join the MAVNI program. Unlike in his civilian life, where officials such as the visa counselor in the Toronto embassy, who doubted his education, experience, and overall intentions, were unwelcoming, recruitment officers and military leaders accepted him with open arms. Vikrant rapidly became the poster boy of the MAVNI program. He had a master's degree from an (American) Ivy League university, was of Indian origin and thus spoke multiple languages deemed vital by the Army, and was eager to fit into the military community. Military leaders applauded his choice, the mass media surrounded him at the enlistment ceremony (putting his name in one of the world's most prestigious newspapers), and the magazine of his former American school also interviewed him. He was on top of the world and very grateful.

Vikrant's Military Experience through Performative Practices

For Vikrant, the transformation from being "an alien" to being an American soldier took place through formal and informal training. His formal training is visible in the transformation of his body and in learning the values and ideology of the group; informally, he was educated through relationships with other members of the military. Just as when he was a civilian, after becoming a soldier Vikrant continued to engage in practices intended to demonstrate that he belonged to his new community. One of the most remarkable of these performers was changing the way he spoke after his military enlistment. My first encounters with Vikrant took place over the phone. While he was well spoken, with an educated mannerism and vast vocabulary, I had a hard time understanding him. During the first few months, depending on his schedule and general availability, we talked on the telephone once or twice a week. His Indian accent was strong, and his manner of speaking was rather fast. He jumped from one subject to another and was generous with details, which made the conversations thought provoking but difficult to follow.

After a few months of military service, however, Vikrant's manner of speech changed significantly. This transition was apparent in his online posts, as well as in our interviews. His online entries changed both quantitatively and qualitatively. His statements became shorter and firmer. As early as the beginning of 2010, a few months after beginning active duty, Vikrant posted comments about his "buddies," whom he often called "bro," in distinct contrast to his earlier civilian way of speaking, when he used to address people—especially colleagues, family, and friends—by their first name. In addition, consistent with this new form of speech was his novel way of shortening words in the typical style of texting—"r u drunk?" or "u r rite?"—signaling a change in his social environment.

One of the benchmarks of Indian immigrants' assimilation is a "greater familiarity with English" (Chakravorty, Kapur, and Singh 2016, xix), but English, like any other language, is not monolithic. While Vikrant's formal English was good even before he enlisted, enabling him to perform well in academic and professional settings, his informal English set him apart. But in the military, he learned the vernacular and was eager to employ it.

When we resumed our phone interviews after he came back from his deployment, Vikrant's voice was clearer, and his accent, while still distinguishable, was no longer an impediment to our communication. His voice was firm, and he spoke quietly. He paused for a long time and waited patiently for my questions. If, by any chance, we started speaking at the same time, he immediately reacted and apologized, allowing me to speak first. This change in how he used language meant Vikrant could adjust better to both professional and more casual environments; it also gave him the flexibility to vary his vocabulary and syntax depending on the circumstances. On the one hand, these linguistic practices enabled Vikrant to perform professionally in the military and avoid unnecessary conflicts; on the other, they allowed him to adjust better socially and to reinforce his social ties to the host country.

This change in his way of speaking reverberated further in his interactions with others. Prior to his enlistment his social media interactions were mainly with members of his ethnic community—people back home or members of the Indian diaspora. But now Vikrant widened his social media connections to include more native-born Americans and military folk. A year after his enlistment, people in his old social circle reacted in awe: "Hi Vikrant, it seems you are a creature from another world, not the one whom we knew," one of his friends from India remarked: "Wow, Congratulations!!! proud of you Man!! now the real Man!!" another stated in surprise. But Vikrant kept his replies to these enthusiastic appraisals of his newfound identity and masculinity short, rarely initiating conversations with Indians. Instead, he was eager to converse with and talk about his new military "buddies": "We have gotten to know each other pretty well here and impressions have changed. I have grown to respect the skills and attitudes of 18-year-old 'battle buddies,' some of whom have helped in family trade—like my battle buddy—and through his earnings bought 8 different motorbikes in 2 years. . . . Here all in the infantry are guys," he wrote on his social media. This post, not unlike many others he displayed during this time, makes his transition clear. He simultaneously acknowledged that it took him time to understand and accept his "battle buddies," because they were so different from him, and that they all shared a common identity now. He was a part of a larger group; they were "all infantry now," in spite of their difference in matters such as age, marital status, family background, or educational level.

Vikrant proudly and publicly acknowledged his new membership of the military. In another post, he thanked his "first platoon" for accepting his membership: "Really miss platoon! the first day away from the 1st was a strange feeling. miss my 'Gangster' squad leader—expert in martial arts, street fighting, purple heart winner, speed demon on bikes and all the good things, miss my team leader who lifts twice of what I do, went on 33 hr trip this winter to get married, was at my citizenship oath ceremony, my platoon sergeant and platoon leader both very supportive and Ranger School grads. They say change is the only constant!! Buddies forever!" Through his public display of solidarity, Vikrant emphasized his membership in the new group and distanced himself from the other Indians and from his diasporic networks. When Vikrant uploaded or was tagged in social media pictures showing his nonmilitary adventures with his military buddies, a different dynamic surfaced, for these pictures were quite different from the socially awkward pictures he posted from his civilian life—now all members were posing comfortably, close to one another, and seemed to have been engaged in pleasant activities.

The linchpin of immigrants' incorporation into a new country is obtaining legal status and, ultimately, citizenship. Vikrant's situation differed from that of Lily and Alexa, who already had permanent-resident status when they joined the U.S. armed forces. His temporary work visa limited his employment and his overall career choices. Losing a job meant losing his legal standing in the United States and could lead to deportation. Over the years, he worried a great deal about his immigration status, and so as soon as he could apply for American citizenship, he did so. Five months after his enlistment, he posted on social media, "passed U.S. citizenship interview . . .—rite here at The Infantry School—thanks to the U.S. Army. Oath ceremony on the graduation day." The citizenship ceremony is the formal, solemn way to symbolize one's naturalization. It is an important moment in immigrants' lives, even more so if citizenship is awarded after a strenuous and precarious immigration process like the one Vikrant endured.

Unsurprisingly, Vikrant was excited about his new national membership and was eager to make it public via social media: "Invitation: YOU R INVITED TO ATTEND MY OATH OF NATURALIZATION (CITIZENSHIP) CEREMONY AT 2PM ON MONDAY FEB 1, 2010 AT USCIS BUILDING 595 ALA MOANA BLVD, HONOLULU. They said friends and family are welcome [original spelling and typing]."

Just a day later, after he officially became a U.S. citizen, Vikrant rushed to change his Social Security number to reflect his newly acquired citizenship, and he enthusiastically posted, "Took the Oath! Now doubly ready to fight for the country!! . . . Thanks guys! Ready to vote, serve on the jury and doubly ready to fight for the country!" Vikrant's post reflects his eagerness to participate in all the required citizenship duties. While these are a part of what constitutes being an American, Vikrant regarded them as privileges and wanted others to publicly acknowledge his "double readiness" to fight for the host country.

Like Lily, Vikrant took the symbolic representations of his inclusion seriously. He accepted and behaved according to military ideology, coupled with the national discourse of citizenship; he shared with his social media world his allegiance to and complete alignment with the values officially promoted by the Army: "yes !! I graduated. I AM THE INFANTRY. I AM THE HEART OF THE FIGHT, WHEREVER, WHENEVER . . . I AM PHYSICALLY STRONG, MENTALLY TOUGH AND MORALLY STRAIGHT. As the Infantryman's Creed says [original spelling and typing]."[18] His post was referring to his recent success in becoming a member of the military, which Vikrant acknowledged and identified with through its creed.

Vikrant was aiming to (re)write his story. His fervor to make his assimilation/integration visible was twofold. He had become a full legal member of the host country and a member of its military. It had been possible for him to go from being an "alien" on a temporary work visa to being an American citizen, skipping over the legal residency status necessary for any civilian "naturalization." Some readers might find his enthusiasm a sign of overcompensation for being an immigrant soldier, but the military staff connected with him on social media approved of and supported his behavior.

To establish his sole allegiance to the United States and to mark the split with his Indian citizenship, Vikrant publicly renounced his Indian passport. "Got cancelled Indian passport back today. Now it is official (on FB) that we are going to Iraq—Operation New Dawn!" he posted one year after he became a soldier. In the same post, Vikrant renounced one identity, his Indian citizenship, and emphasized another allegiance, as a soldier fighting for his new country. This eagerness was soon to be seen during his deployment to a war zone.

Renouncing his passport was a measure required by the Indian government; Indians acquiring citizenship elsewhere have to do this,[19] but Vikrant went further than most. He publicly and emphatically announced his renouncement. Furthermore, just like Lily, who used the American flag and the national anthem to perform her membership of an "imagined community" (Anderson 1991), Vikrant adopted informal national emblems, like popular country songs, the commemoration of 9/11, and the World Trade Center—symbols that have the performative power to unite and to divide the world into "us" and "them."

One such song is "Where Were You" by Alan Jackson, which portrays the suffering of the American community during the attacks of September 11:

> Did you burst out with pride
> For the red, white, and blue
> And the heroes who died
> Just doin' what they do?
> Did you look up to heaven for some kind of answer
> And look at yourself and what really matters?
> I'm just a singer of simple songs
> I'm not a real political man

I watch CNN but I'm not sure I can tell you
The difference in Iraq and Iran
But I know Jesus and I talk to God
And I remember this from when I was young
Faith, Hope and Love are some good things He gave us
And the greatest is love.

While deployed to Iraq, Vikrant reflected and posted on his social media account:

This song by Alan Jackson (heard him for the first time while at Infantry School) (http://www.azlyrics.com/lyrics/alanjackson/wherewereyouwhen theworldstoppedturning.html) made me stop the PT and started musing Dr Watson style. Sherlock Holmes perhaps could have guessed that I was thinking about what I was doing when the planes hit WTC Towers on Sep 11 . . . *I was sitting at home watching TV while my mom made tea in the next room. I actually saw the second plane hit the tower. I had just got back from school after working with school-kids—just like the song lyrics* [emphasis added].

Ironically, Vikrant acknowledged that he was not in the United States in 2001 and that his life was not even connected to the country, as he was "going by his day" in India, riding motorcycles, and having tea with his mother. But he failed to see the irony. Instead, he used the memory to refashion the past in the light of the present. Musing on the song, he created a contemporary unity between events disconnected in time. Neither was Vikrant in the country when the 9/11 events took place, nor was he American when the song became popular. Although he was geographically removed and did not belong to the community commemorated in the song, Vikrant used it to create ties and to emphasize his membership as he continued: "I always thought Pearl Harbor attacks were the biggest ones on the U.S. psyche. But this song confirms Sep 11 attacks were even more so. Today I completed a 4 day course on how to catch bad guys and help the good guys. It will be fun! doing the right thing! [original spelling]." The song empowered him not only to reinforce his membership of his host-country community but also to make a statement of his newly adopted values, which divide the world into "bad" and "good" guys. This polarizing division of the world gave Vikrant a sense of security in his identity, as someone doing the "right thing." Through his posts, Vikrant reconstructed history. As Hannah Arendt (2006) and Agnes Heller (2000) put it, he was caught between the past and the future; he reconstructed his past in order to legitimize his current community membership.

Before he enlisted, Vikrant wrote critically about the American educational system in his blogs, raising questions about its practicality. But once he enlisted, his inquisitiveness rapidly subsided, giving way to an eager display of compliance with military and national ideals. His efforts were not futile. If in his civilian life his attempts to demonstrate his community membership were seen as suspicious or misplaced (as in the example above about wearing an American-flag necktie), within the military these exaggerated symbolic performances were welcomed and encouraged by peers and superiors alike. Through his military service, Vikrant found a new voice, and that voice was singing patriotic country songs. He discovered a place in which he could act without being relegated to the margins. While in civilian life he was an outsider, in the military he found a way of asserting his membership of the institution and willingness to belong. But—as we will see next—his desire to assimilate or integrate, to become a full member, was not enough. While military leaders welcomed him with open arms, his gender, race/ethnicity, and class acted both as facilitators and as obstacles to his assimilation.

Class: Vikrant's Downward Economic Mobility

Indian presence in the United States can be traced as far back as the early nineteenth century, when the first Indians were officially recorded as immigrants.[20] Their presence increased dramatically after the Immigration Act of 1965, leading to an Indian immigrant population in the United States of 26,300 in 1988 (Helweg and Helweg 1991), and by the beginning of the new millennium the Indian diaspora around the world was estimated to be about 20 million (Kapur 2010, 53), with almost 3 million in the United States.[21] Typically, Indian immigrants come from the Indian urban middle class. Even if sometimes their origins are rural, they are likely to have had a university education and be comfortable in a cosmopolitan atmosphere (Helweg and Helweg 1991). Once in the United States, Indian immigrants live across the country, following the general population distribution. Within each state, they tend to gravitate around big cities. For example, in the 1980s, one-third of Indian immigrants lived in New York, Chicago, and Washington, DC (Rangaswamy 2000; Chakravorty, Kapur, and Singh 2016).

Like the majority of Indians in the United States, Vikrant came from a middle-class, urban, and educated family. In the late twentieth century—in contrast to their compatriots moving internationally in the nineteenth century—Indians immigrating to industrialized countries like the United States typically had a profile that was "high caste, medium-high class, skilled, from the rim states in south or west," urban (Kapur 2010, 83), and young (Chakravorty, Kapur, and Singh 2016, xviii). Even though Vikrant did not come from a high-income family, because he hailed from among "the 'best and the brightest' in India" (Chakravorty, Kapur, and Singh 2016, xv), he was able to migrate, and his decision to become an international student shows the importance that he placed on career- and work-related goals (Hercog and van de Laar 2016). As mentioned previously, he had already obtained an MBA prior to his arrival, so he entered the "highest educated immigrant group" (Chakravorty, Kapur, and Singh 2016, xvi). Vikrant was similar to more than 71 percent of Indian immigrants to the United States who had some college education (Kapur 2010, 75), 69 percent who possessed a college degree or higher (Chakravorty, Kapur, and Singh 2016, xvi), and approximately 40 percent who had a master's degree upon arrival (Kapur 2010, 76).

Even though he already had a master's degree from India, Vikrant applied to an Ivy League school for another master's degree. Thus, like about 25 percent of Indians coming to the United States (Chakravorty, Kapur, and Singh 2016, xvi), Vikrant applied for a student visa.

As mentioned before, he was admitted to an elite academic program, but faced the great challenge that most international students need to resolve: studies in the United States are costly, and international students must show that they have the necessary funds to support themselves throughout their studies before they enter the country.[22] This financial requirement is purposefully instituted to block the entrance of both students who lack the necessary funds and those who plan to use their student status to gain employment once they arrive. Given the costs of living and education, Vikrant was not able to provide proof of financial sufficiency on his own,[23] and as a result he failed to qualify for a U.S. student visa. To solve this, he asked for help from a family friend, an Indian immigrant who practiced medicine in Los Angeles. This person became his sponsor and vouched $35,000 for support, and by combining this guarantee with the money from the fellowship given by the American university, Vikrant was able to show proof of sufficient funds to conduct his studies.

American embassy employees scrutinize student visa applications, often making the process unpredictable. Aware that his situation was extremely fragile, Vikrant took the process of obtaining his American visa and traveling to the United States very seriously indeed, and the solemnity of this moment is clear from his detailed account of the process on his blog:

[Knowing that you just] placed your entire fortune (monetary and otherwise) at stake on the decision of one person (such as a visa officer in a US consulate in Asia—who is the sole decision maker in this regard—even US President cannot reverse his judgement), the desire to develop perfect arguments increases many fold [original spelling and typing].

I was able to convince the US visa officer at Delhi that I have great and pressing interest in coming to India (and that I am telling the truth) and that I can pay the exorbitant $35,000 loan while working in India on my return—even though I was (&am) a single, South Asian male with negligible personal assets in India and a great friend in US who sponsored my student loan and would certainly desire that I get married and settle down in US—to make repayment of the loan easier.

Once his visa had been granted, Vikrant embarked on a journey across oceans and thousands of miles and arrived in the United States. His student experience was similar to that of many other Indian students abroad. First, he passed through a process of adjustment to the new environment—for many, this new experience involves getting used to the food and a new financial position in the host country (Helweg and Helweg 1991, 98–99). Resembling many other Indian students, he tried to make the most of the experience. He worked hard and networked with other South Asian student organizations.

"Coming from India, America was seen as the land of opportunity. . . . Some Indian students, especially from a business family, saw ways of making money that they felt they could not pass up" (Helweg and Helweg 1991, 101). Helweg and Helweg argue that some use their student status to maximize their financial assets, taking minimal course loads or changing majors to delay graduation and remain in the United States to work and make money; in addition, they study U.S. immigration laws and look for loopholes that might allow them to remain in the country. Many Indian immigrants, like Vikrant, do not see obtaining an American education as a goal in itself. During the early waves of immigration in the 1970s, Indian students focused on obtaining an American education and then returning to "mold India,"[24] but from the 1980s onward the goal of Indian students shifted to staying in the United States (107). More recently, Indian immigrants have been adjusting to transnationalism, which includes traveling back and forth between the home country and the country of origin, and to ensure they can be mobile, today's Indians often naturalize and hold U.S. passports, renouncing their Indian citizenship. Throughout his graduate studies, Vikrant focused on making his stay in the United States permanent. He applied for a PhD program and proposed a project comparing the American and Indian educational systems; when his application was rejected, he began exploring other ways to immigrate permanently.[25]

Typically, late-twentieth- and early-twenty-first-century Indian immigrants (Bacon 1996; Jensen 1988; Joshi 2006; Leonard 1997; M. Sheth 2006) follow one of three general (documented) paths in order to remain in the United States: using the Family Reunion Act, staying as a student, or applying for a work visa. To upgrade their status from temporary (with a student visa) to permanent (that is, holding a green card), Indians like Vikrant apply for H1B visas used by U.S. businesses to employ foreign workers in specialty occupations that require theoretical or technical expertise in specialized fields, such as scientists, engineers, or computer programmers."[26] While Indian immigrants who enter through the Family Reunion Act typically work in low-skilled jobs within their own community, those on student or work visas often work in specialized fields like computers, finance, or health care, which supports a middle- to upper-class position. Thus, following the "segmented assimilation" argument (Portes and Zhou 1993b), one would expect that—given his ethnic, class, and educational background—Vikrant would enter the middle- or upper-class segment that Indian immigrants typically enter and would have an annual household income of approximately $88,000 (as most of Indian Americans had in 2010).[27] However, in contrast to many of his compatriots, Vikrant chose a different "naturalization" path, which gave him an annual income under $30,000 (plus benefits)[28] and placed him in a lower-class segment within the host country. However, it is also worth mentioning that at the time of this study, Vikrant's career in the military was only just beginning, and in the long run it could prove to be a lucrative endeavor and a path to upward social mobility.

The Battle with Ethnicity and Race: (Mis)fittings in American Civilian Life

Vikrant rarely talked about race or ethnicity, encountering prejudice, or practices of discrimination or *othering*[29] (Chakravorty, Kapur, and Singh 2016), and like many of his compatriots—as it transpired through our conversations—Vikrant considered that his ethnicity made him a "good American" (Rudrappa 2004). Even when I asked him directly about race and ethnicity, he denied that he noticed any differences in treatment along these lines. However, categories of race and ethnicity, as well as the dynamics they

generate, were visible in ways that he could not ignore. A few months before
he enlisted in the U.S. military, Vikrant told me about an event that took
place when he was tutoring young children. One child in his care, a five-year-
old girl, "said something which might shock even the most hardened," he
blogged. The little girl told him, "Your skin is brown, peach and black. I am
white and pink and peach. We are different types of people." His response
to this blunt and unexpected "othering" based on the color of his skin was
"Shocking !! you must admit. How can anyone say that? How can anyone
highlight the differences between different races. Is this a statement from a
white supremacist? Isn't this blatant racial profiling?" In spite of his outrage,
Vikrant took his time and tried to make sense of this event. "I looked at her
self-portrait," he wrote, describing the picture the young girl drew before
she made the statement that moved Vikrant, and showed him that in spite
of his efforts, his "color" was visible and placed him in the host country's
hierarchy. "Her self-portrait is something no Indian girl can make: an oval
head slanting, straight shoulder-length red hair (which ends in sharp curls)
and bright blue eyes and a wide smiley mouth. No Indian girl can boast of
red hair and blue eyes. She can say and do. 'You are brown, black and peach
and I am white, pink and peach,'" Vikrant continued in his blog.

Even though Vikrant's tone expressed his outrage, his words in effect supported the girl's claim of color difference, for by saying that what the young girl
drew was something no Indian girl could have sketched as a self-portrait, he
implicitly said that no Indian girl could have the same physical characteristics
as the young American one. While a gross overgeneralization considering the
great diversity of the immigrants from the South Asian subcontinent, his comment brought to light the complicated politics of India with respect to color
and race. Racial differences in India are often discussed in linguistic or caste
terms[30] (and gender terms; see Beteille 1990). While taking for granted the
racial difference between American and Indian girls, Vikrant took the whiteness hierarchy on board by talking of a young girl "boasting" of having blue
eyes and red hair. The incident drove him to reflect upon racial differences,
which most of the time were not addressed. Indian immigrants' integration in
a racialized society has been explored in several studies (Bhatia 2007; Mishra
1996; Prasad 2000; Ruggiero and Taylor 1997), and scholars found that immigrants are generally not inclined to see discrimination as a cause of negative outcomes because admitting to being discriminated against "lowers their
social self-esteem and the perceived personal control over their performances
and outcomes" (Naujoks 2012, personal correspondence, citing Ruggiero and

Taylor 1997). Furthermore, on the basis of field research among members of the Indian diaspora, Naujoks argues, "There seems to be a strong tendency in the Indian-American community to not display any problem with discrimination. This displays particular 'strength' and enhances the image of the community. In other words, if Indians voice these concerns, they fear that it would become a self-fulfilling prophecy. Being a 'model community'[31] implies that one is successful and well-integrated etc." (2012, personal correspondence). Likewise, while Vikrant did not directly bring to view any discriminatory practices that he might have encountered in the United States, the voice of a five-year-old girl brought racial distinctions to the fore, making them both visible and recognizable to Vikrant and compelling him to reflect on his race within the host country.

In addition to his vast amounts of writing, Vikrant posted many photographs of his civilian life in the United States online. In many of these, he is alone, posing next to tourist sites such as the Bubba Gump Shrimp Company restaurant in Times Square. The photos were clearly taken by other people, revealing that Vikrant likely visited those sites by himself, though in some pictures he is accompanied by Indian friends or he is in his office in the company of his colleagues. While the photos have a positive atmosphere, they also indicate a certain awkwardness, with people in the office pictures sitting well away from one another, smiling nervously.

In civilian life, Vikrant was successful. He obtained his second graduate degree from one of the most prestigious universities in the world and obtained a job that secured his legal standing. But his status was still precarious, because his visa depended on his employer; often a better job did not come with visa sponsorship. As a result, he was aware of his limited possibilities for social and economic mobility. He could work only for the tutoring company that had sponsored his H1B visa, and this job did not pay him enough to cover the student loans guaranteed by his Indian mentor. Hence, in his civilian life, his economic situation was precarious at best.

Similarly, his social life was plagued with obstacles. He had acquaintances among the natives of the host country, but he was not really accepted—despite his best efforts. He tried to assimilate, and formed different relationships, but they were mostly with other Indian immigrants. However, this pattern changed when he enlisted in the military and lived in close proximity with other Americans, working together and depending on one another, sometimes trusting one another with their lives—especially while in deployment in Iraq.

* * *

I was personally connected to Lily and Alexa over several years, but I met Vikrant in person only once. Most of my research was conducted either by means of telephone interviews or through analysis of his social media sites. As a result, my access was to his public persona, to the persona that he created. Vikrant was aware of, and reflected on, the power that social media has of projecting and performing a certain image. Because I did not have extensive access to his persona outside of these sites, a question remained unresolved: What practices did he privately engage in? How did he perform when the usually watchful eye of military power was (at least partially) averted?

On social media, Vikrant followed behavioral norms for this form of interaction, in particular "overdisplaying" the image of a model soldier who enjoyed and took pride in being a member of the armed forces and in being a perfect U.S. citizen.[32] Unlike the other two participants in my research, he never criticized his military life and did not reflect upon the role played by his economic background or his race/ethnicity. However, in spite of his obliviousness, his racial/ethnic identity was visible to others, and, just as for Alexa and Lily, ethnicity was a double-edged sword for Vikrant. On one side was his ethnic identification, as he saw it; on the other were the perceptions of outsiders, the ways in which other military members saw him as "the other." Overall, in spite of his assiduous efforts, Vikrant found it difficult to be seen as a full member by the host group. The only occasion on which he addressed the impact of his ethnicity was when he told me in the course of a phone conversation that his "buddies" call him Osama—at the time, Osama bin Laden had not been apprehended and killed and was the United States' number-one terrorist. I asked Vikrant why his buddies would address him that way, and he answered that it was because of his looks, as "they do not know," and then he changed the subject. I tried to investigate further how this made him feel, but he brushed it off, saying it happens in the military, that everyone has a nickname.

Vikrant's reaction was similar to Alexa's dismissal of being assumed to be an undocumented migrant afraid of the American deportation police. Just like Alexa, Vikrant wanted to share this experience with me; both emphasized that they were not negatively affected, that they understood these were jokes peers played on each other. While name-calling is a common practice not specific to immigrants or foreigners in the American military, the choice of names is telling. For Alexa, the joke alluded to her immigration status, which because of her presumed Latina/Mexican origin was assumed to be "illegal." For Vikrant, his racial/ethnic appearance made him similar to the enemy, the armed forces' number-one target. And while calling him Osama made plain, as Vikrant rightly said, the ignorance of his "buddies" in terms of race, ethnicity, geography, and religion, it nevertheless pointed to the fact that Vikrant was not yet seen as an integral member of the group and was still perceived as different.[33]

Before enlisting Vikrant had some skepticism about American life and social structure and often expressed his views from an outsider's perspective. In his blogs, he discussed American culture from the "objective viewpoint" of a researcher. Like other Indian immigrants, he shared his view of the host country on online forums. He wrote many posts about the American educational system and compared it to the Indian one. When he talked about his trips to U.S. cities, he always used the tone of a tourist or investigator. After he enlisted, he fully embraced both the military and American culture.

At first glance, it appeared that Vikrant engaged in a conscious process of assimilation, embracing the new group identity while leaving behind his former ethnic one. However, this theory assumes that the immigrant's and the host country's identities are entirely different, without any overlapping, while in reality these identities are arguably not so different and can have overlapping areas that immigrants inhabit comfortably without engaging in a transformative process. For example, while some immigration scholars argue that Indian immigrants emphasize group identity, not the individual one cherished in the United States, other scholars (such as Rangaswamy 2000) contend that Indians do value individualism, which could be seen as an American characteristic as well. Also, just as in the host country, "acquiring wealth, succeeding in one's career, being dedicated to one's job or to a particular cause—traits associated with individualism and Protestantism—are also highly valued by the Indian, whether Hindu, Jain, Muslim or Sikh" (Rangaswamy 2000, 33). Therefore, Vikrant's efforts to succeed economically and socially can be seen as reinforcing his ethnic background and as inhabiting this intersecting ethnic space.

After enlisting in the U.S. military, Vikrant exhibited a preoccupation with the Indian-Pakistani conflict in his online posts. In just six weeks of deployment, he posted nine links and commentaries on Pakistan—next to military training, family, and his new personal life, the increased tensions between the two countries drew most of his attention. This overemphasis seemed to go hand in hand with the attention the United States was paying to Pakistan during this time, for in 2011 and 2012 commentators on U.S. foreign policy were expressing concerns about South Asia.

Taking an interest in the region and focusing on the "protracted conflict" that generates feelings of "animosity and distrust" (Ahmad 2019), he was in line with mainstream Indian understanding of the complex and tumultuous relation between Pakistan and India.[34] When Vikrant was deployed to Iraq, Pakistan's foreign and domestic positions were mostly at odds with the preferred U.S. political line, and the situation was further complicated by the fact that Pakistan also played a strategic role in the region and was considered an (unorthodox) ally in the United States' "Global War on Terror." This ambivalent relationship became even clearer when Osama bin Laden, America's most wanted terrorist, was discovered and killed in Pakistan.

Vikrant's social media commentaries, while diplomatic and tactful, were also politically charged. They were sometimes written in a condescending tone, demeaning the Pakistani heritage, such as in the following comment posted on social media: "Pakistan has some very intelligent people, descendants of ancient Indus Valley civilization, trying to find their identity in a nation whose history started just 70 years ago. A tough situation no doubt, in trying to gain the respect of its neighbors and surviving as a nation." While he seems to sympathize with a nation in turmoil, his empathy goes only so far. Intelligence is the attribute of not all Pakistanis, but to "some," specifically those who share the same historical heritage as today's Indians: "descendants of ancient Indus Valley civilization." While India and Pakistan share the same birth year (that is, 1947) as independent republics, Vikrant referred to Pakistan as a nation with a short history: "just 70 years ago," lacking the "respect" of its neighbors, that is, India.

These seemingly out-of-the-blue social media postings, made while he was being deployed in Iraq, highlight Vikrant's newfound preoccupation with distinguishing himself from Pakistani identity and bring to the fore the fact that "regardless of politics between India and Pakistan . . . immigrants from South Asia are racialized in similar ways upon their arrival into the United States" (Rudrappa 2004, 16). Vikrant's effort to be seen as different from Pakistanis is apparent in his discussions presenting Pakistan as a problem that needed to be addressed, as a country in which terrorists are seen as important social figures. "If passionate cricket fans could remove the Taliban in their country—I would do all it takes to help them win the next Cricket World Cup," he said on social media, commenting on a link that described how Pakistan lost a cricket match. A few months later, Vikrant posted an article discussing a Pakistani Taliban leader who vowed to start a new war, and commented: "Looks like a terrorist." His preoccupation with Pakistan and criticism of its people, while rooted in an Indian nationalist mainstream view, was a way to distance himself from the "other" that he closely resembled, for pointing out how someone looked "like a terrorist" diverted attention from his own looks, from the fact that he shared the profile often associated with the American enemy. In doing so, Vikrant forged his separation from the others, attempting to draw an (untraceable) line between himself and the terrorist profile.

This racialized labeling of people from the Middle East and South Asia still persists in the American imaginary in spite of the fact that after 1965, there has been an "increasing presence of [South Asian immigrant] followers of non-Christian faith, such as Hinduism, Islam, and Sikhism [that] has reverberates nationwide in urban, suburban, and rural America" (Joshi 2006, 1). Today, in the aftermath of the September 11, 2001, attacks on the United States and in the profiling of the "enemy," South Asian immigrants are "frequently identified as Arab (and/or Muslim as the difference between these two identities is still blurred) and are, therefore, automatically deemed terrorists and are starts of xenophobia in airports, streets, and neighborhoods" (Rudrappa 2004).[35] Rudrappa argues that everyone who has the phenotype of being Arab is questioned: "We are either with them or we are against them, we are told" (5). This labeling is supported by the fact that people are identified as South Asians, which is "an ascriptive term indicat[ing] a larger racial grouping of persons from Bangladesh, India, Nepal, Pakistan and Sri Lanka" (16), and this categorization blurred Vikrant's ethnic identity, placing him within the circle of possible dangerous "others," increasing the fragility of his newly developed U.S. military identity.

Vikrant was therefore faced with a choice that he found (too) easy to make, and he engaged in intense efforts to show that he was "with them/ us." To show where he stood and to dispel any doubts about his (questionable) identity and therefore assumed allegiance, he focused on presenting the Arab/Muslim identity as the enemy. Vikrant used this identity as a proxy, aiming to enlarge the space between himself and others, and thus to shorten the distance between himself and the host country. Being accepted in a new environment is not a simple declarative gesture, dictated by clear rules and laws. This is a continuous process, throughout which migrants—as new members—need to interpret confusing and complex norms and rules, while carefully conducting their lives through minute, everyday gestures.

Vikrant was aware that he needed to continuously reinforce and perform his identity within the "us" versus "them" paradigm. And because "regardless of politics between India and Pakistan, for example immigrants from South Asia are racialized in similar ways upon their arrival into the United States" (Rudrappa 2004, 16), Vikrant tried to change this and struggled to be seen as different from Pakistanis. Thus, by emphatically and uncritically appropriating the American discourse on its enemies (that is, referring to them as "terrorists"), he hoped to gain recognition in his host country and its military.[36]

Even though Vikrant's interest in distancing himself from Pakistan predated Osama bin Laden's capture, his posts on this topic increased in number when the al-Qaeda leader was found and shot in Pakistan. "Was Osama Bin Laden a guest faculty at Pakistan military Academy 400 meters from his 8 room gilded mansion, where he stayed with his 2 wives, son etc, right in the heart of Pakistan, 30 miles from its capital Islamabad? Heaven help the graduates there, if true. Saw the news on BBC in our base's Iraqi shop," he wrote on social media, reflecting on an event that was rapidly covered by the mainstream media across the globe. He followed up a couple of days later: "Osama was just 100 miles from the Indian border in Kashmir and 250 miles from Afghanistan—no wonder his hosts were terrorists fighting in Indian Kashmir." He was bringing tensions about Kashmir into the conversation, placing Kashmir into the paradigm of the War on Terror, legitimizing the Indian's government action in the contested territory. His focus on Pakistan, its conflict with India, and its ties to terrorists reinforced many of the stereotypes articulated both in India and in the United States and also worked to secure a place for Vikrant among the American soldiers, at a far remove from possible enemies.

Vikrant's attempts to depict himself as a member of the host country and the military, and to be recognized as such, were matched by a (shrinking) number of posts regarding his ethnic and cultural practices. He reflected on the evaporation from his life of events of importance in his Indian community: "Diwali in Hawaii? Just another day. Moral of Diwali: survive in the jungle, avoid running after dazzling deer, do not disrespect someone's sister, do not kidnap someone else's wife." Vikrant's social media post expressed the importance that the Hindu Festival of Lights Diwali represented for him, but also the fact that he was far away from the place that celebrated these festivities. He was now located in a place where this day was not commemorated, where it was "just another day."

Just like Lily, who was happy and proud to be identified both as a soldier and as an American, but was preoccupied with home country's social life, Vikrant was eager to show images of his favorite Indian cuisine in his online postings. He posted pictures of his food in an Indian restaurant and commented: "Eating some butter naan, roti and samosa at the Taj Mahal in Columbus Georgia."

While Vikrant was not particularly religious, and before his military life he was not interested in publicly sharing anything about his spirituality, he asked a friend to send him a copy of the Bhagavad Gita as the one book he was allowed to have during his military training. The Bhagavad Gita is one of the most important books in the Hindu tradition, a part of the epic the Mahabharata. The book is a seven-hundred-verse scripture containing a conversation on theological and philosophical issues between Pandava— Prince Arjuna—and his guide, Lord Krishna. Vikrant's turn to his country's sacred texts after his enlistment and during his basic training is rather similar to the experiences of other Indian immigrants in the United States. Fenton argues that many Indian immigrants coming to the United States are not particularly religious when they arrive, but "secular, urban, modern and technologically educated" (1988, vii). Yet many become more religious while in the United States: "Some Indians say that they are more religious in America than they were in India, and being religious here is much more conscious deliberate behavior than it would have been for them in India" (viii–ix). Religious life is often a way for new migrants to form ethnic ties within the new host country. However, when Vikrant expressed an interest in his Hindu background and Indian religious/spiritual tradition after enlisting in the U.S. armed forces, he was not trying to bring himself closer to other Indian migrants; it was part of his struggle to reinforce his (precarious and diminishing) ethnic identity.

The U.S. military is officially tolerant of and flexible about religious beliefs, but the majority of its recruits are of the Christian faith, with 76 percent of the military personnel declaring themselves in the 2017 survey of Barna Group as "faithful Christians."[37] The dominance of one religious tradition is clear from the choice of the reading materials available for new recruits on military bases during basic training, where copies of the Bible are found. Thus, even though Vikrant was able to ask for a copy of the Gita, he told me that because during boot camp he could find only copies of the Bible on base he read parts of it. While the U.S. military extols religious diversity in its forces,[38] in effect it is structurally skewed toward Christianity.

All three participants in this study reinforced their religious affiliations and sentiments—even exaggerated their beliefs—but it is important to understand that all three exhibited a new interest in religion only after military training. It could be that this enthusiasm for religion arose when they were exposed to the possibility that they might die. However, it is likely that the presence of religious symbols such as the Bible and chapel encouraged Lily, Alexa, and Vikrant to display their own forms of spirituality while reinforcing their different ethnic and religious backgrounds.[39]

Although Vikrant began his military service by forcefully trying to emphasize how much he belonged in the U.S. military and to downplay any similarities he might have had with possible "others," through the years of fieldwork I carried out for this book additional dimensions of his ethnic identity emerged. During a telephone interview, I asked Vikrant about his deployment in Iraq, and he told me that he had become close friends with another soldier from his unit; he informed me that his new buddy had a Middle Eastern background, and they had many things in common. "Such as?" I asked. "Our color," he said bluntly. "Also," he continued, "the food we eat and other things, we are not so different." Vikrant told me that because they had so much in common culturally and ethnically, the two friends spent a considerable amount of time together during their deployment—and remained close. Combat brings soldiers together, and the ties developed during these times are known to endure. Moreover, faced with the imminent presence of the enemy, bonding within the group/unit is a powerful survival tool. Relationships among soldiers during deployment are nurtured not only to successfully achieve tasks, but also to allow for the development of empathy and support among soldiers. Vikrant's friendship further reflects his preference for those who were of a similar racial and ethnic background or people who could understand him without questions about their differences. While Vikrant's race/ethnicity put him at odds with many of his American-born "buddies," it also enabled other liaisons and relationships to form with minority soldiers.

Vikrant's complex racial/ethnic ambivalence further points to a key difficulty faced by the contemporary U.S. military. They have to create a cohesive unit while supporting diversity among their personnel.[40] These competing aims permeate everyday military life and allow for the coexistence of seemingly opposing practices. Vikrant was the type of recruit that the U.S. military needs to accomplish its new goals and military tactics. He was highly educated and had the linguistic skills required to improve U.S.

military performance in the field. But while his profile was in high demand, his ethnic background, age, and language abilities made him stand out, giving rise to tensions in everyday military interactions. The very reason he was admitted into the military is also the reason for the lack of unity and uniformity. As a result, his process of acquiring membership in the host country was neither smooth nor linear. Rather, he engaged in divergent practices that either overemphasized his allegiance to the United States, or its military, or reinforced his ethnic characteristics.

Gender: Being a Man in a Masculine Institution

Soon after he enlisted in the Army, Vikrant became the poster child of the MAVNI program. He had an MA from an American Ivy League University, was of (diverse) Indian origin, spoke multiple languages deemed vital by the U.S. Army, and was eager to become like the larger community. Vikrant was delighted to be sought after and gladly talked about his new military experience; he enjoyed being portrayed in the media and interviewed. He was featured in national newspaper coverage of the swearing-in ceremony in Times Square, which said that Vikrant held a master's degree and that this was his second attempt to enlist, after failing three years earlier because of his Indian citizenship. The reporter added that Vikrant's motivation to serve was because he wanted to help developing countries: "If I'm in the Army, I want to be really involved," he said to the journalist interviewing him on his enlistment ceremony day.

He was described as a model soldier, ready to fight, eager to serve the country, not challenging the system that was in place. While the other two participants in this project needed to negotiate their gender within the military, Vikrant was a comfortable fit. In a sense, Vikrant's gender was equivalent to Lily's race in terms of our analysis. Lily was white, and her race was invisible to her and to many people she served with. She did not reflect upon it or articulate the role her race played in her mobility. Lily took for granted the fact that she was regarded with respect and never had any substantial issues. Similarly, because his gender identity was unchallenging,[41] Vikrant took for granted his place within the Army, especially the fact that he could serve in every aspect of the military, including on combat missions (a privilege awarded to men only). Shortly after he enlisted, Vikrant was sent on deployment, but before he left, he went through a rigorous training program. The Vikrant I met in New York City right after he was sworn in was hardly recognizable a few months later in the photographs he shared on social media. Once, he was featured in an official Army magazine next to his buddies during a field exercise in which they were all wearing fatigues, and even though I was familiar with Vikrant's image from the countless hours I had spent analyzing, classifying, and interpreting it, I experienced a few moments of confusion when I realized that in fatigues and sunglasses Vikrant was almost indistinguishable from his peers. At least at the visual, aesthetic level, he had achieved incorporation in the new community, as he desired.

Changing one's body and bodily image is not an easy task, but the military emphasizes a high level of fitness for undergoing its operations, and Vikrant made use of physical training (PT) sessions to alter his physical appearance. His interest, bordering on obsession, was detailed on his social media posts, like this one he proudly shared on social media:

My first PT Schedule—1st revision
MONDAY: 6 mile run—treadmill (2–3 incline), 200 pushups, 200 crunches, 20 pull ups
TUESDAY: Arms/Chest: Bench Press, Curls, Flyers: 10x3 sets each. 50 dips, 100 crunches, 20 pull ups

Upon enlisting, Vikrant quickly understood that he was at a clear age disadvantage compared to his "buddies": "For long I was by far the oldest at 37 (average age 20), another 37-year-old had 15 years of experience in Honduras army and is already an expert marksman. I had to learn the skill from the scratch," he posted a year into his service. Joining the Army when he was nearly forty, when almost all his peers were in their twenties, posed a challenge that Vikrant embraced wholeheartedly. Not only did he submit his body to rigorous exercises when on the base, but he also invested in fitness machines and created his own private fitness center where he could exercise after hours. As if designing a military physical fitness manual, Vikrant kept a record of the activities that remodeled him. His commitment to this training was not limited to the times set aside for exercise on the base. Having internalized the expectations of the military, Vikrant subjected himself to military discipline even when he was not being formally observed.[42]

Once Vikrant enlisted, his life similarly became subordinated to (the assumed) all-seeing eye of the military. While other recruits might question the military's power in and over their lives, Vikrant was happy to act according to the rules of the new system. He took it upon himself to perform as his superior officers would expect even when he was outside of the Army environment, regulating his own behavior through the (imagined) eyes of the other. He continued his physical training on his own by creating a home gym where he was able to perfect his performative practices of the same athletic routine, transforming his body into one resembling the other ideal American infantrymen.

These performative acts and practices were not limited merely to changing his body shape. Just as Vikrant's body and appearance changed in a matter of months, so did his persona—from a shy, slim figure, he became a larger, athletic man, carrying himself with confidence. When I met him, he was thin and wiry, with a thick, dark mustache. He wore his hair longer in front and shorter in the back. Vikrant wore slightly oversize clothes, held his shoulders in a somewhat hunched posture, and carried his head tilted and faintly bowed, so he looked at people from the corner of his eyes. But in the few months after his enlistment, as his public pictures showed, his muscles bulged, he developed strong abdominal muscles ("a six-pack"), and his body transformed so that his military uniform fitted him to the inch. His hair was cut short, and his mustache disappeared into his Indian past. Vikrant's transformation was far-reaching and minutely described: "We get a haircut every week," he told me in our 2009 telephone interview. "Here they have a small Army mall and a barbershop. . . . The hair needs to be trimmed near the skin. It is not just a plain cut." He enjoyed his ritualistic trips to the Army barber. As his short and clean haircut was visible and reinforced, he belonged to the military and gladly embraced the new style.

Such intense focus on physical appearance and performance has always been part of military discipline, and although these procedures were new to him, Vikrant was proud of the attention that was paid to his body. Through this detailed training, his physical self was gradually altered while the program, strict and focused on achieving fixed goals, made him similar to other American soldiers. Five months after his enlistment, Vikrant described his first training. This excerpt was taken directly from his social media postings, and it shows both the attention and the pride that Vikrant took with respect to practices of his body:

My life at THE INFANTRY SCHOOL
Hi,
Today I completed 9 weeks of training to become a soldier, now on to the AIT (Advanced Individual Training) 5 week portion—which for the

infantry is a combined 14 week program. As each week progresses we have been learning new skills—initially it is focused on muscle building and army procedures and discipline—most guys are fresh out of high school and mostly leaving home for the first time.

After this introduction, he described how difficult it was for him to learn how to use weapons and to qualify for the Basic Rifle Marksmanship, then went on to outline his training for physical battle, which he again embraced happily: "I did not know how to block punches with my arms (I learnt a few techniques from others and drill sergeants), so others were afraid that I might find it tough. I got my upper lip cut a bit and a bit scratch on the eyebrow, but I am glad that like most of us (some had bloody noses) I did not step back and did what was expected."

Through these formal and informal daily physical practices, Vikrant began his bodily transformation and started to resemble the norm of the host military group more and more. However, his past still blended into his new developing identity. In early 2011, Vikrant posted a photo of his newly tattooed arm. While the habit of painting one's body is a military practice and a Hawaiian/Polynesian practice (as Vikrant acknowledged in his post), the choice of his tattoo brought him back to his ethnic roots—the tattoo was an Indian warrior symbol of the Sikh tradition, a "Khanda," as he explained to his audience. Vikrant's gesture is double-sided. The tattoo brought the Indian image to life on his body, while the act of tattooing reinforced his ties to the military, creating bonds with his new peers.

Vikrant: Bodily Practices as Male Bonding Techniques

The effect of this transformation was visible in a picture, taken nearly two years after Vikrant's enlistment and posted on social media by one of his military "buddies," as Vikrant preferred to call his fellow soldiers. It showed Vikrant as a part of a group of five similar men at the end of a marathon, medals hanging from their necks, giving the thumbs-up. The men looked alike, with their athletic bodies dressed in T-shirts, shorts, and sneakers and with their short haircuts, and the image showed how the military training had not only enabled Vikrant's body to perform the required military tasks but also made him part of a larger host-country group and empowered him to create the bonds that he was craving. It was also obvious that these bonds extended beyond the military realm and that Vikrant now engaged in leisure activities with his buddies, the military men with whom by now he shared a similar look.

Like Alexa, Vikrant struggled to assimilate to the dominant culture and appropriated the behavior of the members of the group in which he was integrating while striving to transform his physicality (Rudrappa 2004). And, as Vikrant's body was transformed,[43] so was his sense of masculinity, which needed to adapt to the masculinity preserved within the military structure (Xavia Karner 1998, 229). According to Brandon T. Locke: "the military consistently depicted its men as white, straight, cissexual, physically well-built, and emblematic of white, middle class norms and values" (2013, 4). As a result, military enlistment is typically associated with masculine values of strength and bravery. For Vikrant, this newly developed masculine identity facilitated the process by which he was accepted by the other soldiers. This enabled him to develop strong ties with the members of his platoon; these ties extended beyond training and working together. For example, when he was deployed in Iraq, his wife had an accident, and one of the sergeants back home visited and supported her at the hospital. Hearing about this, Vikrant wrote on social media: "Sgt, Thank you for being there for us. My wife and her parents were so delighted that one of my friends met them at the hospital. An army chaplain met her the next day. Now she is back home but of course has a long way to go before she can walk again without crutches. . . . Very Respectfully."

This new gendered social web of primarily military ties enabled Vikrant both to integrate and to have better access to the host system's resources. Being part of this male social network also made it possible for him to learn how to behave, just like learning a new language. In turn, engaging in socially accepted practices secured his recognition as a member of the group. Performance practices of the body (Wedeen 2008) are multiple and not reducible to mere muscular transformation. In Vikrant's case, they shaped his masculinity and molded him within the expected and accepted military gender identity. In Alexa's case, as we saw earlier, her limited physical abilities as a woman placed her at the margins of her group and created in her a feeling of anxiety about her military experience. Conversely, by "marching together in time" (McNeill 1995; Shils and Janowitz 1948), by being able and willing to perform in tandem with his "buddies," Vikrant performed according to the military's preferred gender and became an integral part of his group. He regularly posted pictures and comments on the drills and marches of his unit. In a 2011 photo, he proudly explained that the picture had been taken after many hours of marching. It showed an exhausted Vikrant, sweaty and barely standing, bent over after his strenuous effort, at the end of a line of soldiers dressed in fatigues. It also revealed the close relationships of the soldiers, who were bonding through intensive physical exercises.

If Alexa felt excluded from "marching together in time" as a result of her medical condition, Vikrant's eager participation in all the Army's physical activities brought him recognition and acceptance. During military exercises, dramatic changes in his muscle tone took place, and this made it easier for him to take part in group-bonding activities. Furthermore, his willingness to assimilate into the U.S. military was visible beyond his bodily training and could be seen in the way in which he displayed his allegiance to the military values[44] even more forcefully during his deployment. "Impossible is a word in the dictionary of fools thank god I don't [have] a dictionary," Vikrant wrote while in Iraq. He later continued: "We are all terminators here! We kill the bad guys!" These statements, in a newly developed writing style, were quite different from his earlier social media posts written as a graduate student or an educator and were symbolic gestures of adapting to his new environment. He used these public discursive practices to show his commitment, to indicate his desire to belong to the group, and to be recognized by others as an equal group member, which in turn empowered his accession to the military.

Overall, Vikrant's newfound masculinity fitted well with the American military ideals: the insistence on physical fitness, close relationship with other male members of the military, forming of brotherly ties, helping and counting on one another, and preparing to fight for the country made him into a model soldier. Compared to Lily and Alexa, who both had limited success within the military, Vikrant excelled. His gender enabled him to explore manliness, to fight, to be in combat, and, moreover, to be recognized for his accomplishments and portrayed as a success. This reaction encouraged him even further and facilitated his integration into both the Army and the host country.

Conclusion: Is Vikrant a Different Indian Immigrant?

Over the years he spent in the United States, Vikrant engaged in a variety of performative practices to be seen as belonging, and even though he did not entirely relinquish his former ethnic identity, he navigated between its different sides and tried his best to access resources and recognition. The thread running through Vikrant's life was his struggle to find a unique path for himself, different from that of the other Indian immigrants, while also being seen as a full member of the host society. He was helped in reaching his final position by the intersection of his gender, class, and ethnicity/race, and especially because his gender placed him in a position of uncontested privilege.

He was successful in a career that put him outside the typical Indian immigrant experience. Not many immigrants decide to join the U.S. military, and even fewer Indian migrants are inclined to follow such a path. So, while not unique, Vikrant broke the Indian migration mold. However, his decision to enlist was not the only act that placed him on the fringes of his diasporic group, for even before he joined the military, he had made less common choices. He decided to go to an Ivy League school, but he pursued a career in a different field from the majority of Indian immigrants who come to the United States on a work visa and are usually seeking to find success in IT, business, or medicine (Chakravorty, Kapur, and Singh 2016). Instead, he chose to come to the United States as a student and to follow a career in education, and this placed him in a more precarious social, legal, and economic situation than an average Indian immigrant of his class, caste, and education. To overcome this difficulty, Vikrant enlisted in the armed forces, which gave him a permanent legal status as well as a form of employment that would enable him to pay back his student loans and to make a living. As a result, he did not join the "top 1 percent" in U.S. society and did not have a similar economic trajectory to other members of his immigrant group (Chakravorty, Kapur, and Singh 2016), instead carving a different path for himself.

Moreover, in contrast to many first-generation Indian immigrants, after a few years in the military Vikrant decided to marry outside his ethnic group, marrying an East Asian American woman with Philippine roots, and they made Hawaii their home. All of these traits make him a special individual, an outlier (but not exceptional) in his community. However, like the majority of recent Indian immigrants, Vikrant also came to the United States with a higher education than most of his American-born counterparts in the military and with a diploma from a prestigious university. Furthermore, he aimed to assimilate in the host country as many Indian immigrants do, applying for a work visa and hoping to stabilize his legal status. Only when this option failed did he look at the Army as an alternative. Once in the military, he performed well and worked hard in order to be recognized and to acquire full membership.

At first glance, Vikrant's is a classic story of assimilation, of a person who shuns previous identities and acquires new ones. As Vikrant rarely directly addressed his religion, ethnicity, class, or race and never reflected on his gender, it might be easy to assume that these identities were not important and that his life was focused on his great educational achievements as well as his military identity. In this way, he is much like other Indian immigrants for whom "money (and/or education) made white" (Chakravorty, Kapur, and Singh 2016), in other words for whom their race or ethnical identity was marginal. Vikrant clearly tried to portray himself in this way and persevered in assimilating into the new host country, striving to change his body, to marry outside of the community, to (publicly) renounce his Indian citizenship. But, as for Alexa and Lily, his willingness to assimilate was not without resistance. Even though he did not directly address them, Vikrant encountered situations in which his race and ethnicity played important roles and underscored the fact that he was different. From the little girl in his premilitary life who pointed out that his skin color was different from hers, to his military buddies who called him Osama, he was still strange in the eyes of the others.

By choosing the Army as the branch of the military in which to enlist, he was similar to Alexa, and his educational background made him similar to Lily. While he was the only male participant whose life story I tell in this study, he presented the clearest version of a successful naturalization narrative. Vikrant's gender eased his incorporation into the military and finally into the host country, as he was the ideal gender candidate, did not challenge any gender norms, did not need any special accommodation, and was allowed to perform all jobs in the Army. Although class did not play a large part in his story, his race/ethnicity worked against his inclusion in the host country, but his gender aided his inclusion.

As I finished working on this research project in 2014, Vikrant was still enlisted in the U.S. Army and undergoing special training. His life took an unexpected turn when his wife passed away. Right before her passing, he talked to me about it and seemed overwhelmed. But his resilience endured. Last I heard he had remarried and seemed to be doing well as an American infantryman.

Conclusion

Did their military experiences Americanize Lily, Alexa, and Vikrant by making them into members of a community? In many ways, they did. But a more accurate description might be that the three immigrant soldiers "negotiated" the Americanization process. They learned new practices of patriotism and national loyalty, but also reaffirmed their own identities and traditions.

My encounters with the participants in this study showed that each of them went through a transformative process in which their military identity grew stronger. Vikrant's military training changed his body; Lily learned new national emotions when she performed ceremonies honoring the American flag; Alexa, in spite of becoming aware of the divisions within American society and changing the way she saw and reacted to the role she was often assigned, held high the assumed values of the U.S. military. Their stories demonstrated that military enlistment and service are powerful transformative tools for immigrants, but did not show that the military "strips them all down, to build them back up"—as Lily argued. Their narratives revealed that their "naturalization" process was continuous but incomplete, depending on the branch of the military, type of duty (that is, active or reserve), and their race/ethnicity, class, and gender. In other words, like the subway riders in New York City in the work of Tonnelat and Kornblum (2017) who in spite of sharing the same identities of "riders" experience the public

154 / Conclusion

spaces differently, and also maintain their distinct racial ethnical, gender and class identities, the three participants did not have a uniform experience of "naturalization" within the American armed forces. Rather, their experiences were shaped by whether they were male or female; white, Asian, or Latino; Romanian, South American, or Indian; highly or medium educated.

Intersectionality studies show that race/ethnicity, class, and gender do not operate individually, or in a vacuum, but are markers constructed and embedded in the complex contexts in which they intersect. This understanding clarifies how "the dual and systematic discriminations of racism and sexism remain pervasive" (D. King 1988, 43) and highlights how they often translate in inequality and forms of oppression. As intersectionality is fundamental (both important and primary) to understanding how power operates, "there is some debate as to whether intersectionality is a theory, paradigm or method" (Few-Demo 2014, 170). There are benefits to using intersectionality in any of these three forms, but, in line with Few-Demo, for this project intersectionality is a "theoretical framework that guides methodological considerations and data interpretations" (170)—in short, as theory/methodology. This theory/methodology approach enables us to engage in thick descriptions (Geertz 1973) that highlight the singular experiences (Hancock 2007) of the participants in this work, by examining "the fluidity, variability, and temporality of interactive processes that occur between and within multiple social groups, institutions, [individuals] and social practices" (Few-Demo 2014, 170). Thus, we must think of intersectionality "as simultaneously political, symbolic, categorical, relational and locational" (170) and focus our attention on how processes like those of gendering and racializing take place (Yuval-Davis 2006; Choo and Ferree 2010) for immigrants within the military.

In line with pioneers and leading figures in intersectionality (see Collins 2000; Crenshaw 1995; Few-Demo 2014; Hancock 2007; D. King 1988; Mohanty 1988; and Moraga and Anzaldúa 1984), the three life stories showed how individuals (as well as groups) inhabit multiple ever-changing social locations and share overlapping and at times even conflicting contexts, in which they continuously negotiate "privilege, oppression, opportunity, conflict" (Few-Demo 2014, 171).[1]

Furthermore, these stories highlighted how immigrant soldiers' experiences are connected to but different from those of immigrant civilians. In civilian life, none of the three participants felt compelled to assimilate into any community, but in the military they all expected to be immersed in the new group and accepted the process. However, their ethnicity/race, class, and gender were significant factors in determining how their attempts to find a place for themselves in the new country played out—this is as true in the military as in a civilian context. Moreover, their race/ethnicity, gender, and class placed them at a crux, facilitating or obstructing their naturalization process and their access to social and economic mobility.

"Segmented Assimilation" and Class

As Portes and Zhou (1993a, 1993b,), Zhou (1997a, 1997b), Portes (2007), and Rumbaut (1994) have observed, while many immigrants come to the United States hoping for a shot at the American dream, they enter a highly segmented society, sometimes at the bottom of the social scale. These studies argue that the United States is diverse as well as segmented, with an underclass residing in central cities, where a large portion of immigrants assimilate. Immigrants may follow the traditional model and assimilate into the white middle class ("straight-line"), attain upward mobility via a tightly knit immigrant community ("upward"), or take a less prosperous path and assimilate into the underclass ("downward"). For Lily, Alexa, and Vikrant, their class—reflected in their financial means and educational level—was a significant determinant of their social and economic mobility.[2] When they enlisted, all were un- (or under)employed and faced dire economic prospects. They used military service as their main source of income, and while they had complex personal reasons, such as parental military heritage for Vikrant, or, for Lily, wanting to get over a broken heart, their main motivation was finding stable employment. Allegiance to the host country came only later.

The U.S. military's role as an employer has been a delicate matter since conscription ended in 1973. Previously, military service was considered to be a vocation and a duty that brought its own rewards quite distinct from monetary gain, but after the end of conscription the U.S. armed forces had to compete in the labor market. Many Americans and immigrants joined the military for financial reasons, as well as to access benefits and training, and the military became one of the nation's largest employers. Alexa, Lily, and Vikrant enlisted because they were struggling to find civilian jobs—and they found this form of employment beneficial.

Lily joined the American military with a bachelor's degree in hand. While serving as a reservist, she earned a master of science degree, which enabled her to pursue her dream career. During her years of service in the armed forces, her economic situation steadily improved, as she received a promotion and was able to afford a house in the suburbs. The financial award she received for her service supplemented her civilian income and made it possible for her to access the American middle class. Lily's master's degree, from a prestigious American university in which she enrolled using the GI Bill, was the key driver of her improved economic well-being: while she did not rely on the U.S. military for her financial security, her economic achievements were directly tied to the promotion she received after she earned an advanced degree. Thus, her financial success was (indirectly) correlated to her military service. However, despite her educational credentials, military experience, and the support of her supervisors, she was not able to progress smoothly upward through the military ranks and become an officer in the Air Force. Her assiduous efforts enabled her to secure a job and make progress—even though, as she often reminded me, she had many setbacks because of her "accent"—but they did not help her reach officer rank. Lily's success in her civilian career might also be attributed to her being a reservist, because she did not have to disrupt her studies or interrupt her civilian employment to serve the country. In addition, her economic success is linked to the fact that she was perceived as white and to the fact that she did not need to challenge any civilian or military hierarchies.

In contrast to the other two participants, who both had at least a bachelor's degree upon enlistment, Alexa joined the military with only an accredited high school diploma and some college credits from Europe that were not formally recognized. She hoped that military service would help her obtain an American undergraduate degree. For many years, Alexa worked as a live-in nanny, earning cash and with her accommodation and meals included, so she was living with almost no expenses. But when she enlisted, she lost many of these financial privileges—and had to live a simpler life in proximity to her military base. She also had to provide for a sister who was entirely reliant on her for financial support. Because Alexa received a small salary in the military, they had to search for and rely on food banks and soup kitchens. Despite these difficulties, she saw her military enlistment as her ticket to attaining higher education. She always sought information about community colleges and other affordable schools. At the time of writing, she had not yet been successful in achieving her goal of enrolling at and attending college. While serving in the Army, Alexa tried to take classes sponsored by the military and to pursue a degree; she encouraged her sister to take English courses at the local church and classes offered for military families on her base. Alexa was painfully aware that her lack of formal and recognized higher education impacted her social mobility. Even when she became a veteran and had both U.S. citizenship and military experience, for more than a year she could not find suitable employment in a field suitable for starting a civilian career and as a result still struggled to make ends meet.

Of the three participants, Vikrant had the highest level of education at the time of his enlistment, with both a graduate degree from India and an MA from an American Ivy League university. While his educational qualifications had initially enabled him to come to the United States, they had not helped him to find a stable job and to remain in the country legally. His decision to join the armed forces was motivated not by the opportunity to continue his studies, as it was for Lily and Alexa, but by the possibility of finding a secure and rewarding job and of developing his skills and expertise. Despite his advanced degrees, Vikrant was in a very difficult position: he desperately needed both to streamline his immigration status and to find a job that would enable him to pay back the student loans that an Indian immigrant friend had cosigned. His military salary and benefits satisfied these needs, and he took advantage of many financial offers provided for soldiers, including low-interest credit cards and discounted goods. Nevertheless, he had lower economic and social status than other Indian immigrants to the United States. In contrast to many Indians, who come to the United States after graduating from top Indian universities and—often after continuing their studies at major U.S. institutions—find employment in highly lucrative jobs (Chakravorty, Kapur, and Singh 2016), Vikrant chose to work in the less well-paid field of education and joined the lower-middle class, the social level from which a large number of U.S.-born military recruits come.

Overall, the military facilitated Lily's, Alexa's, and Vikrant's educational and economic mobility and in doing so helped them enter the American lower-middle to middle class, but none of them enjoyed simple, straightforward, or smooth access. In Alexa's case, enlisting in the military meant taking a pay cut, but it gave her officially recognized experience and the possibility of bettering her situation by obtaining her BA degree. While she had not achieved this by the time this research was completed, doing so remained a possibility. Similarly, Vikrant's military service did not place him on a socioeconomic level equal to most Indian immigrants, but his economic mobility took a downturn for a number of years. In the long run, his newly achieved U.S. citizenship and military service might drive Vikrant's socioeconomic status upward, but when I finished this research, he was still enlisted as an E4, a status considerably below his educational and experiential level. Lily faced a similar situation: in spite of her avid desire to become an officer, she encountered many obstacles that slowed or blocked her social and hierarchical mobility within the military.

These life stories reveal that it is difficult to draw broad-brush conclusions. For all three participants, the military incontestably acted as a driver of social mobility, but this mobility could be downward as well as upward. Alexa, Vikrant, and Lily did not have a direct or smooth accession to a new desired social level, and their process of naturalization was definitely not complete. All three became U.S. citizens, and this opened up social and economic possibilities, including access to employment and benefits, but in their different ways none of them really succeeded in improving their economic situation.

Race/Ethnicity

While wanting to access economic benefits, Lily, Alexa, and Vikrant were also seeking recognition as equals in the military—and, implicitly, in the host country. Recognition implies the involvement of two sides: the individual or group demanding recognition and the host group that grants (or denies) the recognition. When demanding recognition in the civilian world, the participants joined ethnically centered groups. For example, Lily joined a Romanian business professionals' group. But when the three enlisted in the host country's armed forces, they expected to directly assimilate in the military and be recognized as soldiers and full members of the organization. Their experiences showed a different reality. Instead of being recognized solely as American soldiers, they were cast into ethnic/racial, linguistic, or gender groups; their different racial/ethnic identities placed them on different paths. These processes exposed the friction between the official position of the military, which views itself as an institution in which all personnel are treated equally based on individual skills and performance and the impact that race/ethnicity still has on military integration.

Alexa's South American heritage meant that she was visibly identified as "Latina" or "Hispanic," which was accompanied by hazing practices, such as when her military colleagues jokingly yelled, "*Migra, migra!*"—the cry of alarm used among undocumented immigrants to alert their friends that immigration officers are on their way. Alexa accepted the hazing lightheartedly, but she firmly refused to perceive herself as a "Latina" because she did not identify with that ethnic socioeconomic group. She saw little connection between herself and other Spanish-speaking immigrants, whom she described as doing menial jobs and coming to the country undocumented. Her struggle to deny this identity was an attempt to affirm herself as a different type of immigrant. So, in an attempt to own her recognition, she strongly insisted on being recognized as a South American.

When Vikrant arrived in the United States, he imagined himself as part of the new American community, but was shocked to discover how others, even children, perceived him to be racially different. Over the years, both in his civilian and in his military life, Vikrant made consistent and remarkable efforts to assimilate and to be accepted, but despite this he was kept at arm's length. While serving he was called names such as "Osama" based on his overall physical appearance, he tried hard to change this labeling/misrecognition, and he engaged in a series of practices. He adopted his colleagues' language and changed his body shape to better fit in with the host group. He cut his hair short. He became a U.S. citizen and (publicly) renounced his Indian passport. And he strongly emphasized his preference for the American memory of historical events (such as 9/11) and patriotic songs. Yet, while he was committed to becoming more like the ideal American soldier, the features that marked him as different did not disappear.

Compared to other immigrant groups, Romanians have a minimal presence both in American society and in the U.S. military. When Lily was asked directly where she was from, her response was often met with confusion, and she was rarely placed in the correct ethnic group. This gave her space to reaffirm her identity as "white," in a society in which racial entitlements and privileges still run deep. Of the three participants, Lily received results most based on individual achievement and least influenced by feelings about racial/ethnic background. Thus, she fit into the meritocratic aspiration of the military, and her military performances were acknowledged to be due to her personality and skill. Lily was promoted, and this benefited both her civilian and her military careers. However, it is important to add that in addition to Lily being seen as white, she was educated and had good English skills (while she still had a strong accent) and had an ethnic background—that is, east European—mostly considered unproblematic in today's overall American cohesion.

Lily, Alexa, and Vikrant worked hard to be assimilated and to be regarded as equal members of American society, and they hoped that they would be granted this recognition when they entered military service. As with class, it is difficult to draw sweeping conclusions about the effects of race/ethnicity on the treatment of newcomers within the U.S. military, even for the three research participants. It could be said that they were better recognized as equal members in the military than they were in their civilian lives. Vikrant enjoyed close social relations with his "buddies," Lily's accent did not matter as much when she was asked to perform military tasks, and Alexa enlisted on an equal footing with her native-born American counterparts. However, in their daily interactions, their racial/ethnic identities prevented their access to equal recognition: Lily could not cross what at times appeared to be a caste-line division between the enlisted and the officers, because her foreign degree was not recognized, Vikrant was called "Osama," and Alexa was assumed to be an "illegal" immigrant.

While both Lily and Vikrant worked to be accepted, they were eager to make friends and wanted to resemble those around them. Differently, Alexa—who of the three faced the most obstacles related to race and ethnic origin—was hostile to being assimilated, often criticizing "the Americans" and generalizing about what she saw as their negative behavior. Showing subtle disdain toward narrow national identifications, she demanded that she be recognized as a "South American" and expressed concern and disdain when asked if she would like to become a U.S. citizen. Alexa's behavior might be interpreted as a sign of her desire to maintain her own ethnic identity, but it was also a response to the systematic ethnic misrecognition she encountered.

In spite of the differences between the three, one overall insight can be drawn. The participants' experiences with regard to their ethnicities proved that identity is dialogical (C. Taylor 1994), constructed through many varied actions and responses. It is not enough for a person to want to be assimilated if the receiving community engages in formal and informal practices that deny assimilation. While Lily, Alexa, and Vikrant were not interested in practicing identity politics, and hoped to be recognized as individuals in the host military and national communities, identity politics had already categorized them.

Gender

Vikrant, Alexa, and Lily enlisted in an institution in which gender has historically been a dominant factor. It was therefore only to be expected that the three participants' gender would play a role in their assimilation; what was to be determined was how big or small the role and where was it taking them. Thus, it is probably not surprising that the one participant who conformed to the institution's (structurally) preferred gender, Vikrant, was the one whose assimilation was the most successful. To diminish the differences between himself and native-born soldiers, Vikrant took physical exercise very seriously, trained assiduously in the use of firearms, and was actively keen to go on deployment.

Vikrant did not discuss his gender at all. For him, as for the host system, it was a nonissue—and therefore invisible. Vikrant's gender was the equivalent of Lily's race. Being male and being white often go under the institutional radar, as they are the expected status quo identity in the American military The bearers of these identities often conform to the "normal," enjoying its privileges without reflecting upon them.

Lily and Alexa had a different experience of their gender in the military.[3] On joining the Army, Alexa was eager to work on an aircraft, but she was never given the option to do so and felt that this was because she was a woman. Moreover, when her health deteriorated, and her health issues were related to her reproductive organs, and she was not able to control her body and perform all the necessary work-related tasks, she felt further marginalized.

Like Alexa, when talking about her gender Lily often felt that she was a misfit in military culture, since she was not a "whore or a dyke." But while Alexa lamented the institution's gender dynamics, Lily made the best of them. She did not challenge the masculine hierarchy in her unit and beyond; she looked for a more "feminine" field within military service and opted to work in education. Accepting the feminized position did give Lily an advantage. She had a smaller chance of being deployed, ensuring limited disturbances to her life and further enabling her to advance her civilian career. Moreover, Lily capitalized on the subordinate space shaped by her gender. She used the subaltern position to "get things done": men carried her bags when they were too heavy, advised her on matters she did not understand, and solved issues such as procuring food while bending regulations. While taking different stands as to their gender identity, both women were confronted by the limits of their agency within the military and felt compelled to "reproduce traditional femininity and male privilege" (Silva 2008, 937).

It is important to mention that all three participants also conformed to the military's heteronormativity. The three were heterosexuals, and all got married while serving. While the U.S. military still struggles to fully accept different sexual orientations among its members, it clearly prefers its soldiers to have monogamous relationships, and—through incentives like housing or increased pay—it encourages marriage. As these preferences aligned with Lily's, Alexa's, and Vikrant's personal desires, they never questioned or critically engaged with these pressures. They welcomed them.

Different intersections led to different results in people's lives, with a more mainstream position leading to less discrimination. For example, Vikrant's American education coupled with his male gender led to his acceptance in the military, while Alexa's lack of American education and her female gender created a different space and therefore a different experience of military service.

A Descriptive Argument

It is not the aim of this book to lay out a general argument about immigrants in the military based on these three participants' experiences. Neither does this work aim to produce an overarching theory. It simply aims to detail how the "naturalization" processes of Lily, Alexa, and Vikrant took place given the intersection of their race/ethnicity, class, and gender. Following and paraphrasing Pachirat's pioneer approach in the study of politics, the accounts presented in these pages were not "incidental or illustrative of a more theoretical argument" about "naturalization" of immigrants in the military; "they are the argument" (2011, 9).

I have been tempted many times to argue that immigrants in the contemporary U.S. military do this or that or get this or that. Accepting this research direction would have fallen closely (or at least more closely) in line with the expectations often voiced in social sciences. However, it is my strong belief that it would have been wrong to do this. These stories are so intricate, so individual, that extrapolating from them to reach for overarching arguments capable of predicting future developments would be precarious at best and false or dangerous at worst. It is nevertheless my hope that the three life stories inspire fellow researchers, academics, and members of the public to look deeper into stories of migration and the role that institutionalized forms of discrimination (or acceptance) play in the lives of newcomers, if necessary, coupling these inquiries with large quantitative studies from which conclusions can be drawn based on solid data sets, and in so doing minimize any chances of misrepresentation.

* * *

After years of work on this book, I am still impressed by how Lily, Alexa, and Vikrant negotiated their place in the host country, while honoring their differences, accommodating them, in an ongoing and at times laborious and circuitous process of American naturalization.

I stopped research on this book in March 2014. At that time, Lily was frustrated that she could not make it to the officer ranks within the Air Force, was married, and was living in the suburbs of New York City, serving as a reservist and successfully pursuing her career in tourism. Alexa lived across the Hudson River, close to Manhattan with her husband, Ben, and her sister. Ben and Alexa were both veterans, but had difficulty finding any form of employment. Alexa was dealing with severe medical issues and received minimal help from the Veterans Association. She still hoped to get a BA degree. Vikrant's wife passed away at a very young age, while he was still serving. Soon afterward, he remarried. He was content with his military service, but once he returned from deployment, he realized how much he missed his unit and was eager to go back.

With the lives of all the participants in full motion, my decision to stop research on this book was not easy; the three continued to be engaged in different ways in military service, and my work felt somewhat incomplete. In "The Roads of Life," a section in the 1937 memoir *Out of Africa* by Danish author Karen Blixen (who wrote under the name Isak Dinesen), Blixen tells the story of a man who lived by a pond and one night was awakened by a loud noise. Confused, he ventured outside, into the cold, snow, and mud. In the darkness, he ran back and forth, stumbling and falling, until at last he found a leak in a dyke, which he fixed, and returned to bed. Upon waking up at sunrise, he looked through the window and, to his surprise, saw that in his chaotic movement, his footsteps had traced the shape of a stork on the muddy ground. Blixen used this story to meditate about life and to wonder if its meaning could be discerned only after all the "steps" have been taken, the journey has ended, and we have become spectators. Hannah Arendt reflected upon this story as well: "No one has a life worthy of consideration about which a story cannot be told" (1979, 170). These thoughts on the importance of life stories inspired and motivated much of this book. Each life is unique and precious and full of acts that seem random, difficult, unforeseeable, and uncontrollable, but when, like the man in the story, we look at them at sunrise, we can discern meaningful narratives.

Alexa's, Lily's, and Vikrant's lives and processes of naturalization are far from over. I am aware that—just like the man in Blixen's story—they are still to take many steps that could transform their lives into different naturalization outcomes, results not recorded in this book. I see how incomplete these life stories are and hope that Lily, Alexa, and Vikrant will accept my limited account of their rich and ever-expansive lives. They bravely committed to fight for a country that was not (yet) theirs and hoped to become equal citizens. In protecting their host country, they were expected to battle the enemies of the United States. However, what they did not expect to have to fight was a dire battle against intermingling stereotypes about their race/ethnicity, gender, and class identities.

Appendix

Creating Social Research

Intersectionality and Research

Intersectionality as method shaped the research design of this project. In line with intersectionality scholars (Hawkesworth 2006), I contend that researchers' positions are not fixed but change as they engage with the different segments of the communities they study. Researchers' multifaceted identities[1] construct, enable, and sustain what we know and what we do not know, cogenerating data,[2] and can also lead to a "systemic ignorance."[3] Thus, by revealing the researchers' identity, integrating their voice/narrative into a study, and interrogating their positionality vis-à-vis the field (Dragomir 2018), we can reorganize and evaluate the stories we tell (Code 1991).

In writing this book, I used a "situated" methodology: I place myself as a researcher in the study, disclosing who I am and how I came to know what I know—and, implicitly, what I do not know. I further contextualized the stories of my participants and provide transparency (Yanow 2006), to enable the reader to see how and from what perspective the work was produced and to invite other researchers to embark upon a similar task so they can complement these stories. This is not to say that I elevate my own voice above that of my participants or the voice of the scholars who inspired this study. Quite the contrary. By placing myself in the story, I hope to democratize and create "a non-hierarchical, non-manipulative research relationship" (England 1994). Furthermore, in researching the book, I used ethnographic tools to get an in-depth understanding of how immigrants in the U.S. military "make sense of their lived reality" (Hesse-Biber and Levy 2006, 230, cited by Buch and Staller 2014, 107).

Feminist Ethnography

Ethnography can be deployed in different ways, and the version I use is informed by feminist theory. Feminist ethnography—as the field is typically described—has no fixed definition (Buch and Staller 2014, 113) and cannot have one, for feminist ethnographic tools need to be understood as forms of knowledge that produce, reflect, and incentivize our "thinking through tensions and contradictions" (Davis and Craven 2016, 1). The field can be traced back to 1837 (xvi) and has taken many forms, but today most scholars agree that it is a form of ethnography that "attends to the dynamics of power in social interaction" (9). It usually focuses "on women's lives, activities, and experiences or on highly gendered settings," employing methods and writing styles informed by feminist theories and ethics and deploys an "analysis that uses a feminist theoretical lens and/or attends to the interplays between gender and other forms of power and difference" (Buch and Staller 2014, 113).

As two of my participants are women in the military, my work focuses both on women and on how gender operates in a "highly gendered setting." It uses a feminist theoretical interpretation of intersectionality to describe and analyze the cogenerated data and is thus integrated within the field of feminist ethnography. As "feminist ethnography produces knowledge about people and situations in specific contexts with attention on power differentials and inequities" (Davis and Craven 2016, 9), it is an appropriate way to "acknowledge and reflect upon power relations" (11) in military settings. Following Hawkesworth (2006), in doing so I challenge long-established biases and contest the dominant paradigm in understanding power by focusing on immigrants in the U.S. military. I interrogate the commonsense view of immigrant recruits as moldable "tabula rasa" entering a meritocratic institution and becoming heroic national figures.

While ethnographic, including feminist, approaches have been used in social science for decades, they are still a novel and marginal tool within the study of politics. Considering that through detailed analysis and data cogeneration this method is capable of uncovering power structures and their functioning, it is rather puzzling that to date ethnographers have produced limited interventions in the field. Nevertheless, "ethnographic approaches have long informed political science—albeit from the margins" (Schatz 2009, 3), continuously challenging the field with work (Pachirat 2009; De Volo 2009; Wedeen 2008), not only exposing the methodological limitations of orthodox qualitative methodology, but also highlighting the need for an "ethnographic immersion" (Schatz 2009) in the study of politics.

This work therefore used feminist ethnography in examining politics and the structures of power, and overall has been inspired by the strides made in interpretative methodology in political science, such as work on large-scale violence, war, and genocide (Fujii 2009, 2010); identity and nation building (Wedeen 2008); industrialized killing (Pachirat 2011); the construction of "race" and "ethnicity" in America (Yanow 2003); race, class, and gender in political analysis (Hawkesworth 2016a, 2016b); the agency of citizen-subjects (Turner 2014); and the emerging field of political ethnography (Billaud 2015; Bornstein 2003; Hromadžić 2015). This body of work took the narrow field of political science by storm and integrated the interpretative perspective into the study of power.

Furthermore, along similar lines, assuming that reality is not "out there," that truth is cocreated through interpretation of complex social dynamics, this book refrains from passing judgment on the truth value of my participants' testimonies (Wedeen 2008). It takes "people's world views seriously" (Schatz 2009, 13) and offers an interpretation of the process of naturalization via the military of the three participants.

Typically, the study of migration in political science falls under the umbrella of policy analysis or the study of public policy. This approach reveals the political and conceptual underpinnings of immigration legislation and its practices and could give us an understanding of how these policies come into being and into effect. However, employing an ethnographic approach in the study of migration offers the "possibility to care for people on a continual basis" and to keep the research and reader "in touch with the people affected by [the] power relations" (Schatz 2009, 12) inherent in immigration policies. By taking this approach, this work hopes to connect the reader with the participants in this study, and in so doing to empower sensitive and sensible immigration policies and political action.

Ethnographic research also comes in many styles, and mine is inspired by the work of Terry Williams (1990) who in his ethnographic studies creates powerful characters and subtly woven narratives that both transport the reader into the social web of the participants and take an in-depth look into typically marginalized settings while using "collage ethnography" (T. Williams and Milton 2015).

Starting from the premise that we "weave not only the physical world in which we live, but the very identities we construct for ourselves" (Yanow 2006, 6), this research was based on my previous experience as an immigrant. Learning firsthand what it means to naturalize in the United States empowered me to understand the process my participants were going through. I was able to see the difficulties in terms of obtaining entry to the host country, the precariousness of one's legal immigration status, and the anxiety of ensuring that one has the correct documents. While I have not been enlisted in the military, I understand the process of being naturalized through a powerful state institution due both to my studies of American government and to my previous work (both historical and ethnographic) on the role uniforms play in creating unity and discipline. This prior knowledge informed my work in the field and fed into my conversations with my participants, which led to a unique cogeneration of data (Yanow 2006; Pachirat 2009).

Research Timescale

My research for this book involved detailed work with the participants in repeated meetings and over several years. The main part took place in 2008–12 when I was working intensely with the three participants, Lily, Alexa, and Vikrant, on a regular (almost daily) basis. I encountered the three in different ways over several years. I first met Lily in 2008 at a Romanian social event. It was a loud bar, in which about thirty Romanians had gathered to celebrate their friend's birthday. Soon afterward, I started my work with her, and we conducted hundreds of hours of interviews in informal settings. We spent countless hours together and became close. She invited me to many of her social events, and I got to know her father, brother, and (first) husband. She invited me to her bridal shower and American wedding (she had another one back in Romania). She asked me to spend weekends at her home and with her on her military base, where she took me around and introduced me to her supervisors.

Differently, I had known Alexa for almost a decade before this research started, going back to when she first arrived in New York in 2000 and I was in charge of the cultural exchange program that brought her to the United States. Upon finding out that I came from eastern Europe, but—like her—spoke Spanish, she quickly became my friend. In 2009, when she enlisted, she became my participant in this research as well. My interactions with her, many and regular, took place both face-to-face and by telephone when her military life took her to sometimes distant locations. Soon after she enlisted, she visited me (together with her fiancé), invited me to her base, and introduced me to her colleagues. Over many years, I got to know Alexa really well, both in her civilian life, when she worked as a nanny, and in her military life. I visited the families for whom she worked and interacted with the children she cared for; I knew her mother, and I became friends with her sister and, later on, with her husband. Our talks started out as conversations, but were transformed into interviews when Alexa gave me permission to record them and to tell her overall life story. In my research, I reflected on the many memories Alexa and I share of civilian life and analyzed the hundreds of hours we spent together over the years.

Of the three participants, Vikrant was the one I met most formally—and only after he had enlisted in the U.S. military. I met him face-to-face only once, when he came to New York City, but we established a professional relationship and spoke regularly by telephone for months—as time and the demands of his military service permitted. Our regular phone calls, which lasted hours, were interrupted when he was in basic training or in deployment, but while in deployment Vikrant, who was an avid social media user, posted often and regularly shared his views on aspects of his new military life. With his permission, I was able to follow his life story through his own words as he wanted it to be known. Moreover, he posted many photos of himself serving in the U.S. Army, as well as pictures of his civilian life in the United States and from his past in India, which helped my analysis. His public story represents his preferred version of events, but only to the same extent as the stories of Alexa and Lily. While I could verify the "truth claims" of Lily and Alexa by juxtaposing them to their daily "reality," this "reality" was missing for Vikrant—and it could be argued that his "truth" is unverified. To corroborate Vikrant's claims, I juxtapose them with the replies posted to his social media posts and analyze the internal consistency of his story by carefully piecing together the details of his narrative.

With all three participants, I spent time in informal, public, or intimate settings. With the exception of Lily, who invited me to observe one of her physical training sessions on the base, I did not spend time with participants when they were directly performing their military duties. I have only their accounts of this part of their experience, at times supported by (public) photographs taken by military officials at these events. To qualify them as "valid" (rather than "truth") claims, I compare them with other descriptions given by the same participants, with the interactions I was able to observe myself, and with the story others corroborated (or did not confirm) about them. This process was not one of discourse versus reality but of interpreting discourses and, as described above, of cogenerating data through claims within discursive systems.

My connection with Lily, Alexa, and Vikrant over several years meant that I grew to know and understand them well, but equally resulted in my becoming deeply involved with them. The methodology does not deliver neutral and objective data collection or one devoid of emotions. Through my long-lasting emotional engagement with the participants, I was exposed to the details of their lives. I learned about their joys (such as getting married) and their sorrows (such as losing a dear person), and this also meant that I engaged in emotional responses (De Volo 2009).

Another aspect of my engagement with my subjects' lives is that the research delivered results that are not objectively true. The participants' accounts, together with my reflections on their stories and with others' view on the events, created narratives that are open to interpretation (Pachirat 2011; De Volo 2009). They do not claim to generate general answers to questions of naturalization via the military, but to deepen our understanding of this process by having a long and intimate look at the lives of three people. Following Yanow, I focused my work on understanding the meaning produced in the context of the participants' lives, and I do not claim that the findings of this research are universal (2006, 9). Moreover, these stories do not aim to create normative prescriptions applicable to all foreigners in the U.S. military. Instead, they offer a detailed picture of how these three immigrants live and highlight the role that the dynamics of race, ethnicity, gender, and class played in their "naturalization."

Limits and Constraints

Just like any other methodology, the research design of ethnographic interpretive research has its limits. This work presents three life stories of people who are in their prime, whose lives and careers are likely to progress, change, and continue. Thus, by focusing only on a part of their lives, it is incomplete. The decision to write about a segment of their lives was a difficult one. In an ideal format, this work would continue, like a reality show that follows people and reports almost in real time. Of course, this is not possible—and, moreover, this continuous approach is not desirable because it would not permit reflection, analysis, and writing. Thus, after four years, I reluctantly brought the intensive fieldwork for this project to an end. Four years is typically the amount of time needed for military enlistment of recruits for service for the country. As a result, it seems a good limit for the fieldwork as well. Moreover, this description of a section of the participants' lives keeps the field of analysis and interpretation open, as it allows for further adjustments or possible later interventions. While I acknowledge that the research presents only a slice of life, it leaves the research project open for different interpretations, developments, and endings.

When I designed the research for this project, I did not set out to look at three participants. Rather, I decided to look at how the field was constructed and see what was needed to give a comprehensive, in-depth understanding of the process of naturalization via the military. Early on I had to make a rather difficult decision: to work with the military directly or to work with the participants and tell their life stories as they wanted them to be told. There are benefits to both avenues, and of course a combination of the two ways would have been best. I explored different possibilities for conducting this work and reached out to military bases. The military personnel were supportive and helpful. I went to one Air Force and one National Guard base, where the receiving officers even selected a group of enlisted immigrants and gave me the physical space to conduct focus groups. These encounters were highly valuable, and they greatly informed my work.

But I decided to direct my attention and efforts toward telling life stories, weaving the narratives through experiences, memories, and verbal statements and/or postings on social media, and represented the military as an institution only briefly in the background. This might be seen as a shortcoming, but my hope is that this work will inspire future research that looks at the military more closely as an institution.

It is my belief that even one life story told in detail would deepen our understanding of how race/ethnicity, class, and gender act in the experience of migrants in the U.S. military. However, having three participants allowed for differences related to gender, race/ethnicity, and class to become more apparent. I hope these presentations enable the reader to explore these stories and to compare the experiences of Lily, Alexa, and Vikrant in their own ways—as they see fit. In addition to extensive interviews and research into the life of my three participants, I also interviewed several other foreigners in the U.S. military. On Lily's advice, I contacted her military base, where I was able to conduct a group interview with ten immigrants who were enlisted in the Air Force. Their superiors selected the Air Force respondents, and they articulated their views with care. Additionally, I had interviews with other immigrants in the U.S. military whose stories are not told. For example, I worked with a fellow academic colleague, who, while American, has spent his life abroad and returned to the United States to serve in the military. His experience of being a "stranger" in the U.S. military, coupled with his in-depth academic knowledge, facilitated and furthered my work on this topic.

Another participant who fulfilled multiple roles in this research was the late Professor Aristide Zolberg. Ari—as students, friends, and family used to call him—was a great scholar and professor in the field of comparative politics and immigration and citizenship studies; he was my mentor, my friend, my professor, and my dissertation adviser at the New School for Social Research, and he was also an American immigrant who obtained his citizenship by serving in the Korean War as an enlisted soldier. Ari was not only a great academic support and a staunch critic but also a great participant in this study. Over the three years that we worked together, Ari shared with me many stories of the time when he served and made me understand the impact of race, ethnicity, and citizenship status in his military service. One of his favorite stories was to tell me how his supervisors, knowing that he was capable and highly educated, often wanted to entrust him with many tasks, but because he was not an American citizen yet and could not pass the clearance test, he was often relegated to menial office tasks. Ari regularly read my work and critically engaged with it, pushing me to ask questions that I otherwise would not have asked.

As mentioned above, in addition to interviews, I conducted research on social media sites, following the life stories of participants. I also joined social media[4] groups focused on immigrants or women (or both) in the U.S. military forces. I closely followed what other immigrant soldiers were posting on media sites and reflected on their participations. This method of research was unorthodox at the time and raised a lot of questions about the accuracy of data collected through this media. Since then work on the use of social media while enlisted, and especially during deployment, has been expanding, showing how the military has been used to keep a flow of vital information (Silvestri 2015).

Accompanied by Lily, I went to a veterans' meeting at her school and encountered other people who served in the military. Also, this fieldwork was supported by a detailed investigation of official military sources, which are declassified and widely available, mainly regarding the military's demographics, recruitment, and commitment to diversity. This archival research was supplemented by academic and scholarly research pertaining to immigration and naturalization, as well as to African Americans, Latinos/as/x, and women in the military.

The U.S. military has different branches and different ways for people to serve in it. The three participants are from different branches and from different backgrounds and have different genders, providing a broad palette of experiences of immigrant soldiers in today's America. Of course, a different number of participants would have led to a different outcome, and more life stories are needed to deliver a more comprehensive view of these experiences. This work is by no means exhaustive, because it does not present the narratives of recruits in each branch. However, it has two active members and one reserve, two serving in the Army and one in the Air Force, and two enlisting through regular recruitment and one through MAVNI, the Pentagon-designed program for immigrants. The participants come from Eastern Europe, South Asia, and South America, and they are two females and one male. While small, the group of participants in this research is diverse, covering different immigrant experiences within the U.S. military.

Having a limited number of participants brought benefits. Following Crouch and McKenzie, I argue that having three research subjects facilitated my close "association with the respondents, and enhance[d] the validity of fine-grained, [and] in-depth inquiry." Furthermore, I contend that "since such a research project scrutinizes the dynamic qualities of a situation (rather than elucidating the proportionate relationships among its constituents), the issue of sample size—as well as representativeness—has little bearing on the project's basic logic" (2006, 483). Thus, using this research design, this book does not claim to cover all of the experiences, but allows for layered participant experiences to come to the fore.

As a result of this research design, many perspectives of American immigrant soldiers are not represented and are therefore silenced. These are not the only silences within the book. Within the stories of my participants, there were visible and often frustrating moments when they were silent "by choice" (Ybema et al. 2009, 286), moments whose meanings were "multiple and contradictory," both hiding and revealing (Fujii 2010, 237), and thus they "require[d] careful handling since one explanation does not fit all" (238). Silences were mostly visible in Lily's narrative. Lily, who was proud and happy to share her experiences in the military, performed verbal acrobatics to avoid sharing any information that might make the military look bad. Realizing Lily's discomfort with possibly diverging from the story that she wanted to tell, I took her attitude seriously and reflected on the importance that "the right" narrative had for her. Imagined or real, the repercussions of sharing information were shadowing my participants' behavior and stories. Thus, I made note of these silences, but—like Fujii (2010)—decided to respect my participants' boundaries and not push them into areas of discomfort.

This book is not many things, and to present all of them would take lifetimes. But as academic fields of studies have their rigors and standards, it is now a good moment to reflect and spell out the main avenues that my research did not take. This is not a military study. While I make historical references to the institution of military, they are only to ground the analysis and to support the reader's quest further. As expressed earlier, while I looked at the naturalization process of three immigrants via the military service, I considered the U.S. military as one of the institutions of the state, one that has precise processes and employs tools and practices that hold its staff to high standards. These characteristics make transformations easy to follow.

Finally, while grounded in migration scholarly work, this book is not a public policy work. But, put differently, by presenting the transformation of immigrants into U.S. soldiers, it hopes to support policy makers to create and enact a valuable and sensible legal framework that would empower immigrants who enlist into the U.S. military forces.

Ethical Concerns

These lingering silences bring me to my final points regarding methodological decisions. I will end this explanation of my research design by adding a few words about ethical concerns. Needless to say, writing the life stories of people in the armed forces is not an easy task. The U.S. military—like any other military—asks for complete allegiance and creates environments in which the authorities can control or at least account for all variables. Detailing the lives of these immigrants while keeping their identity protected is (to say the least) a difficult task. The participants were ambivalent about their life stories becoming public. This attitude is of course not unusual among participants in qualitative/ethnographic studies. In their work with con men in New York City, Terry Williams and Trevor B. Milton show how difficult it is to walk the fine line of identity protection. They were faced with situations in which they had to promise anonymity to some of their informants, while others "were over eager to share their stories, especially knowing that they would be recorded in literary history" (2015, 21) and were in search of recognition. As one of the key participants in their study, Alibi, put it: "I want the world to know what has happened to me" (21–22). When I was interviewing her, Lily echoed Alibi and was happy to tell her peers and supervisors about her military experience being immortalized in scholarly work. However, she readily chose another name for herself when given the chance. "Lily," she promptly answered when I asked what I should call her in my book. In contrast, Alexa shrugged her shoulders whenever I asked her to pick a name. She genuinely did not take this aspect of the endeavor too seriously. In the end, I picked a name for her, and when I told her she just smiled. But each time I asked her how I should protect her anonymity, she changed her mind. At times she wanted to publicly tell her story, she wanted to say it all, but at others she was pondering if her country of origin should be left out of the story. My ambivalence toward revealing much of her past mimics her indecision. Vikrant was proud to share his story in great detail. He was pleased to be interviewed and proud to be in the research project. Out of respect for his work, I decided to give him another name, even though his identity and many of his stories are widely shared on social media and in the mass media.

Lily, Alexa, and Vikrant were excited about their life stories becoming part of a book, but there were certain points, mainly with regard to their long-standing gray immigration status, that I decided not to pursue. Incomplete information and unresolved questions are an integral part of the legal difficulties immigrants encounter when attempting to establish their status in a host country. I decided to treat this topic carefully, and, after long reflection on how to explore this area of the research without breaking ethical conventions, I decided that if I described my participants' positions more explicitly, it might have an adverse effect on their status. I believe the reader should engage with and take notice of the lingering silences within the book.

Last, it is my hope that these stories will reach academic readers and a wider audience. Having this in mind, I avoided academic jargon while still conducting analysis and placing these narratives in a larger context. As a result, many of the academic references come in the footnotes and through references to the scholarly work used to support the analysis. In this way, the participants' stories are presented as a continuous narrative, and the reader can engage with the text in a different way at different times in the reading process.

Navigating this terrain has not been an easy task, but it has enabled me to hear my participants' narratives, see through the cracks in well-rehearsed discourses, and observe the daily practices that, at times, tell a different story. Showing my participants in a variety of settings over a long period—when they were happy, when they were frustrated or angry, and when they were melancholic and pensive—I assembled a multidimensional profile of each participant's life. Seeing their experiences from different angles and assuming different perspectives helped me create "life-story collages" (Williams and Milton 2015). This perspective led to the creation of an open-ended project, one that welcomes further collaboration. It is my hope that more immigrant soldiers' lives will be depicted and a new perspective will emerge.

Notes

Introduction

1. The term "naturalization" is also used in biology, meaning to bring a plant or animal to a new region, where the new element has to be "brought in conformity to nature. In citizenship and immigration legislation, documents and studies the term denotes the process of becoming a citizen and obtaining the 'rights of a national.'" https://www.merriam-webster.com/dictionary/naturalize, accessed November 23, 2017.

2. https://www.uscis.gov/us-citizenship/citizenship-through-naturalization/path-us-citizenship, accessed November 23, 2017.

3. The naturalization period for spouses of U.S. citizens is three years. See https://www.uscis.gov/us-citizenship/citizenship-through-naturalization/naturalization-spouses-us-citizens, accessed November 23, 2017.

4. https://www.uscis.gov/military/naturalization-through-military-service, accessed November 23, 2017.

5. https://www.brookings.edu/essay/women-warriors-the-ongoing-story-of-integrating-and-diversifying-the-armed-forces/, accessed September 24, 2021.

6. https://www.smithsonianmag.com/smart-news/today-in-1948-the-us-air-force-accepted-its-first-female-member-7671291/, accessed September 24, 2021.

7. https://www.cnas.org/publications/commentary/women-in-combat-five-year-status-update, accessed September 23, 2021.

8. https://www.weareoneamerica.org/immigrants-military-fact-sheet, accessed November 23, 2017.

9. See http://www.goarmy.com/about.html, accessed April 10, 2016.

10. The "Bracero program" was a set of laws and agreements between Mexico and the United States, initiated in 1942, that allowed temporary laborers to legally work in the United States for a limited time. It was shut down in 1951. It was often stated that it created poor job conditions and payment and that its ending led to an increase in irregular migrants who remained in the host country after the program's end. "A new wave of Mexican migrants, following the still persistent labor, crossed the border this time without authorization. Denied access to braceros, U.S. ranchers and farmers did not hire native workers, but turned to the same Mexican workers now rebaptized as clandestine migrants" (Portes and Rumbaut 2014, 24). For more on the Bracero program, see Gritter 2012.

11. Partial information and unresolved questions are an integral part of the difficult legal terrain encountered by immigrants who are in the process of mainstreaming their status in the host country. I chose to speak about their immigration status as a "gray area" after long and careful reflection on how to express something without breaking ethical conventions. I believe the reader should self-consciously experience the lingering silences within the pages, operating within uncertainties, just as migrants often operate within new countries.

12. http://www.qualitative-research.net/index.php/fqs/article/view/1589/3095, accessed October 22, 2016.

13. Under the emblem of cultural exchange programs, companies and nongovernmental organizations operated as recruiters for summer camps and other jobs for which employers could not easily find staff. While participants are full employees, as they are participants in cultural exchange programs, labor laws do not apply to them; therefore, the ads for these positions highlight the entertainment aspects of the job: "Be more than just a tourist. Work, travel, volunteer and play at numerous destinations around the world." See http://www.ccusa.com/Programs/CampCounselorsUSA.aspx, accessed October 1, 2016.

Chapter 1. Conceptual Work

1. https://www.idf.il/en/minisites/how-to-join-us-and-voluntary-programs/how-to-join/, accessed March 7, 2020.

2. According to Hattiangadi, as of 2004, roughly 8,000 immigrants/noncitizens enlist every year. The Navy admits the highest percentage of immigrants, followed closely by the Marine Corps and the Army. The Defense Manpower Data Center estimates that about 35,000 immigrants currently serve in the active military, with an additional 12,000 serving in the Guard and Reserve. In 2003, the four services had the following numbers of immigrants: Navy—15,880 immigrant sailors; Marine Corps—6,440 immigrant Marines; Army—5,596 immigrant soldiers; Air Force—3,056 immigrant airmen. Also, "since Oct. 1, 2002, USCIS has naturalized 102,266 members of the military, with 11,548 of those service members becoming citizens during USCIS naturalization ceremonies in 34 foreign countries: Afghanistan, Albania, Australia, Bahrain, China (Hong Kong), Cuba (Guantanamo), Djibouti, El Salvador, Georgia, Germany, Greece, Haiti, Honduras, Iceland, Iraq, Italy,

Jamaica, Japan, Jordan, Kenya, Korea, Kosovo, Kuwait, Kyrgyzstan, Libya, Mexico, the Philippines, Qatar, South Korea, Spain, Thailand, Turkey, United Arab Emirates and the United Kingdom." See appendix 1, from http://www.uscis.gov/news/fact -sheets/naturalization-through-military-service-fact-sheet, accessed April 15, 2015; and appendix # 2, https://www.weareoneamerica.org/sites/default/files/OneAm-ercaFactSheet_Immigrants_in_the_Military.pdf, accessed April 15, 2015; http://www .migrationpolicy.org/article/immigrants-us-armed-forces, accessed April 15,2015; or https://www.americanprogress.org/issues/immigration/report/2013/11/08/79116/ new-americans-in-our-nations-military/, accessed April 15, 2015.

3. Additionally, according to Zong and Batalova from the Migration and Policy Institute, "almost 1.9 million veterans are the US-born children of immigrants." See https://www.migrationpolicy.org/article/immigrant-veterans-united-statesl, accessed March 7, 2020.

4. Since its launch, the MAVNI program has been controversial and has been suspended at times, only to be relaunched soon after (see https://dod.defense.gov/ news/mavni-fact-sheet.pdf, accessed November 19, 2021; and https://studyinthe states.dhs.gov/what-is-mavni-information-for-designated-school-officials, accessed March 8, 2020), with its recruits at times being stuck in legal and logistical limbo, incurring delays in their military employment and acquiring U.S. citizenship. See https://www.militarytimes.com/news/your-military/2019/08/15/immigrant-recruit -stuck-in-mavni-limbo/, accessed March 8, 2020.

5. More recent legal changes allow undocumented migrants who qualify for the policy known as Deferred Action for Childhood Arrivals (DACA) to join the U.S. armed forces. See http://www.usatoday.com/story/news/nation/2014/09/25/policy-to -allow-undocumented-immigrants-in-military/16225135/, accessed April 15, 2015; and http://www.nytimes.com/2014/09/26/us/military-path-opened-for-young-immigrants .html?_r=0, accessed April 15, 2015.

6. The program is sometimes open, sometimes closed, but typically invites ap-plicants in one of the following immigration categories at the time of enlistment: asylee, refugee, Temporary Protected Status, or nonimmigrant categories E, F, H, I, J, K, L, M, O, P, Q, R, S, T, TC, TD, TN, U, or V (for more info, see http://www .mavni.info/) and more recently DACA participants (see appendix 3 or http://www .goarmy.com/content/dam/goarmy/downloaded_assets/mavni/mavni-language.pdf, accessed April 15, 2015).

7. Although military service grants immigrant soldiers' rapid access to naturaliza-tion and all the rights that American citizenship entails, not all immigrant soldiers become citizens. According to Margaret Stock, in 2009, 59 percent of the foreign-born soldiers were not naturalized as a result of their service. The low number of naturalization cases is often due to administrative or legal issues, such as long delays in the process, the usage of fictive names to enlist, or the personal decision to not become American citizens. See Margaret Stock, Immigration Policy Center, "Im-migrant in the Military: Eight Years after 9/11," http://immigrationpolicy.org/sites/ default/files/docs/Immigrants_in_the_Military_-_Stock_110909_0.pdf, November 2009, accessed March 20, 2010.

8. In her work, Crenshaw (1991) identifies three types of intersectionality: structural, political, and representational. Structural intersectionality analyzes how individuals and groups are affected differently by social systems and structures, specifically how the systems and structures inherently oppress some and privilege others. Political intersectionality highlights how "racism as experienced by people of color who are of a particular gender—male—tends to determine the parameters of antiracist strategies, just as sexism as experienced by women who are of particular race—white—tends to ground the women's movement" (1991, 1252). Thus, political intersectionality shows how traditional "feminist and antiracist politics have contributed to the marginalization of racial/ethnic minority women" (Few-Demo 2014, 171). Finally, representational intersectionality refers to how political agendas and legal structures are influenced by cultural constructions of racial/ethnic minority women's description in the mass media, texts, images, and so on.

9. McCall argues that there are three main approaches to the study of intersectionality: anticategorical complexity, intracategorical complexity, and intercategorical complexity (2005, 1772–73).

10. According to the Pew Research Center, the American middle class has been continuously shrinking over the past thirty years. See http://www.pewsocialtrends.org/2015/12/09/the-american-middle-class-is-losing-ground/ and http://money.cnn.com/2016/05/11/news/economy/middle-class-shrinking/, accessed September 29, 2016.

11. The myth of an automatic entrance into the middle class has been dismantled by Blau (1992), Blau and Duncan (1992), and Portes and Böröcz (1989), who analyzed how ethnical hierarchies systematically limit immigrants' access to jobs, housing, and education (Zhou 1997a).

12. These analyses typically agree that in the beginning, there was an era of "open immigration," which allowed all those who undertook the transatlantic journey to settle in the new land (Tichenor 2002), and that this era was followed by a gradual tightening of immigration controls. According to this argument, the closer to the year 1776, the more open the country was to receiving immigrants. On the other hand, Aristide Zolberg argues that the United States never had an era of open-door immigration: it has used systematic rules, laws, practices, and policies to choose immigrants from the very beginning. Zolberg states that even though America is a nation of immigrants, it is "not just of any immigrants" (2006b, 3). Taking a different path to European countries, the United States established programs and policies to decide who got to come and stay in the country. And, most important, throughout the country's history, these acts took into consideration race, ethnicity, class, and gender—which all became important factors in accessing U.S. citizenship.

13. http://www.lehigh.edu/~ineng/VirtualAmericana/chineseimmigrationact.html, accessed April 16, 2016. For more on how the policy was created and adopted, see Tichenor 2002.

14. The 1924 act created specific quotas, providing immigration visas to 2 percent of the total number of people of each nationality present in the United States as of

the 1890 national census and excluded immigrants from Asia. https://history.state .gov/milestones/1921-1936/immigration-act, accessed April 17, 2016.

15. From 1901 to 1920, 86 percent of immigrants entered from Europe and only 4 percent from Asia, 3 percent from Latin America, 6 percent from Canada, and 1 percent other places, whereas in the period 1980–93 43 percent of immigrants came from Latin America, 39 percent from Asia, 13 percent from Europe, 2 percent from Canada, and 3 percent from other countries. http://cis.org/1965ImmigrationAct -MassImmigration, accessed September 29, 2016.

16. For example, Molina (2014) examines Mexican Americans from 1924 onward and describes how the understanding of race and ethnicity was creating *racial scripts*, which influence perceptions about Mexican Americans.

17. According to Kapur, "Nearly 90 percent of all households with a member outside of the country report that the member left after 1990" (2010, 60), "an over-whelming majority of households reported that the family members who lived abroad were male (81.8 percent)" (61), and the "highly educated migrate to industrialized countries while the less educated go to the Middle East" (62), with 19.7 percent of the total Indian emigrants present in the United States (64). Regarding religion, Indian Americans are Muslim, 14.27 percent; Christian, 14.92 percent; Hindu, 38.7 percent; and unidentified, 36.73 percent.

18. For example, the median annual household income for Indian Americans in 2010 was $88,000 (higher than U.S. households at $49,800), while only 9 percent of adult Indian Americans live in poverty, compared to 13 percent of the U.S. popula-tion. In 2010 the Pew Research Center found that 28 percent of Indian Americans worked in science and engineering fields, and the 2013 American Community Sur-vey found that 69.3 percent of Indian Americans sixteen and older were in man-agement, business, science, and arts occupations. http://www.pewresearch.org/fact -tank/2014/09/30/5-facts-about-indian-americans/, accessed October 12, 2016.

19. https://www.ourdocuments.gov/doc_large_image.php?flash=false&doc=84, accessed September 10, 2021

20. African Americans have served in the U.S. military since the Civil War. Then they were allowed to serve in the Union's troops, within racially segregated units. They accounted for about 10 percent of Army personnel. In the Navy, African Americans served on integrated crews, although primarily at the lowest ranks and in menial jobs, making up about a quarter of Navy personnel. By the end of the war, Congress established four black regiments: the Twenty-Fourth and Twenty-Fifth Infantries and the Ninth and Tenth Cavalries. This represented about 10 percent of Army personnel (M. Segal et al. 2007). African Americans have served since in segregated units. On July 26, 1948, President Truman issued Executive Order 9981, meant to abolish racial discrimination in the armed forces and eventually lead to the end of segregation in the service. http://www.trumanlibrary.org/9981.htm, accessed August 1, 2013.

21. http://www.defense.gov/home/features/2007/blackhistorymonth/index.html, accessed August 1, 2013. Scholars, such as Janowitz and Moskos (1979), refer to the U.S. military as a model of good race relations. Although throughout the years vis-

ible progress occurred in race relations, especially since the establishment of the all-volunteer force (AVF), recent researchers, such as Kirby, Harrell, and Sloan (2000) as well as Burk and Espinoza (2012), challenged this comfortable claim and argued that disparities in military allocations of goods and burdens sometimes disadvantage racial minorities. However, as is the case with women, the African American presence in the U.S. military is not uniform, as more African Americans tend to be at the "enlisted" level and only a few are officers (R. Segal 2004).

22. "2014 Demographics: Profile of the Military Community," report published by the Office of the Deputy Assistant Secretary of Defense (Military Community and Family Policy), http://download.militaryonesource.mil/12038/MOS/Reports/2014 -Demographics-Report.pdf, accessed October 12, 2016.

23. For example, African Americans are more likely than other racial groups to be in functional support, administrative duties, and service or supply occupations and less likely to be in electronic, electrical, or mechanical equipment repair or combat specialties. More recent studies argue that "in an environment where racial stratification has been substantially reduced, traditional racial disparities across a variety of well-being dimensions reverse themselves. By including Latinos [next to African Americans and women], I [Hickes Lundquist] show that minority groups clearly benefit from the meritocratic conditions of military in similar ways as blacks" (Hickes-Lundquist 2008, 493).

24. According to M. Segal et al., "Since the start of the AVF in 1973, African Americans have served in the U.S. military, especially in the Army, in numbers greater than their percent of the population. This disproportionate representation has been especially clear among military women. Recently, accessions of African Americans have declined. At the same time, Hispanics, who constitute a growing segment of the US population, have been underrepresented in the military, especially among the officer corps. Hispanics now comprise a larger percentage of military women than men. We analyze the trends in representation over time and the differences among the US armed forces" (2007, 48).

25. One step in the direction of addressing this situation and offering Latinos (and other immigrants) in the United States the opportunity to serve in return for temporarily streaming their immigration status took place when President Obama signed the Deferred Action for Childhood Arrivals in 2014, granting exemption from deportation and a two-year work permit to those who arrived in the United States as children. For more details, see https://www.uscis.gov/humanitarian/consideration -deferred-action-childhood-arrivals-daca, accessed October 12, 2016. However, legal changes to DACA have been taking place under recent (both Trump and Biden) administrations, making the enlistment of DACA recipients within the military improbable for the foreseeable future.

26. "Women and Migration: Exploring the Data," https://blogs.worldbank.org/ opendata/women-and-migration-exploring-data, accessed July 23, 2019.

27. http://www2.powayusd.com/online/usonline/worddoc/ellisislandsite.htm, accessed April 17, 2016.

28. https://memory.loc.gov/ammem/awhhtml/awlaw3/immigration.html, accessed April 17, 2016.

29. Women were legally targeted in the Cable Act of 1922, also known as the "Married Woman's Act," http://immigrationtounitedstates.org/397-cable-act-of-1922.html, which rectified the act of 1907 that stated that a woman could take a man's nationality upon marriage. The 1922 Cable Act stated that, even if married, a man who was forbidden to become an American citizen because of his race would not become American if he married a woman who was an American citizen. Furthermore, women were sometimes caught at the intersection of gender and race/ethnicity in immigration policies. The 1882 Chinese Exclusion Act was applied to both Chinese females and males but had a greater impact on Chinese women, who entered and settled in the United States in lower numbers than Chinese men. This created a gender gap within the Chinese community. "The number of Chinese females fluctuated between 3.6 percent (in 1980) and 7.2 percent (in 1870) of the total Chinese population" (Chan 1994). Chan argues that these discrepancies were not only the result of women being confronted with "patriarchal cultural values, a sojourning mentality, differentials in the cost of living, and hazardous conditions of the American West" (94) but also because "from early 1870s onward, [there were] efforts by various levels of American government to restrict the immigration of Chinese women" (95). In effect, Chinese women faced immigration legislation that curbed their possibility of becoming Americans, based not only on their race but also on their gender. For an analysis of contemporary gender and immigration, see http://www.immigrationpolicy.org/just-facts/immigrant-women-united-states-portrait-demographic-diversity, accessed April 17, 2016.

30. A Pew Research Center project on Hispanic trends, conducted in 2006, found that while "women around the world have been migrating more in recent decades and . . . have made up ever larger shares of legal immigrants to the United States in recent years . . ., an increasing flow of mostly male unauthorized migrants has more than counterbalanced the feminization of legal migration." http://www.pewhispanic .org/2006/07/05/gender-and-migration/, accessed September 30, 2016.

31. "U.S. Immigration Law Treats Women and Men Differently," http://www .huffingtonpost.com/2013/06/05/us-immigration-women_n_3390540.html, accessed September 30, 2016.

32. http://voxeu.org/article/do-female-immigrants-assimilate-us-labour-market, accessed September 30, 2016.

33. For example, Schoeni (1998) shows that, empowered by their gender traditions, women immigrating from countries such as Japan, Korea, and China experience a high degree of assimilation during the first ten years.

Another criterion for understanding immigrant women assimilation patterns is fertility. It is assumed that "Hispanic" women, especially those migrating from Mexico, will have a higher fertility rate than the native population, which will result in their failure to become similar to women in the host country. However, research by Parrado and Morgan points out that "Hispanic and Mexican fertility is converging with that of whites, and that it is similarly responsive to period conditions and to women's level of education" (2008, 651), and concludes that immigrant women are in effect quite similar to native ones.

34. The military is mostly associated with values attributed to masculinity (force, authority, structure, and violence), but Regina Titunik presents a different perspective.

She argues that "the prevailing view of the military as hypermasculine is misguided. Not unhindered aggressiveness, but camaraderie, discipline, and service are the qualities instilled in soldiers. These qualities foster military effectiveness and counterbalance sexist tendencies, producing a complex institutional culture congenial to women in significant respects" (2008, 137). Hence, the military might not be so "macho" as it might seem, since it incorporates values often associated with the feminine and as a result might create spaces in which women can develop and even flourish. While Titunik's view is interesting, military practices overwhelmingly point in the opposite direction, exposing the inherent male structure and bias of the armed forces.

35. This is not to dismiss the occurrence of sexual assaults within the American military. For example, according to the Department of Defense Annual Report on Sexual Assault in the Military of 2012, "There were 3,374 reports of sexual assault involving Service members. These reports involved one or more Service members as either the victim or subject (alleged perpetrator) of an investigation. The 3,374 reports involved a range of crimes prohibited by the Uniform Code of Military Justice (UCMJ), from abusive sexual contact to rape. This represents a 6 percent increase over the 3,192 reports of sexual assault received in FY11, thus providing the Department greater opportunities to provide victim care and to ensure appropriate offender accountability." http://www.sapr.mil/public/docs/reports/FY12_DoD_SAPRO_Annual_Report_on_Sexual_Assault-volume_one.pdf. For more recent data, see http://www.defense.gov/News/Transcripts/Transcript-View/Article/607047/department-of-defense-press-briefing-on-sexual-assault-in-the-military-in-the-p, accessed September 30, 2016. Moreover, scholars such as T. S. Nelson have a strong position on this topic and argue that "sexual assault and harassment are deeply rooted in today's armed forces. The problem is further complicated by a system that has been unable or unwilling to effectively address this issue over the years" (2002, 3).

Chapter 2. Lily

1. https://georgewbush-whitehouse.archives.gov/news/releases/2002/07/20020703-24.html, accessed December 21, 2019.

2. Scorpions, "Wind of Change," 1990, https://www.youtube.com/watch?v=n4RjJKxsamQ, accessed July 24, 2019.

3. This process of distinguishing between the two waves of immigrants is more visible in Europe, where many more Eastern European immigrants settled. In the early 1990s, it was easier to travel to Germany and France "illegally," riding trains, swimming, preparing false papers. To go to the United States, immigrants had to have a larger sum of money at their disposal and they had to have a visa, which was difficult to obtain under the communist regime.

4. According to the official website of the U.S. embassy in Bucharest, when applying for "non-immigrant visa applicants may also bring any documents that demonstrate personal and economic ties to Romania. Examples include: proof of current employment and past work history; evidence of financial support (including bank statements, salary history or pension statements if retired); proof of property ownership (that is home, land, business); and business statements and accounts (if you own a firm)."

http://romania.usembassy.gov/visas/non-immigrant_forms.html, accessed April 9, 2016.

5. The J1 program was launched in 1961 and as of now includes fourteen different exchange-visitor categories, including "professor and researcher scholar" and "physician" categories, in addition to its "cultural exchange." http://travel.state.gov/content/visas/english/study-exchange/exchange.html, accessed July 30, 2014; http://jlvisa.state.gov/, accessed April 11, 2015.

6. "The Two-Year Home Residency Requirement is often referred as the 212(e). Only the U.S. Department of State can determine if a J1 and/or J2 is subject to the 212(e). If subject, a J-visa holder will have to physically reside within their last country of legal permanent residence for two years before s/he may return to the U.S. as an H-1B visa holder, L visa holder, K visa holder or as a permanent resident. If subject, J-visitors are unable to apply for a change of status within the U.S.A." https://isso.ucsf.edu/immigration-visas/for-scholars/j-1-scholars/j-1-two-year-home-residence, accessed April 9, 2016.

7. When Lily came to the United States, the trend of female migration was slightly declining (from 50.6 percent to 50.2 percent).

8. Pew Hispanic, http://www.pewhispanic.org/2006/07/05/gender-and-migration/, accessed November 24, 2017.

9. International Organization for Migration, https://www.iom.int/sites/default/files/about-iom/Gender-migration-remittances-infosheet.pdf, accessed November 24, 2017.

10. Lily's answer to the question about enlisting is similar to that given for decades by the majority of American-born recruits. According to Charles C. Moskos, reasons for joining the armed forces are, in the following order of importance, personal, that is, to get away from home, mature, and travel; patriotic, that is, to serve one's country; draft, that is, being motivated to choose the time of entry or branch service; and self-advancement, that is, to learn a trade and receive an education (1970, 49). As these motivations set *longue-durée* trends, military recruiters are aware of the recruits' motivations for enlistment. Nowadays, military websites promote as incentives for joining the armed forces furthering one's education, getting a stable salary, satisfying a sense of adventure, achieving physical fitness, and gaining recognition/accessing social mobility. https://www.afreserve.com/news-article/5-reasons-to-join-the-air-force-reserve, accessed November 24, 2017. Moreover, like other women who enlisted in the U.S. military, Lily's response suggests that enlisting in the military could being seen as an exciting prospect, which could give women the opportunity to be independent (Sullivan 2011). This was a decision based primarily on personal reasons, but one that may create "a legacy of courage, patriotic service" (2).

11. https://www.afreserve.com/news-article/5-reasons-to-join-the-air-force-reserve, accessed November 24, 2017.

12. According to the 1965 Immigration and Nationality Act, a.k.a. the Hart-Cellar Act, Public Law 89-236, October 3, 1965, https://www.congress.gov/bill/115th-congress/house-bill/6183/all-info, accessed June 13, 2013, family reunification is possible under certain conditions, which includes the ability of the U.S. citizen

petitioner to support the family member(s) at 125 percent of the poverty level and provide proof of their family relationship. For more details, see http://www.uscis .gov/family/family-us-citizens, accessed June 13, 2013.

13. Migration Policy, https://www.migrationpolicy.org/article/family-reunification, accessed November 24, 2017.

14. My understanding of "performative practice" follows Lisa Weeden's description. She defines practices as unique to humans and as "actions or deeds that are repeated over time, [which] are leaned, reproduced and subjected to risk through social interaction" (2008, 87). Furthermore, she refers to "performative" following J. L. Austin and J. Derrida as an "iterable practice," which interprets "self-formation through the character of speech and bodily practices, which constitutes individuals as particular kinds of special beings or 'subjects'" (88). For more on performative practices, see J. Butler 1993, 1997; and Bourdieu 1979.

15. For example, even those who are not (yet) members of the nation have to defend it with their life: "THE AIRMAN'S CREED: I am an American Airman. I am a warrior. I have answered my nation's call. I am an American Airman. My mission is to fly, fight and win. I am faithful to a proud heritage. A tradition of honor. And a legacy of valor. I am an American Airman. Guardian of freedom and justice, My nation's sword and shield. Its sentry and avenger. I defend my country with my life. I am an American Airman. Wingman, Leader, Warrior. I will never leave an airman behind. I will never falter. And I will not fail." Airmen's Guide, https://static.e-publishing .af.mil/production/1/af_a1/publication/afhandbook1/afhandbook1.pdf, accessed April 20 2020.

16. Benedict Anderson revealed in *Imagined Communities* that "regardless of the actual inequality and exploitation that may prevail in each, the nation is always conceived as a deep, horizontal comradeship. Ultimately it is this fraternity that makes it possible, over the past two centuries, for so many millions of people, not so much to kill, as willingly die for such limited imaginings" (1991, 7).

17. Creating and emphasizing citizenry and allegiance is not new or specific to foreign-born soldiers. The flag has also been used by native-born soldiers to express their allegiance to the country, their solidarity, and their comradeship: "A small group of Union soldiers, held prisoners by the Confederates, made a Stars and Stripes from their own clothing, flew it for a few minutes from the rafters of the old warehouse in which they were imprisoned, and then tore it into 22 pieces, one for each man who helped make it. Everyone then hid the piece of flag in his clothing and took it with him when released from prison. In the years following the war, the pieces were finally recovered and sewed together again to form the flag, which is still in existence." "The Soldier's Guide," 1952, https://openlibrary.org/books/OL35746357M/ The_Soldier's_Guide.

18. "Correctly" singing the national anthem is a powerful symbol of respecting the nation, and deviance often produces immediate dissent—see how in 2016 American footballer Colin Kaepernick's refusal to stand during the anthem, instead "taking the knee," led to a pervasive political controversy. https://www.youtube.com/ watch?v=bBdoDOXMWkg, accessed March 13, 2020.

19. In the U.S. Air Force, a "wing" is an organizational unit, a level of command below the numbered Air Force or higher headquarters, which has a distinct mission with a significant scope. http://www.afhra.af.mil/factsheets/factsheet.asp?id=10946, accessed June 18, 2014.

20. In contrast, Moskos argues, "Though every soldier is an integral part of a tremendously large organization that is the United States military, his social horizon is largely circumscribed by activities occurring at the level of the company" (1970, 66). However, we can see that in Lily's case, allegiance to the smaller and larger units was deeply intertwined, and at least at the level of her personal reflection, military and nationalistic identifications merged. Lily learned about American citizenry practices and the military in general by being socialized within a small horizon, the horizon of her wing/unit. Without having this first experience, her allegiance to the larger community might have not grown.

21. This was not the first or last time that I heard Lily saying this. For example, while we were in a bar in West Village, after a few drinks, Lily met two of her female friends. The conversation heated up when Lily tried to defend a budget increase for the military. She argued, using similar words and logic as we have seen above, "If we are not there [that is, in Afghanistan and Iraq], they will come after us here [in the United States]." The two women, who had just taken master's degrees in international relations, were strong opponents of an increased military budget, so Lily's arguments encountered robust opposition. In response, she just repeated the "danger argument," which left the two women dissatisfied.

22. The training of female recruits to perform different tasks within the military is a frequently contested topic. While we see how important these practices are in Lily's case, and how much they impacted on her sense of belonging and her overall commitment and willingness to participate, women soldiers do not always benefit from the same training as their male counterparts, which in turn could impact their performance and career advancement. For example, in her memoir *Fight Like a Girl: The Truth behind How Female Marines Are Trained*, Lieutenant Colonel Kate Germano describes how she was a top-flight Marine officer and a battalion commander, but was fired due to her vision—at odds with the official line—for training female Marines. In doing so, she exposes how the myth that "women can't fight" leads to a limited training, which in turn creates a legacy of second-class treatment for women in the military (Germano and Kennedy 2018).

23. Additionally, different branches of the U.S. military developed video games that informally trained soldiers both in furthering their community cohesion and in performing specific military tasks. This was not without controversy, as critics argue that effects of war such as physical and mental disabilities are utterly downplayed in the games. For more, see Derby 2014, citing R. Allen 2011.

24. The transition to a system based on volunteerism took place at the same time the U.S. armed forces were also withdrawing from the long Vietnam War (Griffith 1998). The change from mandatory service to an all-volunteer force was not an easy process or one embraced by all military personnel: "Men who loved their army, men who had committed their lives to its values, men who were losing hundreds of their

soldiers a month in a war that would not be won, who saw respect for their proud institution draining away—such men found it difficult to confront the power of a civilian commission that treated soldiering as just another job, that seemed to presume that the nation's defense could be managed through the supply-and-demand forces of the labor market and that a competitive wage would be sufficient to motivate men into combat" (Bailey 2009, 35–36).

25. "G.I. Bill of Rights. Formally called the Servicemen's Readjustment Act of 1944, the law extended numerous social benefits to returning veterans of World War II. Any veteran who received a discharge status other than dishonorable after at least ninety days of service qualified for extensive unemployment benefits, low-interest guaranteed loans to buy a home, farm, or business, and financial assistance to pursue additional education or training. Until they found a job, veterans could qualify for unemployment benefits of $20 a week for up to one year; the average veteran used only 19.7 weeks' worth of the '52-20 Club,' as the program was called, with only 14 percent exhausting their full entitlement. Twenty-nine percent took advantage of the loan guarantee provisions: 4.3 million purchased homes at low interest rates, and 200,000 purchased farms or businesses. The construction industry received an enormous boost: by 1955, nearly one-third of new housing starts nationwide owed their backing to the Veterans Administration" (Mettler 2005, 6).

26. The view that the U.S. military is a profession rather than a calling attracts strong criticism. Frazier (2006) argues that "the problem surrounding the values of America's youth suggests that we as a nation must do better to prepare young men and women for quality citizenship and the capability of leading our country. Data from studies of Baby Boomer, X and Y generations will be extrapolated to compare them to the values espoused by today's professional military services. Preliminary findings indicate that major differences in values exist among each generation and how they perceive life as a whole. From these differences evidence also suggests incidents involving sex, harassment, race, money, and 'Abu Ghraib' scandals will increase as the military profession continues to rely on current society to fill its ranks. Values education must be reinforced to combat this probable dilemma using creative, diverse, and innovative program designs and delivery strategies." Critics further argue that the prospect of military service being seen as "just another job" is unsettling, and there is a need for the military to be perceived as "something bigger than oneself" or even as "a self-sacrificial Christian calling" (Frickenstein 2005).

27. http://www.goarmy.com/goarmywebapp/GetAdvicceResults.do, accessed November 2012.

28. https://www.weforum.org/agenda/2015/06/worlds-10-biggest-employers/?link =mktw, accessed November 26, 2017.

29. Pierre Bourdieu, "Capital Cultural: Interview at Radio Droit de Ote," published August 2010, https://www.youtube.com/watch?v=cJ4ru3tOEFM, accessed October 5, 2016.

30. According to http://www.military.com/Recruiting/Content/0,13898,diversity _main,00.html, accessed April 19, 2015: "The US Armed Forces are a reflection of America—virtually every possible ethnic and religious group is represented. The

military is a team of men and women from all over the United States working to-gether with a single purpose: to protect our Nation and fight for freedom. Today's service-members are part of a team with a unique character and identity, where each service-member is judged by his or her performance—never by race, color, religion or gender. It has been said that if society as a whole were more like the military in this regard, the US would be a better place. Although diverse, the US military is strengthened by the unified goal of preserving freedom. Learn more about our diverse military and the legends and heroics of those who have served and continue to serve for the cause of freedom." Embracing diversity in the military is seen as "an asset [that] provides a myriad of advantages. Among them are 1) full utilization of human capital; 2) reduced interpersonal conflict; 3) greater innovation and flex-ibility; 4) improved productivity; 5) reduced employee turnover; and 6) improved recruiting opportunities" (Varvel 2000).

31. For more details on the officer program for Air Force Reserve officers, see http://www.arpc.afrc.af.mil/ServiceCenter/Guard-ReserveFactsheets/FactSheets/Display/tabid/310/Article/637906/accessions.aspx, accessed October 4, 2016.

32. Lily's situation is by no means unique. The promotion of women within military ranks is a sensitive and dire topic that has been gaining public attention. For example, the U.S. Air Force official website published in 2014 said: "Today, women make up 19 percent of all USAF military personnel, 30.5 percent of all civilian personnel, with nearly equal representation in both the officer (18.8 percent) and enlisted (19.1 percent) corps. Of the officers, 55 percent of the female officers are line officers, and 45 percent are non-line. Of the 328,423 active duty personnel, 62,316 are women, with 712 female pilots, 259 navigators and 183 air battle managers." https://www.af.mil/News/Article-Display/Article/497548/womens-legacy-parallels-air-force-history/; accessed September 24, 2021.

33. Post-Marxists, like Antonio Gramsci, might consider Lily's attitude an act of a "false consciousness." In his *Selections from the Prison Notebooks* (1989), Gramsci argued that elites dominate not only the means of production but also their symbolic meaning. Hence, elites control "the ideological sectors" of society: culture, religion, education, and media. Because of this control, they can manufacture consent that further enables their ruling and acts of oppression. In turn, this consent creates a discourse that lays out a standard of accepted values. The subordinates (or the op-pressed) internalize these values, obey them, and perpetuate the power system, despite its not being in their best interests. This submission further prevents revolt or free thinking. In this manner, Gramsci explains the lack of resistance and the oppressed display, even in situations unfavorable to their well-being. In opposition to Gramsci, James C. Scott argues that "false consciousness" depends on the symbolic alignment of the elites with the subordinate classes. However, Scott continues, groups are not homogenous but have diverse and contradictory currents. It is hard, therefore, to assume perfect alignment under these conditions. Whereas for Gramsci resistance is impossible because of elite hegemony, for Scott resistance is possible because false consciousness is not fully realizable. For more details on the debate regarding false consciousness, see Scott 1985, chap. 2.

34. Because we shared the same ethnic background, Lily often made cultural references that were easy for me to understand. During the above-mentioned conversation, she indirectly referred to the discriminatory treatment that Romanians receive when they travel within the European Union and contrasted it with the positive handling she felt she received in the U.S. military.

35. According to Charles Taylor (1994), having one's identity recognized is mandatory in order to achieve social justice. The self is dialogical, he argues, meaning that it is formed both by one's self-definition and by others' views. Hence, respecting others' identity is both an existential and a civic obligation. Consequently, not recognizing or misrecognizing others' identity is a political offense and one addressed to their core individual existence. To remedy this, Taylor advocates for a "politics of recognition," in which the state plays an active role in ensuring that individuals' identities are not misrecognized.

36. Throughout American history, many ethnic immigrant groups who were not yet full members in civilian life received better accommodation after serving in the military. For example, Irish immigrants who served in the Civil War and proved both their courage and their allegiance to the new country were regarded with less suspicion and had better chances to be accepted in the civilian realm (Dragomir 2012).

37. According to Moskos (1970), on July 26, 1948, President Truman issued the executive order addressing racial segregation in the armed forces of the United States. In World War II, desperate shortages of combat personnel resulted in the army asking for African American volunteers. After the war, pressure from African American and liberal groups, coupled with an acknowledgment that African American soldiers were poorly used, led the Army to reexamine its racial policies (Moskos 1970, 110). Moskos argues: "While the percentage of black enlisted men in the army increased only slightly, the likelihood of a black serving in a combat arm is well over two times greater in the 1960's than it was at the end of WWII. . . . Even though integration of the military has led to great improvement in the performance of African American servicemen, the social and particularly educational deprivation suffered by the black in American society can be mitigated, but not eliminated, by the racial egalitarian policies of the armed forces" (115). By signing Executive Order 9981, Truman mandated equality of treatment and opportunity. However, his order did not wipe out segregation in the armed forces, as the *Chicago Defender* reported on July 31, 1948. In fact, desegregation of the military was not completed for several years, and all-black Army units persisted well into the Korean War (1954). In spite of considerable progress, discriminatory practices against minorities were visible in the military even twenty years later (Dudziak 1988).

38. For more information on contemporary leadership diversity, see the final report of the Military Leadership Diversity Commission, https://diversity.defense.gov/Portals/51/Documents/Resources/Commission/docs/Issue%20Papers/Paper%2009%20-%20Military%20Leadership%20Diversity%20Commission%20History.pdf, accessed July 16, 2022.

39. Administrative Appeals Tribunal of Australia, www.mrtrrt.gov.au/Article Documents/171/ROU36062.pdf.aspx, accessed April 19, 2015.

40. "Cenaclul Flacăra" was a music and poetry show that took place in various cities around Romania. Although it was an active youth movement run by Adrian Păunescu, it was also connected with the Communist Party. For more, see Cracana and Păunescu 2007; and Pavelescu 2011.

41. "There is no other country in the world so widely diverse, yet so deeply committed to being unified as the United States of America. The challenges we face today are far too serious, and the implications of failure far too great, for our Air Force to do less than fully and inclusively leverage our nation's greatest strength—our remarkably diverse people. Across the force, diversity of background, experience, demographics, perspective, thought and organization are essential to our ultimate success in an increasingly competitive and dynamic global environment. As airpower advocates, we must be culturally competent and operationally relevant to effectively accomplish our various missions." http://www.af.mil/Diversity.aspx, accessed October 5, 2016. In addition, recent scholarship has also debated many forms of diversity within the U.S. military. See W. Taylor 2016; and Bristol and Stur 2017. See also Deborah Lee James, secretary of the Air Force, on the Air Force diversity official website, http://www.af.mil/Diversity.aspx, accessed October 5, 2016.

42. http://www.af.mil/Diversity.aspx, accessed October 5, 2016.

43. For example, in 2013, 10,569 males and 11,130 females migrated from Romania, according to UNICEF, "Migration Profiles," https://esa.un.org/miggmgprofiles/indicators/files/Romania.pdf, accessed November 26, 2017.

44. According to the Migration Policy report of 2008, the number of female immigrant soldiers serving in all branches of the American armed forces was "11,182, representing 17.2 percent of all foreign-born serving in the military." https://www.migrationpolicy.org/article/immigrants-us-armed-forces#6, accessed November 26, 2017.

45. 2015 Demographics, Profile of Military Community, http://download.military onesource.mil/12038/MOS/Reports/2015-Demographics-Report.pdf, accessed November 26, 2017.

46. Many different styles of life are found in Romanian society. Approaches and expectations vary from one person to another and between genders. Women have many roles, from the traditional housekeeper to the professional businesswoman and the performer, from the mother to the independent woman (Arsene 2012, 374).

47. For example, "Stereotypes such as have been mentioned: the woman must stay in the kitchen, the woman that wants a career is not able to maintain her household, the woman must be subjected to the man, the blond woman is brainless, the divorced woman is blamed, women are weak, girls are geekier than boys. . . . Also, standardised images of the man were presented: the man is the supporter of the household, the man must be in charge, men are the best cooks, the man is a fighter, men are strong, but also behind every powerful man there is a powerful woman" (Arsene 2012, 375).

48. American immigration policies, especially the 1965 Immigration Act, made European migration drop to a record low of 4.8 million, out of the total 42.4 million in 2014. http://www.migrationpolicy.org/article/european-immigrants-united-states, accessed October 7, 2016.

49. In spite of the widespread presence of eastern European migrants in the United States, they are an understudied group in immigration studies (Robila 2007). Romanians in the United States are among the best-educated groups from eastern Europe, with 20.5 percent having a university degree; they are surpassed only by Bulgarians and Russians, and their educational level is far higher than immigrants from other parts of the world. However, 40 percent of Romanian immigrants report that they "speak English less than very well" (117), which leads to slower naturalization. Romanians in the United States are dispersed across the income platform, with 38 percent making between $35,000 and $75,000 and 8.2 percent of families living beneath the poverty level. Similar to most eastern European immigrants, Romanian women earn less than men, with a median income of $29,176 compared to $40,078 among males (120). "The results suggest that there is wide diversity in economic welfare for Eastern European immigrants. Therefore, there is a need for social programs to be developed to support Eastern European immigrants to adapt to the new society. This has been an overlooked immigrant group. However, it faces similar struggles associated with the immigration processes as other groups. Developing support programs to meet its needs would advance their adaptation into society" (123).

50. http://www.domesticworkers.org/sites/default/files/HomeEconomicsEnglish.pdf, accessed October, 9, 2016.

51. In the United States, immigrants are "1.4 time as likely as US-born workers to be employed in the leisure and hospitality sector." http://www.theatlantic.com/politics/archive/2016/01/immigrants-in-the-workforce-state-by-state-and-industry-by-industry/458775/, accessed October 9, 2016; http://www.pewtrusts.org/en/multimedia/data-visualizations/2015/immigrant-employment-by-state-and-industry, accessed October 9, 2016; http://www.nytimes.com/2009/02/25/dining/25feed.html, accessed November 27, 2017.

52. http://popularmilitary.com/no-girls-allowed-three-reasons-why-women-shouldnt-be-integrated-into-combat-arms/, accessed October 9, 2016.

53. I found out later from Lily, and verified the information with the Air Force data, that the typical age for an Air Force reservist is between thirty and forty years old, approximately a decade older than their active counterparts.

54. Along similar lines, Katzenstein's classic work on feminist protest within the military, *Faithful and Fearless*, allows us to understand resistance not only as protests that take place "only on the streets," but as acts that are endemic to institutions. Specifically, Katzenstein draws our attention to "an additional and newer institutional reality: that understanding the emergence of gender, race, and sexual politics in contemporary American society means recognizing the importance of protest inside institutions" (1998, 3).

55. Similarly, Charissa Threat (2015) argues that African American women immediately after World War II benefited from gender typing, which opened opportunities for social and economic mobility.

56. It is important to mention that to date (2014), Lily has not experienced deployment, which is the stage in military service that adds different dimensions into the integration naturalization process, wherein one's gender, ethnicity/race, and class often create experiences. For more, see Thorpe 2015.

Chapter 3. Alexa

1. I refer to Alexa's place of origin as South America, though I am aware that this generalization leaves out important country and local specificities. I understand that the possibility of a common history of South America is thoroughly contested as an idea. While scholars, such as Bolton (1933), propose the idea of the Great Americas while suggesting commonalities such as colonization, conquest, and development that would strengthen the individual countries' perception and history, Hanke (1964) argues that we need to assert individual countries' histories. Intellectually, I am convinced by Hanke's argument, but for the purpose of this book, I will refer to South America, as Alexa herself did, and so respect her wish to be described as a South American rather than a citizen of a particular country.

2. Bearing in mind that generalizations about the continent are likely to produce gross misrepresentation, in order to contextualize Alexa's life and give the reader a better understanding of the political and historical background that shaped her formative years, I will add that in other countries in South America during colonial times, the European settlers lived for generations in an agriculture-based country with the land belonging to the colonists and the church. After independence, these countries went through a turbulent development, which included war, dictatorship, and attempts at rapid industrialization. Today, agriculture is still the main economic activity, yet the economy is dominated by the informal sector, based on reexporting imported goods from neighboring countries.

3. Alexa's ambitions were similar to those of women who have been serving in the armed forces, like Hegar, who from a young age knew that she wanted to be a fighter pilot. In her book *Shoot Like a Girl: One Woman's Dramatic Fight in Afghanistan and on the Home Front* (2017), Hegar shows how despite the sexism, military politics, and emotional setbacks she encountered while serving, she was able to persist in following her dreams and achieved them when she was commissioned in the U.S. Air Force as a combat pilot. However, in contrast to Hegar, Alexa was soon to be discharged and has not (to date) learned how to be a pilot and serve her host country in this way.

4. In her work, Thorpe (2015) addresses the complex web of class and gender in which (native-born) women find themselves when serving their country while looking to obtain tuition benefits that would drive their economic and social mobility. The three women in Thorpe's work enlisted in the National Guard (the branch of the military that is typically reserved for interventions within the United States), but ended up serving in war zones abroad, and thus facing unexpected challenges.

5. The U.S. military has been training women for a variety of jobs within its ranks since World War II. For example, Sullivan says, "When women finished basic training and had identities and trained for particular jobs, they were sent to military posts throughout United States to perform those functions," a position different from men who often were sent to "the fighting fronts" (2011, 4).

6. Since her education took place in Czech Republic and no degree was awarded, the transfer of academic credits was difficult.

7. http://www.armyg1.army.mil/hr/docs/demographics/FY11_ARMY_PROFILE .pdf, accessed August 4, 2013. While the low educational background of U.S. military recruits is a point of controversy, within the U.S. Army we can see that at the level of "enlisted" even as early as the 1970s, "72.3 per cent of all officers had college degrees compared to only 1.3 per cent of enlisted men ... [A] college degree has become a virtual environment for officers while a high school diploma is the modal educational level for enlisted personnel ... The trend data also reveal a growing discrepancy between the educational levels of officers and enlisted men" (Moskos 1970, 42). Another contentious point is the idea that recruits from underprivileged classes are overrepresented in the military (Lutz 2008, 167, citing Kane 2006). Similarly, the Heritage Foundation states that "50 percent of the enlisted recruits (i.e., not including the officers' corps) come from families in the top 40 percent of the income distribution, while only 10 percent come from the bottom 20 percent." https://www .heritage.org/defense/report/who-serves-the-us-military-the-demographics-enlisted -troops-and-officers, accessed July 24, 2022.

8. According to the military website goarmy.com, as an E4, Alexa should be receiving a minimum annually of $22,3165, of which she pays $600/month for rent. http:// www.goarmy.com/benefits/money/basic-pay-active-duty-soldiers.html, accessed October 17, 2016.

9. It is, however, important to mention that in spite of difficulties encountered in the U.S. military in the rapidly changing twentieth and twenty-first centuries, individual (native-born) women have been able to accomplish many things. For example, see Biank and Thompson 2014. My work and its three life stories do not mean to dismiss these successes, but to give a deeper understanding of the obstacles (and success pathways) encountered by these three specific immigrants while serving the host country.

10. Brno is the second largest city in Czech Republic.

11. In her work "Whiteness in Latina Immigrants: A Venezuelan Perspective," which examines the construct of whiteness in Venezuela, Padrón argues that understanding race "requires a framework that differs from the fixed racial categories commonly used in the United States." In a country in which "most citizens are of mixed race and where the concept of race is fluid, race and racism take on more complex forms that include dimensions such as social class, eye color, family, education, and even manners. This means that Whiteness and privilege do not always go hand in hand" (2015, 194). While Alexa is not from Venezuela, the same racial dynamics can be observed in Latin American countries that have a majority of an ethnically and racially mixed population, and therefore we can infer Alexa's racial understanding is rather similar to this.

12. For most of the nineteenth century, Central and South America were dominated by theories of race and racism (Wade 2010a) intimately connected with those of ethnicity. Prevalent racial theories shaped public opinion, policies, and the overall political spectrum. Moreover, classification and the ranking of people according to the color of their skin influenced scientific discourses. Biology, medicine, and psychology have all been "shaped by the evolutionary paradigm" (Graham 1990). For

centuries, racialist thinking shaped political decisions across Latin America. The unfortunate triumph of racist theories and politics led to the decline in the native population, both through immigration (especially from Europe) and through race mixture (Meade 2010, 96). Current studies (Wade 2010a, 2010b, 2014) discuss the two vectors in tandem and aim to distinguish race and ethnicity as a social construction (Moreno Figueroa 2008) that produced the "racialized," rigid, hierarchical context of Central and South American countries (Appelbaum, Macpherson, and Rosemblatt 2003) and implicitly of their emigrants.

13. "The Richies" were a family for whom Alexa worked as a nanny for three years, when she first moved to the United States.

14. Alexa's attitude toward being a nanny resonated with the description found in the scholarship about *domésticas*, which argues that immigrant women providing child care are imagined to be doing their job because they love children, but, in reality, these women typically face labor problems such as long hours, unpaid extra work, lack of opportunities for advancement, and unstable employment (Colen 1990; Hondagneu-Sotelo 1994, 2001; Romero 1992, 1997; Tronto 2002).

15. Waters and Eschbach's 1995 study "Immigration and Ethnic and Racial Inequality in the United States" argued that taking into consideration the impact of three factors—economic restructuring, racial discrimination, and immigration—leads us to observe the current patterns of racial inequality in the United States. Group differences have changed shape rather than disappeared. Based on the 1990 census, they show the continuing inequality among American minority groups, when compared with whites. Of the major racial/ethnic minorities in the United States, only Asians have a higher median family income than whites, with an income of $41,583, compared to $37,630 for non-Hispanic whites. American Indians have the lowest median income with $21,750, followed closely by blacks and Hispanics. Data on unemployment follow this general pattern, with blacks and American Indians the worst off, followed by Hispanics. Moreover, studies of the labor market find that while Hispanics are disadvantaged in the labor market compared to whites, this is due to the low percentage of the Latino community in education (29 percent).

16. In fact, according to Waters and Eschbach, "Each aggregation includes subpopulations that are themselves diverse, both in the social and cultural organization of sending countries and in the average experiences of group members in the United States. For example, the term 'Asian' covers the experiences of so-called 'model minorities' like the Japanese and Koreans who have high socioeconomic standing in the United States, as well as Southeast Asian populations that have experienced more difficulties" (1995, 421).

17. See the nationwide survey of Hispanic adults by the Pew Hispanic Center, a project of the Pew Research Center: http://www.pewhispanic.org/2012/04/04/ ii-identity-pan-ethnicity-and- race/, accessed August 5, 2013. In spite of their problematic use, census strategies still employ these categories to classify the population. In the 2010 Census, 50.5 million (or 16 percent) were accounted as people of Hispanic or Latino origin: http://www.census.gov/prod/cen2010/briefs/c2010br-04 .pdf, accessed August 5, 2013.

18. http://www.pewhispanic.org/files/factsheets/6.pdf, accessed August 5, 2013.

19. According to the Pew Research Center (2019), "The percentage of officers who are women has steadily grown since the 1970s. For example, in 1975, 5% of commissioned officers were women, and, by 2017, that share had risen to 18%." This change is replicated in terms of racial and ethnic diversity, with "the share of racial and ethnic minorities in the military growing steadily in recent decades. Hispanics, in particular, are the fastest growing minority population in the military—a shift that aligns with larger demographic trend in the US." https://www.pewresearch.org/fact -tank/2019/07/08/u-s-hispanic-population-reached-new-high-in-2018-but-growth -has-slowed/, accessed December 23, 2019. While the military is typically considered a pioneer in social mobility, in the civilian realm the U.S. Bureau of Labor Statistics (2007) reported the higher percentages of women in managerial positions by ethnicity: whites, 39 percent; African Americans, 31 percent; Asians, 46 percent; and Latinas, 22 percent (Catalyst 2006). https://www.pewresearch.org/fact-tank/2019/09/10/the -changing-profile-of-the-u-s-military/, accessed December 23, 2019. According to Pentagon data (reported by CNN), in 2011 there were 203,000 enlisted personnel, with 14.5 percent of the active-duty force of nearly 1.4 million. This was divided by branch as follows: 74,000 in the Army, 53,000 in the Navy, 62,000 in the Air Force, and 14,000 in the Marine Corps. Among these, nearly 167,000 women were in the enlisted ranks, making up 14.2 percent of that force, and 36,000 women in the officer corps, equivalent to 16.6 percent. Specifically, in the top ranks, 69 of the 976 generals and admirals, that is, 7.1 percent, were women, with 28 female generals in the Air Force, 19 in the Army, 1 in the Marine Corps, and 21 female admirals in the Navy. Of the 3,698 new female officers in 2011, 579 were graduates of the nation's service academies. In addition, 18 percent of the 722,000 enlisted reservists and National Guard troops and 19 percent of their 113,000 officers are women. In the Coast Guard, now a division of the Department of Homeland Security, women made up 10.5 percent of the total force of 44,000 active-duty and reserve personnel. "By the Numbers: Women in the US Military," CNN, January 24, 2013, https://www.cnn.com/2013/01/24/us/military -women-glance/index.html. For more see Elizabeth M. Trobaugh, "Women, Regardless: Understanding Gender Bias in US Military Integration," *Joint Force Quarterly* 88 (1st Quarter 2018), https://ndupress.ndu.edu/Portals/68/Documents/jfq/jfq-88/jfq -88_46-53_Trobaugh.pdf?ver=2018-01-09-102340-317, accessed December 23, 2019.

20. On a similar note, William A. Taylor (2016) addresses the contentious issue of a volunteer force representation within democracies and concludes that in spite of its inherent problems, an all-voluntary U.S. armed force addresses both the needs and the values of the American democracy.

21. https://aspe.hhs.gov/basic-report/overview-uninsured-united-states-summary -2011-current-population-survey, accessed April 22, 2020.

22. https://home.army.mil/stewart/index.php/download_file/force/7306/434, accessed April 22, 2020.

23. Considering the specific health issues that Alexa was facing at that time, it is difficult to make a swift decision about military policies and their (dis)regard for gender, especially in terms of the training that Germano and Kennedy (2018) advocate. But it is clear that in order to ensure the integration, support, and success

of female (of immigrant background in this case) recruits, complex, detailed, and sensitive policies are needed with a degree of flexibility and supporting resources.

24. http://www.apd.army.mil/pdffiles/r40_501.pdf, accessed August 4, 2013.

25. The physical profile serial system was developed by the military as a medical profile indicator. It is used to determine medical standards for different jobs and to make sure that members of the military are medically qualified to perform the duties of their job. It takes the form of a serial number that provides an index to overall functional capacity. It is the functional capacity of a particular organ or system of the body that is evaluated rather than the defect: "To determine medical standards for different jobs, and to make sure that military members are medically qualified to perform the duties of that job, the military has developed a medical profile indicator for every one of its members." http://usmilitary.about.com/od/joiningthemilitary/l/blpulse.htm, accessed April 19, 2015; http://army.com/info/mos/pulhes, accessed April 19, 2015.

26. Its mission is stated as follows: "1-1. Purpose: This regulation establishes policies and procedures for the implementation of the Army Weight Control Program (AWCP). . . . The primary objective of the AWCP is to ensure that all personnel—(1) Are able to meet the physical demands of their duties under combat conditions. (2) Present a trim military appearance at all times. b. Excessive body fat—Connotes a lack of personal discipline; (2) Detracts from military appearance; (3) May indicate a poor state of health, physical fitness, or stamina; c. Objectives of the AWCP are to: (1) Assist in establishing and maintaining—(a) Discipline. (b) Operational readiness. (c) Optimal physical fitness. (d) Health. (e) Effectiveness of Army personnel through proper weight control. (2) Establish appropriate body fat standards. (3) Provide procedures for which personnel are counseled to assist in meeting the standards prescribed in this regulation. (4) Foster high standards of professional military appearance expected of all personnel" (2006, 1, http://www.apd.army.mil/pdffiles/r600_9.pdf, accessed April 19, 2015).

27. Eggerth et al. argue that "almost half of the Latino immigrants working in the United States are women," and they face an "excessive workload, familiar work/unfamiliar hazards, cultural tensions, lack of health care, pregnancy, sexual harassment, and family obligations/expectations." The authors conclude that "the responses of the Latina workers in this study clearly indicated that they live within a complex web of stressors, both as workers and as women" (2012, 13).

28. The literature on Latin American women primarily discusses their "burden" and economic or political participation (Zetterberg 2009; Chant and Craske 2003).

29. For more on gender and labor relations in Latin America, see also Radcliffe 1999.

30. http://www.nbcnews.com/news/latino/citizen-or-immigrant-latinas-may-have-sign-military-draft-n508396, accessed October 17, 2016.

31. The simplifying, objectifying, and essentializing of women in the military is a topic of intense debate among feminist scholars. For example, Robinson (2011) presents the divisions between feminists who believe in an "ethic of care," the theory that women are inherently life- and caregivers and should not be engaged in acts that might end up taking lives in combat, with feminists who support an "ethic of

198 / Notes to Chapter 3

justice," a theory that argues for women's right to equal treatment under the law, which includes their right to serve alongside men in any job, at any rank, and in combat in the military.

32. This trivializing oversexualization of women, especially of women of color, within the military is not new. Conserving the hypermasculine structure of the military, women's role has often been allocated along the lines of caregiver or sexual object. For example, Stur tells the story of Lily Lee Adams, a half Chinese and half Italian American nurse who served in the military in Vietnam and details how Adams dealt with sexual harassment and racial discrimination: "American women who ventured to Vietnam were expected to fulfill the conventional women's role of caregivers, mothers, and virginal girlfriends even as their concrete experiences told a different story. . . . [A]s an American woman in nurse's attire, she has an accepted, if marginal role in a war zone, but her Chinese ethnicity activates the stereotype that led some troops, both American and Vietnamese, to conclude that she was more likely a *dragon lady* than the *girl next door*" (2011, 3).

33. Furthermore, when compared with their civilian counterparts, family formation rates (that is, fertility) among U.S. military women is comparatively higher, as "upon the transition to an all-volunteer force, the military developed programs specifically for families, which include full family health coverage" (Lundquist and Smith 2005, 2). Alexa did not get pregnant during her service, but this was not because she did not want to—it was because of her medical condition. Her eagerness to have children can be interpreted as being in line with the general trend of U.S. military women.

34. http://www.usarec.army.mil/support/faqs.htm#age, accessed October 18, 2016.

35. Romantic engagements within the military, while frowned upon, are not rare. For example, Germano and Kennedy (2018) declared that without serving in the Marine Corps, she would not ever have met her husband.

36. Jedlicka shows that older women are likely to seek mates in less conventional ways and that regardless of the mode of selection, women are consistently disadvantaged. Most of those in the older age groups will have to remain unmarried after widowhood whether they want to or not. Men, on the other hand, have more freedom in determining their marital status. This inequality is attributed to the persistence of age preferences in favor of men. "Women express preferences for older men and men for younger women. This double standard is the basis of preferential mating in America and it is presented as a fundamental source of sex inequality" (1978, 137). While Jedlika's research is four decades old, it is still pertinent today. Nevertheless, gender dynamics have changed since 1978, permitting more flexibility for women in choosing life partners or mates. While this speaks volumes about Alexa's choices and life determination, it also shows that the U.S. military acted as an equal playing field on which characteristics, such as ethnicity and age, receded into the background, and this made their romantic encounter possible.

37. While this incident illuminates Alexa's dogmatic adherence to Catholicism, and ignorance of other forms of Christianity, it also reveals the difficulties that people of the cloth who serve in the U.S. armed forces might face when working with a diverse body of soldiers. Furthermore, it also sheds light on how the U.S. military,

while diverse, still operates within a very narrow understanding of faith and the spiritual life, primarily having representatives of one religion (Christianity) and of a particular denomination (Protestant Christianity) on bases, in this way limiting the range of advice and spiritual guidance that soldiers receive while serving. For more on this tantalizing debate about religion and politics and church and state, see Hansen 2012 and Stahl 2017.

38. In their study with 639 Latinas in 2015, Bekteshi and van Hook found that next to perceived discrimination, "difficulty visiting family abroad were positively associated with acculturative stress" (2015, 1401). But like many other immigrants, the fact that Alexa was away from her family did not diminish the responsibility she felt to support them. For more about remittances to Latin America, see Orozco 2002.

39. Morales and Saucedo studied "a recent campaign to organize immigrant workers in the male-dominated residential construction industry," where "Latina immigrants spearheaded the demand for labor rights in Las Vegas, Nevada," and found that "masculinity culture and structures that exclude Latina immigrants can facilitate their participation in labor organizing. Indeed, rather than enacting masculinities, these Latina immigrants upheld traditionally feminine norms that created a political opening for labor organizing" (2015, 144).

Chapter 4. Vikrant

1. Silvestri's research reveals how social media has been blurring the distinctions between deployment/front lines and home front, creating both positive and negative ramifications in the life on those who serve: "Since 2006, internet access has become much more widely available to US troops on deployment. Today, although some of the most remote out- posts in the mountains of Afghanistan do not have access to running water, many of them do have access to 'internet cafés,' or as some service members refer to them, 'lounges.' . . . They are portable satellite units where US troops can share a set of computers with satellite feeds to communicate back home. Military officials provide the units, which come equipped with a router, up to eight laptops, and phones, to provide service personnel with free internet access and phone calls home" (2015, 2).

2. His allegiance to these values distinguished Vikrant from "many Indian immigrants [who] believe that Americans do not have strong loyalties to their immediate and extended families. An Indian American man expressed that 'Indians are more attached to their families. We visit our relatives in India which is 10,000 miles apart . . . we are much more family-oriented'" (Rudrappa 2004, 169).

3. For a more detailed account of the diversity among Asian Indian immigrants, see Sheth 2001.

4. For example, in Indian households in United States in the 1990s, "fifteen major regional languages [were spoken], many of which are mutually unintelligible. Although mostly Hindu, about 10 percent of the [population] is Muslim, and there are small Sikh, Jain, Christian, Parsi and Buddhist minorities" (Bacon 1997, 7).

5. According to the Pew Research Center, 2017, Indian Americans composed the third-largest Asian ethnic group in the United States, behind Chinese and Fili-

pinos. https://www.pewresearch.org/fact-tank/2017/09/08/key-facts-about-asian-americans/.

6. It became possible for Indian nationals to migrate to the United States after the passing of the 1965 Immigration Act; previously, Indians' movement to the United States was limited by the 1924 Immigration Act, which restricted immigration from Asia (Bacon 1997). Specifically, "when, in 1946, a restrictive quota was introduced to allow limited immigration, the Asian Indian population numbered a mere 1,500 persons; by 1965, it had grown to 10,000. By 1990, however, there were 450,406 persons born in India living in the United States, and 815,447 persons claiming Asian Indian ancestry" (Bacon 1997, 7). See also Joshi 2006.

7. From http://immigrationtounitedstates.org/360-asian-indian-immigrants.html#Beyond_2000, accessed on April 27, 2019.

8. According to Joshi, "Thirty-three percent of Indian Americans live in the Northeast, 26.2 percent in the South, 24 percent in the West and 17 percent in the Midwest" (2006, 2).

9. According to Waters and Jimenez (2005), there are four primary benchmarks of assimilation: socioeconomic status, spatial concentration, language assimilation, and intermarriage. Education is also an important factor in improving one's socioeconomic status.

10. According to Bacon, Indian migration to the United States was curtailed until 1965, but then it exponentially grew after the adoption of the 1965 Immigration Act, not only in numbers (that is, 1,500 persons by 1965 to 10,000), but also in terms of their social and economic success. Thus, these "social and economic characteristics of Asian Indians, however, place them among the more elite immigrant groups" (1997, 7).

11. For example, Vikrant—like many Indian immigrants—was not particularly religious when he arrived, did not emphasize religion as the "most important aspect of Indian culture" (Fenton 1988, 200), and so the immigrants he chose to integrate with "were secular, urban, modern and technologically educated" (vii).

12. https://www.uscis.gov/working-united-states/students-and-exchange-visitors/students-and-employment/optional-practical-training, accessed November 29, 2017.

13. For more information on applying of H1B work visas to the United States, see https://www.uscis.gov/working-united-states, accessed April 25,2020.

14. To apply for any American visa and to have it stamped in a passport, one needs to be outside of U.S. territory. Many people decide to go back to their country of origin and apply there, as the U.S. government suggests. However, some applicants choose to apply in a third country like Canada or Mexico. Vikrant decided on Toronto because of its proximity to Washington, where he was working at the time.

15. According to the Migration Policy Institute, in 2018 Indian immigrants were not accounted for in the ethnic groups enlisting in the armed force, given that they accounted for less that 2 percent of U.S. armed forces personnel. https://www.migrationpolicy.org/article/immigrant-veterans-united-states#CountryofBirth, accessed January 30, 2020.

16. The first record of an Indian joining the U.S. military dates to the Vietnam War, but that enlistment was not voluntary—the individual was drafted (Helweg

and Helweg 1991). This account of the first Indians serving in the U.S. military is challenged. For example, Dawinder and Gohil (2009) argue that Bhagat Singh Thind served in the U.S. forces during World War I, and Sunny Ramchandani argues that "the initial wave began in the 1970s and early 1980s, when a few Indian immigrants were inspired to serve their adopted home." https://www.indiaspora.org/a-life-of-service-indian-americans-and-the-u-s-armed-forces, accessed March 1, 2020.

17. https://www.goarmy.com/coronavirus.html, accessed April 25, 2020.

18. "Infantry Creed," https://www.youtube.com/watch?v=oLllrADCvP0, accessed November 2, 2016.

19. https://indianembassyusa.gov.in/pdf/menu/RenunciationFAQ.pdf, accessed April 25, 2020.

20. Mary Hanna and Jeanne Batalova, "Indian Immigrants in the United States," Migration Policy Institute, October 16, 2020, https://www.migrationpolicy.org/article/indian-immigrants-united-states, accessed April 25, 2020.

21. According to the U.S. Census of 2010, the Asian Indian population in the United States grew from almost 1,678,765 in 2000 (0.6 percent of the U.S. population) to 2,843,391 in 2010 (0.9 percent of the U.S. population). See also http://usatoday30.usatoday.com/news/nation/census/2011-05-12-asian-indian-population-Census_n.htm, accessed April 20, 2020.

22. According to the Department of State, Indian citizens wanting to apply for a student visa to the United States need to show proof of transcripts, diplomas, degrees, or certificates from schools they attended; standardized test scores required by their U.S. school; their intent to depart the United States upon completion of the course of study; and how they will pay all educational, living, and travel costs. For detailed information on the requirements regarding the student visa, see https://in.usembassy.gov/visas/nonimmigrant-visas/ and http://www.ustraveldocs.com/in/in-niv-typefandm.asp, accessed October 25, 2016.

23. The number of Indian students increased as the immigration expanded, and so did the number of visas. Still, admittance and financial backing to study in the United States proved no guarantee that a visa would be granted. If the officer at the embassy was not convinced that the student would return to India, they did not have to award the visa, and this caused Indians to feel discriminated against (Helweg and Helweg 1991).

24. The South Asian migration process of the twentieth century took place in three waves: the first decade, during the 1970s, and from the late 1990s to the early twenty-first century. This last immigration wave took place after 1965 Immigration Act and is the largest to date, making Indian migrant groups the "third largest Asian immigrant population in the United States. The Asian Indian immigrant population increased by 38 percent between 2000 and 2005, becoming the third-largest immigrant population in the United States. Asian Indians have attained the highest level of education and the highest median income among all national origin groups in the United States. More than 40 percent are medical professionals, scientists, or engineers concentrated in metropolitan areas across the United States." http://immigrationtounitedstates.org/360-asian-indian-immigrants.html#Beyond_2000, accessed April 27, 2019.

25. http://india.blogs.nytimes.com/2012/04/18/so-you-want-to-move-back-to -india/, accessed April 19, 2015; http://www.nytimes.com/2012/04/16/us/more-us -children-of-immigrants-are-leaving-us.html?src=me&ref=us, accessed April 19, 2015.

26. http://www.uscis.gov/portal/site/uscis/menuitem.5af9bb95919f35e66f614176 543f6d1a/?vgnex toid=4b7cdd1d5fd37210VgnVCM100000082ca60aRCRD&vgne xtchannel=73566811264a3210VgnVCM100000b92ca60aRCRD, accessed April 19, 2015.

27. In 2010 the Pew Research Center found that 28 percent of Indian Americans worked in science and engineering fields, and the 2013 American Community Survey found that 69.3 percent of Indian Americans aged sixteen and older were in management, business, science, and arts occupations. http://www.pewresearch.org/ fact-tank/2014/09/30/5-facts-about-indian-americans/, accessed October 12, 2016.

28. According to data compiled from several sources, E4 (Vikrant's rank at the time of this research) has an annual salary of $29,185.20. https://m.goarmy.com/benefits/ money/basic-pay-active-duty-soldiers.m.html, accessed November 30, 2017.

29. Closely related, prejudice and discrimination are two distinct modes of operation. The difference between them is between attitude and acts: prejudice implies an inflexible and irrational attitude and opinion held by members of one group about another, while discrimination refers to unequal treatment based on group membership. S. Williams and Dilworth-Anderson (2002), for example, indicate practices, modes, or behaviors directed against other groups. Prejudices can be positive or negative; one can be prejudiced against another group, but at the same time not discriminate against members of that group.

30. For example, Ghurye (2005) engages in historical analysis of the evolution of caste from the Vedic to the "modern period" and claims that the castes were mostly the result of racial divisions as these were rationalized over hundreds of years of conflict and assimilation. Other work compares the caste/race relations in India to Western racial divisions and explains existing differences in various social systems (Cox 1945; Berreman 1960). In recent years, there have been major changes in India with regard to race relations, but racial hierarchy associated with the caste system and gender differentiation still persists in the wider Indian society and abroad when they immigrate. It is typically understood that upon migrating to the United States, Indian immigrants "tend to identify themselves not with the Indian national origin group but with their particular regional, linguistic, religious, or professional subgroups. After arrival, Bengalis, Punjabis, Marathis, and Tamils tend to maintain their languages, religious practices, foods, and dress." http://immigrationtounitedstates. org/360-asian-indian-immigrants.html#Beyond_2000, accessed April 27, 2019.

31. For example, Bacon asserts that Indian immigrants in the United States are "the wealthiest and most highly educated of all recent immigrants. Almost two-thirds of Indian immigrants have completed at least a Bachelors' degree. Almost half are employed in managerial or professional occupations, and the per capita income is well over twice that of the general population. Two-thirds of Asian Indian immigrants report that they speak English very well, making them among the most English-proficient immigrants" (1996, 7).

32. In conducting analysis on social media, I employed visual analysis. See Rosen and Taubman 1982.

33. Curtailing hazing within the military has been a struggle for some time. For example, in 2013 Dr. Richard Oliver from the Hope Human Relations Research Center and in 2015 the Rand Corporation conducted separate studies on the topic of hazing within military, describing it as "abusive and harmful treatment." https://www.deomi.org/DownloadableFiles/research/documents/31-16TheShiftfromAcceptance toPreventionHazingBehaviorsintheUSMilitary.pdf; https://www.rand.org/content/ dam/rand/pubs/research_reports/RR900/RR941/RAND_RR941.pdf, accessed April 20, 2020.

34. Just after World War II, in 1947, the Indian subcontinent was partitioned into Pakistan and India, and the division resulted in a series of conflicts over the disputed region of Kashmir. On four occasions, the countries fought conventional wars, but at other times the conflict took the form of terrorist attacks. Tensions over Kashmir are embedded in the foreign policies of the two countries and the way in which both sides understand and re-create history. In addition, both India and Pakistan have a long and complicated history with the United States, dating back to the Cold War, when India was an ally of the Soviet Union and Pakistan a partner of the United States.

35. This view is supported by Joshi, who also argues that "Indian American Hindus, Muslims and Sikh, will not melt into whiteness after a generation" (2006, 2).

36. Vikrant's attempt to use racism to be integrated within the preferred racial majority is not specific to South Asian immigrants, but it is often used by migrants who use racial discourses, symbols, and identifications to mark their difference and assert their "superiority" from the "undesirable" natives. See Fox and Mogilnicka 2019.

37. https://www.barna.com/research/faith-influences-military-service/, accessed March 2, 2020.

38. http://www.history.army.mil/html/faq/diversity.html, accessed October 27, 2016.

39. The power of the church within the U.S. military and its role in shaping national politics is not new or pertinent only to migrants who enlist in the American armed forces. It is, rather, part of a complex and *longue-durée* process that highlights and challenges the separation between church and state (see Hansen 2012).

40. https://www.cfr.org/article/demographics-us-military, accessed March 2, 2020.

41. While is it typically assumed that the U.S. military is a masculine institution, literature on masculinity and hypermasculinity within the institution was scarce. Myrttinen, Khattab, and Naujoks acknowledged this lack and showed that "masculinities in conflict-affected and peacebuilding contexts have generally speaking been under-researched. Much of the existing research focuses relatively narrowly on men and their assumed 'violence,' especially that of combatants. Conceptually, much of the policy debate has revolved around either men's 'innate' propensity to violence or relatively simplistic uses of frameworks such as hegemonic, military/ militarized, or 'hyper'-masculinities. These discourses have often been reinforced and reproduced without relating them to their respective local historical, political, and socio-economic contexts. In academic circles, the discussion is more advanced

and progressive, but this has yet to filter through to on-the-ground work" (2017, 103). Additional work on masculinity and military service is focused on sexual identity and focused on "sodomy" (Canaday 2011).

42. In *Discipline and Punish*, Foucault presented a genealogy of the soul and body in the political, judicial, and scientific fields, focusing on the relation of punishment to power over and within the body. "Power relations," he wrote, "have an immediate hold upon the body; they invest it, mark it, train it, torture it, force it to carry out tasks, to perform ceremonies to emit signs—the dense web of power relations is the micro-physicist of power. This power is not exercised simply as an obligation or a prohibition on those who 'do not have it.' It invests in them, is transmitted by them and through them" (1995, 160). While for Foucault these are the ways in which power operates through every aspect of life, they become visible and discernible within state institutions and spaces, such as prisons, schools, hospitals, and the military. Beginning in the eighteenth century, a preoccupation with "docile bodies" developed, aiming to assimilate the body into a mechanics of power in all areas of life. "Soldiers are now trained to march. Factory workers now have posts, skills and timetables. School kids have to sit and write properly. In all areas, insolence, lateness, laziness, dirtiness and impurity are punished" (Foucault 1995, 161). To ensure that bodies are submissive to power and useful, surveillance and observation spread everywhere; as the ideal of complete visibility is impossible to achieve, a new device is invented: "the panopticon." Originally designed by utilitarian philosopher Jeremy Bentham, the panopticon is a tower from which warden, doctor, teacher, or foreman can spy on the inmates, patients, and pupils. They are able to see, and therefore locate, each body in space and in relation to each other, without the subjects' knowing when they are watched. In turn, Bentham suggests that the "watched" assume they are under continuous surveillance and police their own behavior, complying with whatever is requested of them.

43. Most scholars writing about migration (Rudrappa 2004) assume that Indian immigrants assimilate into public life and keep performing their ethnic identity in private. However, as military life does not allow for much privacy, and also because Vikrant took great pains to change his body, this often-accepted distinction between public and private is blurred in his case. Moreover, Kurien argues that when discussing Indian immigrants' integration process, we need to take into account gender, as their migration and settlement are the result of "an interrelated but distinct sequence of gender processes at three analytical levels—the household, the local ethnic community, and the pan-Indian umbrella organizations. The processes occurring at the three levels intermesh in a complicated and contradictory dynamic. The contradictions are manifested in the construction of gendered ethnicity and in gender practice, particularly at the organization level" (Kurien 1999, 649).

44. https://www.army.mil/values/, accessed February 1, 2020.

Conclusion

1. Intersectionality further exposed and dismantled the process of marginalization that operates within institutionalized discourses, legitimizing the existing power structures (Carbado et al. 2013; Crenshaw 1991, 1995).

2. Salary is not the only factor contributing to economic gain. Receiving GI Bill benefits furthers soldiers' academic advancement—and access to these benefits is one of the main reasons for joining the military. For first-generation immigrants, it is very difficult to attend an American university because of the high cost of education and their limited access to funds (loans, fellowships, grants, and the like) for noncitizens (Sassler 2006). Hence, for first-generation immigrants, the chance to use the GI Bill becomes an even more valuable incentive to join the U.S. armed forces.

3. One of the sensitive topics relating to gender in the U.S. military is the large number of sexual assault allegations. In 2014 the Department of Defense received 5,983 reports that led to 3,586 new criminal investigations (http://www.sapr.mil/ public/docs/reports/FY14_POTUS/FY14_DoD_Report_to_POTUS_Appendix_A. pdf, accessed November 29, 2017); in 2015 the number rose to 6,083 reports for sexual assault involving service members (http://sapr.mil/public/docs/reports/FY15 _Annual/FY15_Annual_Report_on_Sexual_Assault_in_the_Military_Full_Report. pdf, accessed November 29, 2017) and in 2016 to 6,172 (https://www.nbcnews.com/ news/us-news/sexual-assault-reports-u-s-military-reach-record-high-pentagon -n753566, accessed November 29, 2017). While this topic deserves in-depth investigation, because none of the participants in this study referred to it in any direct or indirect way, this study does not develop the issue.

Appendix

1. Matilda Aberese-Ako, "'I Won't Take Part!': Exploring the Multiple Identities of the Ethnographer in Two Ghanaian Hospitals," *Ethnography* 18, no. 3 (2016): 300–321; Fabienne Darling-Wolf, "White Bodies and Feminist Dilemmas: On the Complexity of Positionality," *Journal of Communication Inquiry* 22, no. 4 (1998): 410–25; Jonathan Dean et al., "Desert Island Data: An Investigation into Researcher Positionality," *Qualitative Research* 18, no. 3 (2017): 273–89; Calogero Giametta, "Reorienting Participation, Distance and Positionality: Ethnographic Encounters with Gender and Sexual Minority Migrants," *Sexualities* 21, nos. 5–6 (2018): 868–82; Richard Milner IV, "Race, Culture, and Researcher Positionality: Working through Dangers Seen, Unseen, and Unforeseen," *Educational Researcher* 36, no. 7 (2007): 388–400; Michaela Rogers and Anya Ahmed, "Interrogating Trans and Sexual Identities through the Conceptual Lens of Translocational Positionality," *Sociological Research Online* 22, no. 1 (2017): 4; Stefani Relles, "A Call for Qualitative Methods in Action: Enlisting Positionality as an Equity Tool," *Intervention in School and Clinic* 51, no. 5 (2015): 312–17; Urvashi Soni-Sinha, "Dynamic of the Field: Multiple Standpoints, Narrative and Shifting Positionality in Multisited Research," *Qualitative Research* 8, no. 40 (2008): 515–37; Catherine Vanner, "Positionality at the Center: Constructing an Epistemological and Methodological Approach for a Western Feminist Doctoral Candidate Conducting Research in the Postcolonial," *International Journal of Qualitative Methods* 1 (2015): 1–12.

2. Dvora Yanow and Peregrine Schwartz-Shea, *Interpretation and Method: Empirical Research Methods and the Interpretive Turn* (New York: Routledge Press, 2014).

3. Shannon Sullivan and Nancy Tuana, ed., *Race and Epistemologies of Ignorance* (Albany: State University of New York Press, 2011), 4, citing Horkheimer.

4. For use of social media posts, and threads as a method of analysis in life stories of women serving in the U.S. military, see also Silvestri 2015; Thorpe 2015; and Rose 2016.

References

Ahmad, Manzoor. 2019. "Understanding India-Pakistan Relations: Memory Keeps Getting in the Way of History." *Jadavpur Journal of International Relations* 23, no. 1 (June): 69–80. https://doi.org/10.1177/0973598418804289.

"Air Force Guide (2)." n.d. http://www.e-publishing.af.mil/shared/media/epubs/AFPAM10-100.pdf.

Alba, Richard. 1999. "Immigration and the American Realities of Assimilation and Multiculturalism." *Sociological Forum* 14 (1): 3–25.

Alba, Richard, and Nancy Foner. 2015. *Strangers No More: Immigration and the Challenges of Integration in Northern American and Western Europe*. Princeton, NJ: Princeton University Press.

Alba, Richard, and Victor Nee. 1997. "Rethinking Assimilation Theory for a New Era of Immigration." In "Immigrant Adaptation and Native-Born Responses in the Making of Americans." Special issue, *International Migration Review* 31 (4): 826–74.

———. 2003. *Remaking the American Mainstream: Assimilation and Contemporary Immigration*. Cambridge, MA: Harvard University Press.

Alexander, L. George. 1971. "Primary Groups, Organization and Military Performance." In *Handbook of Military Institutions*, edited by R. W. Little. Beverly Hills: Sage.

Allen, R. 2010. "The Unreal Enemy of America's Army." *Games and Culture* 6:38–60. https://doi.org/10.1177/1555412010377321.

Allen, Theodore. 2012. "The Invention of the White Race." In vol. 1 of *Racial Oppression and Social Control*. New York: Verso.

Amaya, Hector. 2007a. "Dying American; or, The Violence of Citizenship: Latinos in Iraq." *Latino Studies* 5:3–24. https://doi.org/10.1057/palgrave.lst.8600240.

———. 2007b. "Latino Immigrants in the American Discourses of Citizenship and Nationalism during the Iraqi War." *Critical Discourse Studies* 4 (3): 237–56. https://doi.org/10.1080/17405900701656841.

Anderson, Benedict R. O'G. 1991. *Imagined Communities: Reflections on the Origin and Spread of Nationalism*. Rev ed. London: Verso, 2006.

Antecol, Heather. 2000. "An Examination of Cross-Country Differences in the Gender Gap in Labour Force Participation Rates." *Labour Economics* 7 (4): 409–26.

Antecol, Heather, and Kelly Bedard. 2006. "Why Do Immigrants Converge to American Health Status Levels?" *Demography* 43 (2): 337–60.

Antecol, Heather, Peter Khun, and Stephen J. Trejo. 2006. "Assimilation via Prices or Quantities? Sources of immigrant Earnings Growth in Australia, Canada and the United States." *Journal of Human Resources* 41 (4): 821–40.

Appelbaum, Nancy P., Anne S. Macpherson, and Karin Alejandra Rosemblatt, eds. 2003. "Racial Nations." In *Race and Nation in Modern Latin America*. Chapel Hill: University of North Carolina Press.

Appy, Christian G. 1993. *Working-Class War American Combat Soldiers and Vietnam*. Chicago: University of Chicago Press.

Arendt, Hannah. 1979. "Isak Dinesen (1885–1962)." In *Daguerreotypes*. Chicago: University of Chicago Press.

———. 2006. *Between Past and Future*. New York: Penguin Classics.

Arias, Elizabeth. 2002. "Chance in Nuptial Patterns among Urban Cuban Americans: Evidence of Cultural and Structural Assimilation?" *International Migration Review* 35 (2): 525–56.

"Army Profile." 2011. http://www.armyg1.army.mil/hr/docs/demographics/FY11 _ARMY_PROFILE.pdf.

"Army's Guide to Citizenship." n.d. https://www.hrc.army.mil/TAGD/Soldiers%20 Guide%20to%20Citizenship.

Arsene, Andreea. 2012. "Learning the Roles and Rights of the Romanian Women between Traditional Patterns and Globalization (Lifelong Learning in the Romania Gender Context)." *Procedia—Social and Behavioral Sciences* 46:374–78.

Azari, Jaz. 2010. "Cultural Stress: How Interactions with and among Foreign Populations Affect Military Personnel." *Armed Forces & Society* 36 (4): 585–603.

Bacevich, Andrew. 2013. *Breach of Trust: How Americans Failed Their Soldiers and Their Country*. American Empire Project. New York: Metropolitan Books.

Bachman, Jerald G., John D. Blair, and David R. Segal. 1977. *All Volunteer Force: Study of Ideology in the Military*. Ann Arbor: University of Michigan Press.

Bacon, Jean Leslie. 1997. *Life Lines: Community, Family, and Assimilation among Asian Indian Immigrants*. New York: Oxford University Press.

Bailey, Anne J. 2006. *Invisible Southerners: Ethnicity in the Civil War*. Athens: University of Georgia Press.

Bailey, Beth L. 2009. *America's Army: Making the All-Volunteer Force*. Cambridge, MA: Harvard University Press. ProQuest Ebook Central.

Baker, Michael, and Dwayne Benjamin. 1997. "The Role of the Family in Immigrants' Labour-Market Activity: An Evaluation of Alternative Explanations." *American Economic Review* 87 (4): 705–27.

Baldwin, James. 1996. *The Fire Next Time*. New York: Vintage.

Barkawi, Tarak. 2017. *Soldiers of Empire: Indian and British Armies in World War II*. Cambridge: Cambridge University Press.

Barken, Elliott, and Robert Barkan, eds. 2013. *Immigrants in American History: Arrival, Adaptation, and Integration*. Santa Barbara: ABC-Clio.

Barreto, Matt A., and David L. Leal. 2007. "Latinos, Military Service, and Support for Bush and Kerry in 2004." *American Politics Research* 35, no. 2 (March): 224–51. https://doi.org/10.1177/1532673X06298077.

Barth, Ernest A. T., and Donald L. Noel. 1972. "Conceptual Framework for the Analysis of Race Relations: An Evaluation." *Social Force* 50: 333–48.

"Basic Pay: Active Duty Soldiers." n.d. http://www.goarmy.com/benefits/money/basic-pay-active-duty-soldiers.html.

Bauder, Harald. 2014. "Domicile Citizenship, Human Mobility and Territoriality." *Progress in Human Geography* 38 (1): 91–106.

Bekteshi, Venera, and Mary van Hook. 2015. "Contextual Approach to Acculturative Stress among Latina Immigrants in the U.S." *Journal of Immigrant and Minority Health* 17, no. 5 (October): 1401–11.

Bekteshi, Venera, Mary van Hook, and Lenore Matthew. 2015. "Puerto Rican–Born Women in the United States: Contextual Approach to Immigration Challenges." *Health & Social Work* 40, no. 4 (November): 298–306. https://doi.org/10.1093/hsw/hlv070.

Bell, E., and S. Nkomo. 2001. *Our Separate Ways: Black and White Women and the Struggles for Professional Identity*. Cambridge, MA: Harvard Business School Press.

Ben-Ari, B. Eyal. 1998. *Mastering Soldiers: Conflict, Emotions, and the Enemy in Israeli Military Unit*. New York: Berghahn Books.

Berreman, Gerald D. 1960. "Caste in India and the United States." *American Journal of Sociology* 66 (2): 120–27.

Beteille, Andre. 1990. "Race, Caste and Gender." *Man*, n.s., 25 (3): 489–504.

Betters-Reed, B. L., and L. L. Moore. 1995. "Shifting the Management Development Paradigm for Women." *Journal of Management Development* 14:2–24. https://doi.org/10.1108/02621719510078876.

Bevir, Mark. 2006. "How Narratives Explain." In *Interpretation and Method: Empirical Research Methods and Interpretive Turn*, edited by Dvora Yanow and Peregrine Schwartz-Shea. Armonk, NY: M. E. Sharpe.

Bhatia, Sunil. 2007. *American Karma: Race, Culture, and Identity and the Indian Diaspora*. New York: New York University Press.

Bhattacharya, Gauri. 2011. "Global Contexts, Social Capital, and Acculturative Stress: Experiences of Indian Immigrant Men in New York City." *Immigrant Minority Health* 13: 756–65.

Biank, Tanya, and Mark Thompson. 2014. *Undaunted: The Real Story of America's Servicewomen in Today's Military*. New York: Dutton Caliber Press.

Bick, Joanne. 1997. *Ethnic Vision: A Romanian American Experience*. Niwot: University Press of Colorado.

Billaud, Julie. 2015. *Kabul Carnival Gender Politics in Postwar Afghanistan*. Philadelphia: University of Pennsylvania Press.

Bird-Francke, Linda. 1997. *Ground Zero: The Gender Wars in the Military*. New York: Simon and Schuster.

"Black Americans in the U.S. Army." n.d. http://www.army.mil/africanamericans/timeline.html.

Blacksmith, E. A., ed. 1992. *Women in the Military*. New York: Wilson.

Blair, Clay. 1987. *The Forgotten War*. New York: Time Books.

Blau, Francine D. 2015. "Immigrants and Gender Roles: Assimilation vs. Culture." Discussion Paper no. 9534. November. http://ftp.iza.org/dp9534.pdf.

Blau, Francine D., Lawrence M. Kahn, Joan Moriarty, and Andre Souza. 2003. "The Role of the Family in Immigrants' Labour-Market Activity: An Evaluation of Alternative Explanations: Comment." *American Economic Review* 93 (1): 429–47.

Blau, Francine D., Lawrence M. Kahn, and Kerry L. Papps. 2008. "Gender, Source Country Characteristics and Labour Market Assimilation among Immigrants: 1980–2000." NBER Working Paper 14387 (October). http://voxeu.org/article/do-female-immigrants-assimilate-us-labour-market.

———. 2011. "Gender in Country Characteristics and Labor Market Assimilation among Immigrants: 1980–2000." *Review of Economics and Statistics* 93 (1): 43–58.

Blau, Peter M. 1992. "Mobility and Status Attainment." Edited by Peter Blau and Otis Dudley Duncan. *Contemporary Sociology* 21 (5): 596–98. https://doi.org/10.2307/2075538.

Blau, Peter M., and Otis Dudley Duncan. 1967. *The American Occupational Structure*. New York: John Wiley & Sons.

Bloemraad, Irene. 2006. "Becoming a Citizen in the United States and Canada: Structured Mobilization and Immigrant Political Incorporation." *Social Forces* 85 (2): 667–95.

Bobango, Gerald J. 1979. *The Romanian Orthodox America: Episcopate of the First Half Century, 1929–1979*. Jackson, MI: Romanian-American Heritage Center.

Boehm-Philips, Kimberley L. 2012. *War! What Is It Good For? Black Freedom Struggles and the U.S. Military from World War II to Iraq*. John Hope Franklin Series in African American History and Culture. Chapel Hill: University of North Carolina Press.

Boellstorff, Tom. 2010. *Coming of Age in Second Life: An Anthropologist Explores the Virtually Human*. Princeton, NJ: Princeton University Press.

Bohon, Stephanie A. 2005. "Occupational Attainment of Latino Immigrants in the United States." *Geographical Review* 95 (2): 249–66.

Bolton, Herbert E. 1933. "The Epic of Greater America." *American Historical Review* 38:448–74.

Booth, Bradford, et al. 2000. "The Impact of Military Presence in Local Labor Markets on the Employment of Women." *Gender and Society* 14 (2): 318–32.

Bornstein, Avram S. 2003. *Crossing the Green Line between the West Bank and Israel*. Philadelphia: University of Pennsylvania Press.

Borstelmann, Thomas. 1999. "Jim Crow's Coming Out: Race Relations and American Foreign Policy in the Truman Years." *Presidential Studies Quarterly* 29 (3): 549–69.

Bott, Elizabeth. 2013. *Family and Social Network: Roles, Norms and External Relationships in Ordinary Urban Families*. London: Routledge.

Bourdieu, Pierre. 1979. "Les trois états du capital culturel." *Actes de la Recherche en Sciences Sociales* 30:3–5.

Bowers, William T., et al. 2005. *Black Soldier, White Army: The 24th Infantry Regiment in Korea*. N.p.: University Press of the Pacific, 2005.

Boyd, Monica, and Elizabeth Grieco. 2003. "Women and Migration: Incorporating Gender into International Migration Theory." https://www.migrationpolicy.org/article/women-and-migration-incorporating-gender-international-migration-theory.

Brandt, Mark J. 2011. "Sexism and Gender Inequality across 57 Societies." *Psychological Science* 22 (11): 1413–18.

Braudel, Fernand. 1995. *A History of Civilizations*. New York: Penguin Books.

Bristol, Douglas W., and Heather Marie Stur Jr., eds. 2017. *Integrating the US Military*. Kindle ed. Baltimore: Johns Hopkins University Press.

Brown, W. 1995. "Postmodern Exposures, Feminist Hesitations." In *States of Injury: Power and Freedom in Late Modernity*. Princeton, NJ: Princeton University Press.

Brubaker, Rogers. 1992. *Citizenship and Nationhood in France and Germany*. Cambridge, MA: Harvard University Press.

Buch, E., and K. Staller. 2014. "What Is Feminist Ethnography?" In *Feminist Research Practice*. New York: Sage.

Buchanan, Suzanne H. 1979. "Language and Identity: Haitians in New York City." In "International Immigration in Latin America." Special issue, *International Migration Review* 13 (2): 298–313.

Bucur, Maria. 2008. "An Archipelago of Stories: Gender History in Eastern Europe." *American Historical Review* 113 (5): 1375–89.

Burk, James, and Evelyn Espinoza. 2012. "Race Relations within the US Military." *Annual Review of Sociology* 1: 401–22.

Burton, William. 1998. *Melting Pot Soldiers: The Union's Ethnic Regiments*. New York: Fordham University Press.

Bussey, Lt. Col. Charles M. 2002. *Firefight at Yechon: Courage and Racism in the Korean War*. Lincoln, NE: Bison Books.

Butler, John Sibley. 1992. "Affirmative Action in the Military." In "Affirmative Action Revisited." Special issue, *Annals of the American Academy of Political and Social Science* 523 (1): 196–206.

Butler, Judith. 1993. *Bodies That Matter: On the Discourse Limits of Sex*. New York: Routledge.

———. 1997. *Excitable Speech: A Politics of the Performative*. New York: Routledge.

———. 1998. "Performative Acts and Gender Constitution: An Essay in Phenomenology and Feminist Theory." *Theatre Journal* 40 (4): 519–31. http://www.egs.edu/faculty/judith-butler/articles/performative-acts-and-gender-constitution/.

———. 2006. *Gender Trouble: Feminism and the Subversion of Identity*. New York: Routledge.

Campisi, Paul J. 1948. "Ethnic Family Patterns: The Italian Family in the United States." *American Journal of Sociology* 53 (6): 443–49.

Canaday, Margot. 2011. *The Straight State: Sexuality and Citizenship in Twentieth-Century America*. Princeton, NJ: Princeton University Press.

Capozzola, Christopher. 2008. *Uncle Sam Wants You: World War I and the Making of the Modern American Citizen*. New York: Oxford University Press.

Carbado, Devon, et al. 2013. "Intersectionality: Mapping the Movements of a Theory." *Du Bois Review: Social Science Research on Race* 10: 303–12. https://doi.org/10.1017/S1742058X13000349.

Certeau, Michel de. 2002. *The Practice of Everyday Life*. Berkeley: University of California Press.

Chakravorty, Sanjoy, Devesh Kapur, and Nirvikar Singh. 2016. *The Other One Percent: Indians in America*. New York: Oxford University Press.

Chan, Sucheng, ed. 1994. *Entry Denied: Exclusion and the Chinese Community in America, 1882–1943*. Philadelphia: Temple University Press. http://www.lcsc.org/cms/lib6/MN01001004/Centricity/Domain/81/TAH%202.pdf.

Chandrasekhar, Sripati. 1984. *From India to America, a Brief History of Immigration: Problems of Discrimination, Admission and Assimilation*. La Jolla, CA: Population Review.

Chant, Sylvia, and Nikki Craske. 2003. *Gender in Latin America*. New Brunswick, NJ: Rutgers University Press.

Chavez, Leo R. 1997. *Shadowed Lives: Undocumented Immigrants in American Society*. Case Studies in Cultural Anthropology. Belmont, CA: Wadsworth.

Cheng, Shu-ju Ada. 1999. "Labor Migration and International Sexual Division of Labor: A Feminist Perspective." In *Gender and Immigration*, edited by Gregory A. Kelson and Debra L. DeLaet. New York: New York University Press.

Chin, Thomas. 1989. *Bridging the Pacific: San Francisco Chinatown and Its People*. San Francisco: Chinese Historical Society of America.

Cho, Sumi, Kimberlé Williams Crenshaw, and Leslie McCall. 2013. "Toward a Field of Intersectionality Studies: Theory, Applications, and Praxis." *Signs: Journal of Women in Culture and Society* 38 (4): 785–810.

Choo, Hae Yeon, and Myra Marx Ferree. 2010. "Practicing Intersectionality in Sociological Research: A Critical Analysis of Inclusions, Interactions, and Institutions in the Study of Inequalities." *Sociological Theory* 28, no. 2 (June): 129–49.

Clark, W. 2003. *Immigrants and the American Dream: Remaking the Middle Class*. New York: Guilford Press.

Code, Lorraine. 1991. *What Does She Know: Feminist Theory and the Construction of Knowledge*. Ithaca, NY: Cornell University Press.

Colen, S. 1990. "Housekeeping for the Green Card: West Indian Household Workers, the State, and Stratified Reproduction in New York." In *At Work in Homes: Household Workers in World Perspective*, edited by R. Sanjek and S. Colen, 89–118. Washington, DC: American Anthropological Association.

Collins, Patricia Hill. 2000. "It's All in the Family: Intersections of Gender, Race, and Nation." In *Decentering the Center: Philosophy for a Multicultural, Postcolonial, and Feminist World*, edited by Uma Narayan and Sandra Harding, 156–76. Bloomington: Indiana University Press.

Comay, Rebecca. 2015. "Resistance and Repetition: Freud and Hegel." *Research in Phenomenology* 45, no. 2 (September): 237–66.

Conway, Dennis, and Jeffrey Cohen. 1998. "Consequences of Migration and Remittances for Mexican Transnational Communities." *Economic Geography* 74 (1): 26–44.

Cooney, Jerry W. 1980. *Paraguay: A Bibliography of Immigration and Emigration.* Long View, WA: J. W. Cooney.

Cornell, Stephen E., and Douglas Hartmann. 1998. *Ethnicity and Race: Making Identities in a Changing World.* Thousand Oaks, CA: Pine Forge Press.

Corrin, Chris. 1992. *Superwomen and the Double Burden: Women's Experience of Change in Central and Eastern Europe and the Former Soviet Union.* Toronto: Second Story Press.

Cox, Oliver C. 1945. "Race and Caste: A Distinction." *American Journal of Sociology* 50 (5): 360–68.

Cracana, Violina, and Adrian Păunescu. 2007. *Cu și Despre Adrian Păunescu.* Bucharest: Fundația Constantin.

Craven, Christa, and Dana-Ain Davis, eds. 2014 *Feminist Activist Ethnography: Counterpoints to Neoliberalism in North America.* Lanham, MD: Lexington Books.

Crenshaw, Kimberlé. 1989. "Demarginalizing the Intersection of Race and Sex: A Black Feminist Critique of Antidiscrimination Doctrine, Feminist Theory, and Antiracist Politics." *University of Chicago Legal Forum*: 139–67.

———. 1991. "Mapping the Margins: Intersectionality, Identity Politics, and Violence against Women of Color." *Stanford Law Review* 43 (6): 1241–79. https://doi.org/10.2307/1229039.

———. 2010. "Close Encounters of Three Kinds: On Teaching Dominance, Feminism, and Intersectionality." *Tulsa Law Review* 46: 151–89.

Crenshaw, Kimberlé, et al., eds. 1995. *Critical Race Theory.* New York: New Press.

Crocker, Rebecca. 2015. "Emotional Testimonies: An Ethnographic Study of Emotional Suffering Related to Migration from Mexico to Arizona." *Front Public Health.* https://doi.org/10.3389/fpubh.2015.00177.

Crouch, Mira, and Heather McKenzie. 2006. "The Logic of Small Samples in Interview-Based Qualitative Research." *Social Science Information* 45, no. 4 (December): 483–99. doi:10.1177/0539018406069584.

Dalfume, Richard. 1969. *Desegregation of the U.S. Armed Forces.* Columbia: University of Missouri Press.

D'Amico, Francine. 1997. "Policing the U.S. Military's Race and Gender Lines." In *Wives and Warriors: Women and the Military in the United States and Canada*, edited by Laurie Lee Weinstein and Christie C. White. Westport, CT: Bergin & Garvey.

Dandekar, Christopher. 2003. "Diversifying the Uniform? The Participation of Minority Ethnic Personnel in the British Armed Services." *Armed Forces & Society* 29, no. 4 (Summer): 481–507.

Daneshvary, Nasser, et al. 1992. "Job Search and Immigrant Assimilation: An Earnings Frontier Approach." *Review of Economics and Statistics* 74 (3): 482–92.

Daniels, Roger. 2005. *Guarding the Golden Door: American Immigration Policy and Immigrants since 1882.* New York: Hill and Wang.

Dasgupta, Sathi. 1992. "Conjugal Roles and Social Network in Indian Immigrant Families." *Journal of Comparative Family Studies* 23 (3): 465–80.

Dasgupta, Shashmita Das. 1998. "Gender Roles and Cultural Continuity in the Asian Indian Immigrant Community in the U.S." *Sex Roles* 38:953–74. https://doi.org/10.1023/A:1018822525427.

David, Deborah S., and Robert Brannon. 1976. *The Forty-Nine Percent Majority: The Male Sex Role*. Boston: Addison Wesley.

Davis, Dana-Ain, and Christa Craven. 2016. *Feminist Ethnography: Thinking through Methodologies, Challenges and Possibilities*. Lanham, MD: Rowman and Littlefield.

Dawinder, S. Sidhu, and Neha Singh Gohil. 2009. *Civil Rights in Wartime: The Post-9/11 Sikh Experience*. Farnham, UK: Ashgate.

DeGroot, Gerard, and Corrinna Peniston-Bird. 2000. *A Soldier and a Woman: Sexual Integration in the Military*. Harlow, UK: Longman Pearson Education.

DeLaet, Debra L. 1999. "Introduction: The Invisibility of Women in Scholarship in International Migration." In *Gender and Immigration*, edited by Gregory A. Kelson and Debra L. Delaet. New York: New York University Press.

De León, Jason. 2015. *The Land of Open Graves: Living and Dying on the Migrant Trail*. Oakland: University of California Series in Public Anthropology.

Derby, John. 2014. "Violent Video Games and the Military: Recruitment, Training and Treating Mental Disability." *Art and Education* 67 (3): 19–25.

DeSipio, Louis, and Rodolfo De La Garza. 1998. *Making Americans, Remaking America*. Boulder, CO: Westview Press.

Desposato, Scott, and Barbara Norrander. 2008. *The Gender Gap in Latin America: Contextual and Individual Influences on Gender and Political Participation*. Cambridge: Cambridge University Press.

De Volo, Lorraine Bayard. 2009. "Participant Observation, Politics, and Power Relations: Nicaraguan Mothers and U.S. Casino Waitresses." In *Political Ethnography: What Immersion Contributes to the Study of Power*, edited by Edward Schatz, 217–36. Chicago: University of Chicago Press.

De Volo, Lorraine Bayard, and Edward Schatz. 2004. "From the Inside Out: Ethnographic Methods in Political Research." *PS: Political Science and Politics* 37, no. 2 (2004): 267–71. www.jstor.org/stable/4488818.

DeWind, Josh, and Philip Kasinitz. 1997. "Everything Old Is New Again? Processes and Theories of Immigrant Incorporation." In "Immigrant Adaptation and Native-Born Responses in the Making of Americans." Special issue, *International Migration Review* 31, no. 4 (Winter): 1096–1111.

Dietrich, Cheryl. 2018. *In Formation: One Woman's Rise through the Ranks of the U.S. Air Force*. Kindle ed. New York: Yucca.

"Diversity in the Air Force." 1995. http://www.au.af.mil/au/awc/awcgate/dod/d13502p.txt.

Dongxiao, Qin. 2009. *Crossing Borders: International Women Students in American Higher Education*. Lanham, MD: University Press of America.

Dorius, Shawn F., and Glenn Firebaugh. 2010. "Trends in Global Gender Inequality." *Social Forces* 88, no. 5 (July): 1941–68.

Dower, John W. 1986. *War without Mercy: Race and Power in the Pacific War*. New York: Pantheon Books.

Dragomir, Cristina. 2012. "History of Immigrants in the U.S. Military." In *Making Modern Immigration*, edited by Patrick J. Hayes. Santa Barbara: ABC-Clio.

———. 2018. "Identity Is Dialogical: The Naturalization of Immigrants in American Military." *Bulletin of the Transilvania University of Braşov*, ser. 4.

Du Bois, W. E. B. 1898. "The Study of the Negro Problems." *Annals of the American Academy of Political and Social Science* 11: 1–23.

———. 1962. *Black Reconstruction in America, 1860–1880*. 1890. Reprint, New York: S. A. Russell.

Dudziak, Mary L. 1988. "Desegregation as a Cold War Imperative." *Stanford Law Review* 41 (1): 61–120.

Dwyer, Gail O'Sullivan. 2009. *Tough as Nails: One Woman's Journey through West Point*. Kindle ed. Ashland, OR: Hellgate Press.

Eagly, A. H., and L. L. Carli. 2007. *Through the Labyrinth: The Truth about How Women Become Leaders*. Boston: Harvard Business School Press.

Eagly, A. H., and S. J. Karau. 1991. "Gender and the Emergence of Leaders: A Meta-analysis." *Journal of Personality and Social Psychology* 60:685–710. https://doi.org/10.1037/0022-3514.60.5.685.

Eakin, Marshall C. 2004. "Does Latin America Have a Common History?" *Vanderbilt EJournal of Luso-Hispanics Studies* 1. http://ejournals.library.vanderbilt.edu/ojs/index.php/lusohispanic/article/view/3179/1365.

Echevarria, Antulio J., II. 2005. "Fourth-Generation War or Myths." http://www.strategicstudiesinstitute.army.mil/pdffiles/pub632.pdf.

Eggerth, Donald E., Sheli C. Delaney, Michael A. Flynn, and C. Jeff Jacobson. 2012. "Work Experience of Latina Immigrants: A Qualitative Study." *Journal of Career Development* 39, no. 1 (February): 13–30.

Einhorn, Barbara. 1993. *Cinderella Goes to Market: Citizenship, Gender, and Women's Movements in East Central Europe*. London: Verso.

Ellis, Carolyn, Tony E. Adams, and Arthur P. Bochner. 2011. "Autoethnography." *Forum: Qualitative Social Research* 12, no. 1 (January).

Elron, Efrat, Boas Shamir, and Eyal Ben-Ari. 1999. "Why Don't They Fight Each Other? Cultural Diversity and Operational Unity in Multinational Forces." *Armed Forces & Society* 26, no. 1 (Fall): 73–97.

Elshtain, Jean Bethkem. 2000. "'Shooting' at the Wrong Target: A Response to Van Creveld." *Millennium* 29 (2): 443–48.

England, K. V. L. 1994. "Getting Personal: Reflexivity, Positionality, and Feminist Research." *Professional Geographer* 46 (1): 80–89.

Fanon, Frantz. 2005. *The Wretched of the Earth*. New York: Grove Press.

Feaver, Peter D. 1999. "Civil-Military Relations." *Annual Review of Political Science* 2: 211–41.

Fenton, John. 1988. *Transplanting Religious Traditions: Asian Indians in America*. Westport, CT: Praeger.

Few-Demo, April. 2014. "Intersectionality as the 'New' Critical Approach in Feminist Family Studies: Evolving Racial/Ethnic Feminisms and Critical Race Theories." *Journal of Family Theory and Review* 6, no. 2 (June): 169–83.

Fitts, Shanan, and Greg McClure. 2015. "Building Social Capital in Hightown: The Role of *Confianza* in Latina Immigrants' Social Networks in the New South." *Anthropology and Education* 46, no. 3 (September). https://doi.org/10.1111/aeq .12108.

Fitzgerald, Kelly G. 2000. "The Effect of Military Service on Wealth Accumulation." *Research on Aging* 28 (1): 56.

Fontana, A., and R. Rosenheck. 1994. "Traumatic War Stressors and Psychiatric Symptoms among World War II, Korean, and Vietnam War Veterans." *Psychology and Aging* 9: 27–33.

Foote, Nicola, and René D. Harder Horst, eds. 2010. *Military Struggle and Identity Formation in Latin America.* Gainesville: University Press of Florida.

Ford, Nancy Gentile. 2001. *Americans All! Foreign-Born Soldiers in World.* College Station: Texas A&M University Press.

Foucault, Michel. 1980. *Power/ Knowledge.* New York: Pantheon Books.

———. 1995. *Discipline and Punish: The Birth of Prison.* 1975. Reprint, New York: Vintage Books.

Fox, Jon E., and Magda Mogilnicka. 2019. "Pathological Integration; or, How East Europeans Use Racism to Become British." *British Journal of Sociology* 70 (1): 5–23. https://onlinelibrary.wiley.com/doi/pdf/10.1111/1468-4446.12337.

Frankenberg, Ruth. 1993. *White Women, Race Matters: The Social Construction of Whiteness.* Minneapolis: University of Minnesota Press.

Fraser, Nancy. 2000. "Rethinking Recognition." *New Left Review* (May–June).

Fraser, Nancy, Hanne Merlene Dahl, Pauline Stoltz, and Rasmus Willig. 2004. "Recognition, Redistribution and Representation in Capitalist Global Society: An Interview with Nancy Fraser." *Acta Sociologica* 47, no. 4 (December): 374–82.

Fraser, Nancy, and Axel Honneth. 2005. "Redistribution or Recognition? A Political-Philosophical Exchange." *Ethics* 115, no. 2 (January): 397–402.

Fraser, Nancy, and Nancy Naples. 2004. "To Interpret the World Is to Change it: An Interview with Nancy Fraser." *Signs* 29 (4): 1103–24.

Frazier, Joseph J. 2006. "The Military Profession: What Happens When Values Collide." https://apps.dtic.mil/sti/pdfs/ADA449655.pdf.

Frickenstein, Scott G. 2005. "The Concept of 'Calling' and Its Relevance to the Military." Professional Study #4. https://www.ocfusa.org/wp-content/uploads/2017/01/calling_study4_sgf.pdf.

Fujii, Lee Ann. 2009. *Killing Neighbors: Webs of Violence in Rwanda.* Ithaca, NY: Cornell University Press.

———. 2010. "Shades of Truth and Lies: Interpreting Testimonies of War and Violence." *Journal of Peace Research* 47 (2): 231–41.

Funk, Nanette, and Magda Mueller, eds. 1993. *Gender Politics and Post-communism: Reflections from Eastern Europe and the Former Soviet Union.* New York: Routledge.

Gadamer, Hans Georg. 1975. *Truth and Method.* New York: Seabury Press.

———. 1977. *Philosophical Hermeneutics.* Berkeley: University of California Press.

Gadekar, Rahul, Pradeep Krishnatray, and Shubhra Gaur. 2012. "A Descriptive Study of Facebook Uses among Indian Students." *Media Asia: Asian Media Information & Communication Centre* 39, no. 3 (January): 140–47.

Gammage, Sarah. 2006. "Exporting People and Recruiting Remittances: A Development Strategy for El Salvador?" *Latin American Perspectives* 33, no. 6 (November): 75–100.

Geertz, Clifford. 1973. *The Interpretation of Cultures*. New York: Basic Books.

Gerber, David. 2011. *American Immigration: A Very Short Introduction*. New York: Oxford University Press.

Germano, Kate, and Kelly Kennedy. 2018. *Fight Like a Girl: The Truth behind How Female Marines Are Trained*. Kindle ed. Amherst, NY: Prometheus Books.

Gest, Justin. 2016. *The New Minority: White Working Class Politics in an Age of Immigration and Inequality*. New York: Oxford University Press.

Ghosh, Bimal. 2006. *Migrants' Remittances and Development: Myths, Rhetoric and Realities*. Geneva and The Hague: International Organization on Migration and The Hague Process on Refugees and Migration.

Ghurye, G. S. 2005. *Caste and Race in India*. Bombay: Popular Prakashan.

Glazer, Nathan, and Daniel P. Moynihan. 1970. *Beyond the Melting Pot: The Negroes, Puerto Ricans, Jews, Italians and Irish of New York City*. Cambridge, MA: MIT Press.

———. 2000. "On *Beyond the Melting Pot*, 35 Years After." *International Migration Review* 34, no. 1 (Spring): 270–79.

Glenn, Evelyn Nakano. 2002. *Unequal Freedom: How Race and Gender Shaped American Citizenship and Labor*. Cambridge, MA: Harvard University Press.

Goldman, Nancy. 1973. "The Changing Role of Women in the Armed Forces." *American Journal of Sociology* 78, no. 4 (January): 892–911.

Gonzales, Juan L. 2020. "Asian Indian Immigration Patterns: The Origins of the Sikh Community in California." *International Migration Review* 20, no. 1 (1986): 40–54. https://doi.org/10.2307/2545683.

"Google Public Data: Population of Paraguay." n.d. http://www.google.com/publicdata/explore?ds=d5bncppjof8f9_&met_y=sp_p op_totl&idim=country:PRY&dl=en&hl=en&q=paraguay+population.

Gordon, Milton M. 1964. *Assimilation in American Life: The Role of Race, Religion, and National Origins*. New York: Oxford University Press.

Graham, Richard, ed. 1990. *The Idea of Race in Latin America, 1870–1940*. Austin: University of Texas Press.

Gramsci, Antonio. 1989. *Selections from the Prison Notebooks of Antonio Gramsci*. 1971. Reprint, New York: International.

Greene, Robert Ewell. 1974. *Black Defenders of America, 1775–1973*. New York: Johnston.

Grey, Jesse Glen. 1973. *The Warriors: Reflections on Men in Battle*. New York: Harper and Row.

Griffith, J. E. 1988. "The Measurement of Group Cohesion in U.S. Army Units." *Basic and Applied Social Psychology* 9: 149–71.

Griffith, Robert K., and Center of Military History. 1997. *The U.S. Army's Transition to the All-Volunteer Force, 1968–1974*. Washington, DC: Center of Military History, U.S. Army.

Gritter, Matthew. 2012. *The Origins of Anti-discrimination Policy in Texas and the Southwest*. College Station: Texas A&M University Press.

Gropman, Alan L. 1978. *The Air Force Integrates, 1945–1964.* Washington, DC: Office of Air Force History.

Guy-Sheftall, Beverly. 1995. *Words of Fire: An Anthology of African-American Feminist Thought.* New York: New Press.

Hajjar, Remi M. 2010. "A New Angle on the U.S. Military's Emphasis on Developing Cross-Cultural Competence: Connecting in-Ranks' Cultural Diversity to Cross-Cultural Competence." *Armed Forces & Society* 36 (2): 247–63.

Hall, Kathleen D. 2004. "The Ethnography of Imagined Communities: The Cultural Production of Sikh Ethnicity in Britain." *University of Pennsylvania Scholarly Commons.* http://repository.upenn.edu/cgi/viewcontent.cgi?article=1073&context=gse_pubs.

Hamdan, Amani. 2012. "Autoethnography as Genre of Qualitative Research: A Journey Inside Out." *International Journal of Qualitative Methods.* http://journals.sagepub.com/doi/pdf/10.1177/160940691201100505.

Hancock, Ange-Marie. 2007. "Intersexuality as a Normative and Empirical Paradigm." *Politics and Gender* 3, no. 2 (June): 248–54. https://doi.org/10.1017/S1743923X07000062.

Hanke, Lewis. 1964. *Do the Americas Have a Common History? A Critique of the Bolton Theory.* New York: Alfred A. Knopf.

Hansen, Kim Philip. 2012. *Military Chaplains and Religious Diversity.* London: Palgrave.

Harper, Douglas. 2000. "Small N's and Community Case Studies." In *What Is a Case? Exploring the Foundations of Social Inquiry,* edited by Charles C. Ragin and Howard S. Becker. Cambridge: Cambridge University Press.

Hauser, Robert M. 1978. "On Inequality in the Military." *American Sociological Review* 43 (1): 115–18.

Hawkesworth, Mary. 2006. *Globalization and Feminist Activism.* Lanham, MD: Rowman & Littlefield.

———. 2016a. *Embodied Power: Demystifying Disembodied Politics.* New York: Routledge.

———. 2016b. *Feminist Inquiry: From Political Conviction to Methodological Innovation.* New Brunswick, NJ: Rutgers University Press.

Healey, Joseph, and Eileen O'Brien, eds. 2007. *Race, Ethnicity and Gender.* Los Angeles: Sage.

Hegar, Mary Jennings. 2017. *Shoot Like a Girl: One Woman's Dramatic Fight in Afghanistan and on the Home Front.* Kindle ed. New York: New American Library.

Heller, Agnes. 2000. "Between Past and Future." In *Between Past and Future: Revolutions of 1989 and Their Aftermath,* edited by Sorin Antohi. Budapest: Central European University Press.

Helweg, Arthur, and Usha M. Helweg. 1991. *An Immigrant Success Story: East Indians in America.* Philadelphia: University of Pennsylvania Press.

Hendrix, Teresa H. 2006. "The Effects of Military Training on Men's Attitudes toward Intimate Partner Violence." Master's thesis, Ohio State University.

Henry, Frances, and Carol Tator. 2006. *The Colour of Democracy: Racism in Canadian Society.* 3rd ed. Toronto: Nelson.

Herbert, Melissa S. 1998. *Camouflage Isn't Only for Combat: Gender, Sexuality and Women in the Military.* New York: New York University Press.

Hercog, Metka, and Mindel van de Laar. 2016. "Motivations and Constraints of Moving Abroad for Indian Students." *Journal of International Migration and Integration* 18. https://doi.org/10.1007/s12134-016-0499-4.

Hesse-Biber, Sharlene Nagy, eds. 2014. *Feminist Research Practice*. Los Angeles: Sage.

Hickes-Lundquist, Jennifer. 2008. "Ethnic and Gender Satisfaction in the Military: The Effect of a Meritocratic Institution." *American Sociological Review* 73, no. 3 (June): 477–96.

Hickes-Lundquist, Jennifer, and Herbert L. Smith. 2005. "Family Formation among Women in the U.S. Military: Evidence from the NLSY." *Journal of Marriage and Family* 67, no. 1 (February): 1–13.

Higginbotham, Thomas. 2018. "The Military and the Gender Gap: The Air Force and Equality as Security Imperative." *Diplomatic Courier*, September 2. https://www.diplomaticcourier.com/posts/the-military-and-the-gender-gap-the-air-force-and-equality-as-security-imperative.

Highmore, Ben. 2002. "Introduction: Questioning Everyday Life." In *The Everyday Life*. New York: Routledge.

Hing, Bill Ong. 1993. "Beyond the Rhetoric of Assimilation and Cultural Pluralism: Addressing the Tension of Separatism and Conflict in an Immigration-Driven Multi-racial Society." *California Law Review* 81, no. 4 (July): 863–925.

Hingham, John. 2002. *Strangers in the Land: Patterns of American Nativism, 1860–1925.* 1955. Reprint. New Brunswick, NJ: Rutgers University Press.

Hirschman, Charles. 1983. "America's Melting Pot Reconsidered." *Annual Review of Sociology* 9: 397–423.

Hjerm, Mikael. 2005. "Integration to the Social Democratic Welfare State." *Social Indicators Research*: 117–38.

Hoeder, Dirk. 2014. *Migrations and Belonging*. Cambridge, MA: Belknap Press.

Hondagneu-Sotelo, Pierrette. 1994. "Regulating the Unregulated: Domestic Workers' Social Networks." *Social Problems* 41 (February): 50–64.

———. 2001. *"Doméstica": Immigrant Workers Cleaning and Caring in the Shadows of Affluence*. Berkeley: University of California Press.

Honneth, Axel. 1996. *The Struggle for Recognition: The Moral Grammar of Social Conflicts*. Cambridge: Polity Press.

Honneth, Axel, and Nancy Fraser. 2003. *Redistribution or Recognition? A Political-Philosophical Exchange*. New York: Verso.

Honneth, Axel, and Gwynn Markle. 2004. "From Struggles for Recognition to a Plural Concept of Justice: An Interview with Axel Honneth." *Acta Sociologica* 47, no. 4 (December): 383–91.

Horowitz, Murray M. 1978. "Ethnicity and Command: The Civil War Experience." *Military Affairs* 42 (4): 182–89.

Horst, Harder René D. 2010. "Cross, Cactus, and Racial Construction: The Chaco War and Indigenous People in Paraguay." In *Military Struggle and Identity Formation in Latin America*, edited by Nicola Foote and René D. Harder Horst. Gainesville: University Press of Florida.

Hromadžić, Azra. 2015. *Citizens of an Empty Nation: Youth and State-Making in Postwar Bosnia-Herzegovina*. Philadelphia: University of Pennsylvania Press.

Huntington, Samuel. 1957. *The Soldier and the State: The Theory and Politics of Civil-Military Relations*. Cambridge, MA: Harvard University Press.

———. 2004. *Who Are We? The Challenges to America's National Identity*. New York: Simon & Schuster.

Hurtado-de-Mendoza, Alejandra, Adriana Serrano, Felisa A. Gonzales, Nicole C. Fernandez, Mark L. Cabling, and Stacey Kaltman. 2015. "Trauma-Exposed Latina Immigrants' Networks: A Social Network Analysis Approach." *Journal of Latina/o Psychology* (December 21).

Hymowitz, C., and T. D. Schelhardt. 1986. "The Glass-Ceiling: Why Women Can't Seem to Break the Invisible Barrier That Blocks Them from Top Jobs." *Wall Street Journal*, March 24.

Iurcovich, Mark. 1997. *An Immigrant's Journey*. New York: Rivercross.

Jacobson, David, ed. 1998. *The Immigration Reader*. Boston: Blackwell.

———. 1996. *Rights across Borders: Immigration and the Decline of Citizenship*. Baltimore: John Hopkins University Press.

Janowitz, Morris, and Charles C. Moskos. 1979. "Five Years of the All-Volunteer Force: 1973–1978." *Armed Forces & Society* 5, no. 2 (January 1): 171–218. https://doi.org/10.1177/0095327X7900500201.

Jedlicka, Davor. 1978. "Sex Inequality, Aging, and Innovation in Preferential Mate Selection." *Family Coordinator* 27, no. 2 (April): 137–40.

Jelin, Elizabeth, ed. 1990. *Family, Household and Gender Relations in Latin America*. London: Kegan Paul International; Paris: UNESCO.

Jensen, Joan M. 1988. *Passage from India: Asian Indian Immigrants in North America*. New Haven, CT: Yale University Press.

Jimenez, Tomas. 2009. *Replenished Ethnicity: Mexican Americans, Immigration, and Identity*. Berkeley: University of California Press.

Jones, Richard C. 1998. "Remittances and Inequality: A Question of Migration Stage and Geographic Scale." *Economic Geography* 74, no. 1 (January): 8–25.

Jones-Correa, Michael. 1998. "Different Paths: Gender, Immigration and Political Participation." *International Migration Review* 32, no. 2 (Summer): 326–49.

Joshi, Khyati Y. 2006. *New Roots in America's Sacred Ground: Religion, Race, and Ethnicity in Indian America*. New Brunswick, NJ: Rutgers University Press.

Kamarck, Kristy. 2015. "Women in Combat: Issues for Congress." Congressional Research Service Report 7-5700. https://fas.org/sgp/crs/natsec/R42075.pdf.

———. 2017. "Diversity, Inclusion, and Equal Opportunity in the Armed Services: Background and Issues for Congress." https://fas.org/sgp/crs/natsec/R44321.pdf.

Kamath, M. V. 1976. *The United States and India, 1776–1976*. Washington, DC: Embassy of India.

Kamphoefner, Walter D., and Wolfgang Helbich, eds. 2006. *Germans in the Civil War: The Letters They Wrote Home*. Chapel Hill: University of North Carolina Press.

Kao, G., and M. Tienda. 1998. "Educational Aspirations of Minority Youth." *American Journal of Education* 106 (3): 349–84. www.jstor.org/stable/1085583.

Kapur, Devesh. 2010. *Diaspora, Development, and Democracy: The Domestic Impact of International Migration from India*. Princeton, NJ: Princeton University Press.

Karpathakis, Anna. 1999. "Home Society Politics and Immigrant Political Incorporation: The Case of Greek Immigrants in New York City." *International Migration Review* 33, no. 1 (Spring).

Katzenstein, Mary Fainsod. 1998. *Faithful and Fearless: Moving Feminist Protest Inside the Church and Military.* Princeton, NJ: Princeton University Press.

Katznelson, Ira, and Shefter Martin. 2002. *Shaped by Trade and War.* Princeton, NJ: Princeton University Press.

Keely, Charles B., and Tran Bao Nga. 1989. "Remittances from Labor Migration: Evaluations, Performance and Implications." *International Migration Review* 23 (3): 500–525.

Keene, Jennifer D. 2001. *Doughboys, the Great War, and the Remaking of America.* Baltimore: Johns Hopkins University Press.

Kelty, Ryan, Meredith Kleykamp, and David R. Segal. 2010. "The Military and the Transition to Adulthood." *Future of Children* 20, no. 1 (Spring): 181–207.

King, Anthony. 2006. "The Word of Command Communication and Cohesion in the Military." *Armed Forces & Society* 32, no. 4 (July): 493–512.

King, Deborah. 1988. "Multiple Jeopardy, Multiple Consciousness: The Context of a Black Feminist Ideology." *Signs* 14 (1): 42–72.

Kirby, S. N., M. C. Harrell, and J. Sloan. 2000. "Why Don't Minorities Join Special Operations Forces?" *Armed Forces and Society* 26: 523–45.

Klimenkova, Tatiana. 1994. "What Does Our Democracy Offer Society?" In *Women in Russia: A New Era in Russian Feminism,* edited by Anastasia Posadskaya. London: Verso.

Kuo, Wen H., and Nan Lin. 1977. "Assimilation of Chinese-Americans in Washington, D.C." *Sociological Quarterly* 18, no. 3 (June): 340–53.

Kurien, Prema. 1999. "Gendered Ethnicity: Creating a Hindu Indian Identity in the United States." *American Behavioral Scientist* 42: 648–70. https://doi.org/10.1177/00027649921954408.

Kviz, Frederick J. 1978. "Survival in Combat as a Collective Exchange Process." *Journal of Political and Military Sociology* 6 (Fall): 219–32.

LaBrack, B. 1988. "Evolution of Sikh Family Form and Values in Rural California: Continuity and Change, 1904–1980." *Journal of Comparative Family Studies* 19: 287–309.

Laguerre, Michael. 1984. *American Odyssey: Haitians in New York City.* Ithaca, NY: Cornell University Press.

Lambert, Richard D., and Marvin Bressler. 1956. *Indian Students on an American Campus.* Minneapolis: University of Minnesota Press.

Landale, Nancy S., and R. S. Oropesa. 1995. *Immigrant Children and the Children of Immigrants: Inter- and Intra-ethnic Group Differences in the United States.* East Lansing, MI: Population Research Group.

Lee, Jennifer, and Frank D. Bean. 2004. "America's Changing Color Lines: Immigration, Race/Ethnicity, and Multiracial Identification." *Annual Review of Sociology* 30:221–42.

Leonard, Karen Isaksen. 1997. *The South Asian Americans.* Westport, CT: Greenwood Press.

Lerner, S. 2013. "Labor of Love." *Stanford Social Innovation Review* 11 (Summer): 66–71. https://proxy.library.upenn.edu/login?url=http://search.proquest.com/doc view/1431073057?accountid=14707.

Lessinger, Johanna. 1995. *From Ganges to the Hudson: Indian Immigrants in New York City*. Boston: Allyn and Bacon.

Levi, Margret. 1997. *Consent, Dissent, and Patriotism*. New York: Cambridge University Press.

Li, Peter S. 1977. "Occupational Achievement and Kinship Assistance among Chinese Immigrants in Chicago." *Sociological Quarterly* 18 (4): 478–89.

Lieberson, Stanley. 1963. *Ethnic Patterns in American Cities*. New York: Free Press.

———. 1980. *A Piece of the Pie: Blacks and White Immigrants since 1880*. Berkeley: University of California Press.

Lind, William S. 1985. *Maneuver Warfare Handbook*. Boulder, CO: Westview Press.

Linge, David E., ed. 1977. *Philosophical Hermeneutics: Hans-Georg Gadamer*. Berkeley: University of California Press.

Lipsitz, George. 2006. *The Possessive Investment in Whiteness: How White People Profit from Identity Politics*. Philadelphia: Temple University Press.

Livingston, Gretchen. 2006. "Stable Gender, Job Searching, and Employment Outcomes among Mexican Immigrants." *Population Research and Policy Review* 25 (1): 43–66.

Locke, Brandon T. 2013. "The Military-Masculinity Complex: Hegemonic Masculinity and the United States Armed Forces, 1940–1963." PhD diss., University of Nebraska. https://digitalcommons.unl.edu/cgi/viewcontent.cgi?article=1065& context=historydiss.

Lonn, Elizabeth. 1969. *Foreigners in the Union Army and Navy*. New York: Greenwood Press.

Lorde, Audre, and Cheryl Clarke. 2007. *Sister Outsider: Essays and Speeches*. 1984. Reprint, Berkeley, CA: Crossing Press.

Lowe, Tony B., June G. Hopps, and Leatha A. See. 2006. "Challenges and Stressors of African American Armed Service Personnel and Their Families." *Journal of Ethnic & Cultural Diversity in Social Work* 15 (3–4): 51–81. https://doi.org/10.1300/J051v15n03_03.

Lundquist, Jennifer Hickes. 2008. "Ethnic and Gender Satisfaction in the Military: The Effect of a Meritocratic Institution." *American Sociological Review* 73, no. 3 (June): 477–96.

Lundquist, Jennifer Hickes, and Herbert L. Smith. 2005. "Family Formation among Women in the U.S. Military: Evidence from the NLSY." *Journal of Marriage and Family* 67, no. 1 (February): 1–13.

Lutz, Amy. 2008. "Who Joins the Military? A Look at Race, Class, and Immigration Status." *Journal of Political and Military Sociology* 36 (2): 167–88.

Lyman, Stanford. 1972. *The Black American in Sociological Thought: New Perspective on Black America*. New York: Capricorn Books.

MacKenzie, Megan. 2013. "Let Women Fight: Ending the U.S. Military's Female Combat Ban." *Foreign Affairs*, January 23.

———. 2015. *Beyond the Band of Brothers: The US Military and the Myth That Women Can't Fight*. Cambridge: Cambridge University Press.

MacLeish, Kenneth T. 2013. *Making War at Fort Hood: Life and Uncertainty in a Military Community*. Princeton, NJ: Princeton University Press.

Mahler, Sarah J. 1995. *American Dreaming: Immigrant Life on the Margins*. Princeton, NJ: Princeton University Press.

Malavolti, M., N. C. Battistini, M. Dugoni, B. Bagni, I Bagni, and A. Pietrobelli. 2008. "Effect of Intense Military Training on Body Composition." http://www.ncbi.nlm.nih.gov/pubmed/18550967.

Manning, Lori. 2005. *Women in the Military: Where They Stand*. 5th ed. Washington, DC: Women's Research and Education Institute.

Mark, Diane Mei Lin, and Ginger Chih. 1982. *A Place Called Chinese America*. Dubuque, IA: Kendall Hunt.

Massey, Douglas S., Jorge Durand, and Nolan J. Malone. 2002. *Beyond Smoke and Mirrors: Mexican Immigration in an Era of Economic Integration*. New York: Russell Sage Foundation.

Matthews, Lloyd J., and Tinaz Pavri, eds. 1989. "Population Diversity in the U.S. Army." http://www.au.af.mil/au/awc/awcgate/ssi/pop_diversity.pdf.

Mayakovich, Minako K. 1976. "To Stay or Not to Stay: Dimension of Ethnic Assimilation." *International Migration Review* 10, no. 3 (Autumn): 377–88.

McCall, L. 2005. "The Complexity of Intersectionality." *Signs* 30, no. 3 (Spring): 1771–1800.

McCormick, Theresa E. 1984. "Multiculturalism: Some Principles and Issues." *Theory into Practice Multicultural Education* 23, no. 2 (Spring).

McIntosh, Peggy. 2004. "White Privilege: Unpacking the Invisible Knapsack." In *Race, Class, and Gender in the United States*, edited by Paula S. Rothenberg. 6th ed. New York: Worth.

McKay, John. 2007. *Brave Men in Desperate Times: The Lives of Civil War Soldiers*. Guilford, CT: Globe Pequot Press.

McNaughton, James C., Kristen E. Edwards, and Jay M. Price. 2002. "Incontestable Proof Will Be Exacted: Historians, Asian Americans, and the Medal of Honor." *Public Historian* 24, no. 4 (Autumn): 11–33.

McNeill, William H. 1995. *Keeping Together in Time: Dance and Drill in Human History*. Cambridge, MA: Harvard University Press.

McThomas, Mary. 2015. "Performing Citizenship." Paper presented at the Centre for Citizenship Studies, Detroit, March 12.

Meade, Teresa. 2010. *A History of Modern America, 1800 to the Present*. Oxford: Wiley-Blackwell.

Melchert, Norman. 2002. *The Great Conversation: A Historical Introduction to Philosophy*. Boston: McGraw-Hill.

Menjivar, Cecilia, and Olivia Salcido. 2002. "Immigrant Women and Domestic Violence: Common Experiences in Different Countries." *Gender and Society* 16, no. 6 (December): 898–920.

Merhson, Sherie, and Steven Scholssman. 2003. *Foxholes and Color Lines: Desegregating the U.S. Armed Forces*. Baltimore: Johns Hopkins University Press.

Mettler, Suzanne. 2005. *Soldiers to Citizens: The GI Bill and the Making of the Greatest Generation*. New York: Oxford University Press.

"Military Resources: Blacks in the Military." n.d. http://www.archives.gov/research/alic/reference/military/blacks-in-military.html.

Miller, Laura L. 1997. "Not Just Weapons of the Weak: Gender Harassment as a Form of Protest for Army Men." *Social Psychology Quarterly* 60, no. 1 (March): 32–51.

Miller, Richard E. 2004. *The Messman Chronicles: African Americans in the U.S. Navy, 1932–1943*. Annapolis, MD: Naval Institute Press.

Mincer, Jacob. 1978. "Family Migration Decisions." *Journal of Political Economy* 86, no. 1 (October): 749–73.

Mishra, Vijay. 1996. "The Diasporic Imaginary: Theorizing the Indian Diaspora." *Textual Practice* 10 (3): 421–47.

Mittelstadt, Jennifer. 2015. *The Rise of the Military Welfare State*. Cambridge, MA: Harvard University Press.

Moghadam, Valentine, ed. 1993. *Democratic Reform and the Position of Women in Transitional Economies*. Oxford: Clarendon Press.

Mohanty, Chandra Talpade. 1988. "Under Western Eyes: Feminist Scholarship and Colonial Discourses." *Feminist Review* 30 (Autumn): 61–88.

Molina, Natalia. 2014. *How Race Is Made in America: Immigration, Citizenship and the Historical Power of Racial Scripts*. Berkeley: University of California Press.

Montoya, Rosario, et al., eds. 2002. *Gender's Place: Feminist Anthropologies of Latin America*. New York: Palgrave Macmillan.

Moon, Maj. Molly K. 1997. "Understanding the Impact of Cultural Diversity on Organizations." http://www.au.af.mil/au/awc/awcgate/acsc/97-0607c.pdf.

Moraga, Cherríe, and Gloria Anzaldúa, eds. 1984. *This Bridge Called My Back: Writings by Radical Women of Color*. 2nd ed. New York: Kitchen Table Press.

Morales, Maria Cristina, and Leticia Saucedo. 2015. "Disposability and Resistance in a Male Dominated Industry: Latina Immigrants Organizing in Residential Construction." *Human Organization* 74, no. 2 (Summer): 144–53. https://doi.org/10.17730/0018-7259-74.2.144.

Moreno Figueroa, Mónica G. 2008. "Historically Rooted Transnationalism: Slightedness and the Experience of Racism in Mexican Families." *Journal of Intercultural Studies* 29, no. 3 (July): 283–97.

Moskos, Charles C. 1966. "Racial Integration in the Armed Forces." *American Journal of Sociology* 72, no. 2 (September): 132–48.

———. 1970. *The American Enlisted Man*. New York: Russell Sage Foundation.

Myrdal, Gunnar. 1944. *An American Dilemma*. New York: Harper and Row.

Myrttinen, Henri, Lana Khattab, and Jana Naujoks. 2017. "Re-thinking Hegemonic Masculinities in Conflict-Affected Contexts." *Critical Military Studies* 3 (2): 103–19. https://doi.org/10.1080/23337486.2016.1262658.

Naujoks, Daniel. 2012a. "Does Dual Citizenship Increase Naturalization? Evidence from Indian Immigrants in the US." HWWI Research Paper, no. 125. Hamburgisches WeltWirtschaftsinstitut (HWWI), Hamburg.

———. 2012b. *Migration, Citizenship and Development. Diasporic Membership Policies and Overseas Indians in the U.S.* New Delhi: Oxford University Press.

Neckerman, K. M., P. Carter, and J. Lee. 1999. "Segmented Assimilation and Minority Cultures of Mobility." *Ethnic and Racial Studies* 22 (6): 945–65.

Nelson, Dennis D. 1953. "A Report on Military Civil Rights." *Negro History Bulletin* (January): 75–78.

Nelson, T. S. 2002. *For Love of Country: Confronting Rape and Sexual Harassment in the U.S. Military*. Binghamton, NY: Haworth Press.

Ngai, M. 2014. *Impossible Subjects: Illegal Aliens and the Making of Modern America*. Princeton, NJ: Princeton University Press.

"Non-citizens in Today's Military: Final Report." 2005. http://www.cna.org/research/2005/non-citizens-todays-military-final-report.

O'Farrell, Clare. 2005. *Michael Foucault*. Oxford: Sage.

Olzak, Susan. 1983. "Contemporary Ethnic Mobilization." *Annual Review of Sociology* 9: 355–74.

Oropesa, R. S., and Nancy S. Landale. 1997. "In Search of the New Second Generation: Alternative Strategies for Identifying Second Generation Children and Understanding Their Acquisition of English." *Sociological Perspectives* 40, no. 3 (September 1): 429–55. https://doi.org/10.2307/1389451.

Orozco, M., B. Lowell, and J. Schneider. 2006. "Gender-Specific Determinants of Remittances: Differences in Structure and Motivation." http://www.remesasydesarrollo.org/uploads/media/Gender-Specific_Determinants_of_Remittances.pdf.

Orozco, Manuel. 2002. "Globalization and Migration: The Impact of Family Remittances in Latin America." *Latin American Politics and Society* 44, no. 2.

Pachirat, Timothy. 2009. "The Political in Political Ethnography: Dispatches from the Kill Floor." In *Political Ethnography: What Immersion Contributes to the Study of Power*. Chicago: University of Chicago Press.

———. 2011. *Every Twelve Seconds*. New Haven, CT: Yale University Press.

Padrón, Elena. 2015. "Whiteness in Latina Immigrants: A Venezuelan Perspective." *Women & Therapy* 38 (3–4): 194–206. https://doi.org/10.1080/02703149.2015.1059181.

Pagano, A., J. P. Lee, V. Garcia, and P. Recarte. 2018. "Ethnographic Research in Immigrant-Specific Drug Abuse Recovery Houses." *Journal of Ethnicity in Substance Abuse* 17: 79–90. https://doi.org/10.1080/15332640.2017.1362726.

Park, Robert E. 1914. "Racial Assimilation in Secondary Groups with Particular Reference to the Negro." *American Journal of Sociology* 19: 606–23.

———. 1950. *Race and Culture*. Glencoe, IL: Free Press.

Parrado, Emilio A., and Marcela Cerrutti. 2003. "Labor Migration between Developing Countries: The Case of Paraguay and Argentina." *International Migration Review* 37, no. 1 (Spring): 101–32.

Parrado, E. A., and S. P. Morgan. 2008. "Intergenerational Fertility among Hispanic Women: New Evidence of Immigrant Assimilation." *Demography* 45, no. 3 (August): 651–71.

Pascall, Gillian, and Anna Kwak, eds. 2009. *Gender Regimes in Transition in Central and Eastern Europe*. Chicago: University of Chicago Press, 2009.

Patterson, G. James. 1977. *The Romanians of Saskatchewan: Four Generations of Adaptation*. National Museum of Man, Mercury Series, Canadian Centre for Folk Cultural Studies, Paper no. 23. Ottawa: National Museums of Canada.

Pavelescu, Alina. 2011. "Idéologiser la culture alternative: Adrian Păunescu et le Cénacle Flacăra." In *Avatars of Intellectuals under Communism*, vol. 2 of *History of Communism in Europe*, 51–71. Bucharest: Zeta Book.

Peach, Lucina Joy. 1997. "Behind the Front Lines: Feminist Battles over Women in Combat." In *Wives and Warriors: Women and the Military in the United States and Canada*, edited by Laurie Lee Weinstein and Christie C. White. Westport, CT: Bergin & Garvey.

Penn, Shana, and Jill Massino. 2009. *Gender Politics and Everyday Life in State Socialist Eastern and Central Europe*. New York: Palgrave Macmillan.

Peterson, V. Spike. 2007. "Thinking through Intersectionality and War." *Race, Gender & Class* 14 (3–4): 10–27. http://www.jstor.org/stable/41675287.

Plato. 1977. *Timaeus and Critias*. London: Penguin Books. http://classics.mit.edu/Plato/timaeus.html.

Poros, Martisa. 2004. "Networks of Inclusion and Exclusion in the Economic Concentrations of Indian Immigrants in New York and London." *Research in Sociology of Work* 14: 35–61.

Portes, Alejandro. 2007. "Migration, Development, and Segmented Assimilation: A Conceptual Review of the Evidence." *Annals of the American Academy of Political and Social Science* 610 (1): 73–97.

Portes, Alejandro, and Robert L. Bach. 1985. *The Latin Journey: Cuban and Mexican Immigrants in the United States*. Berkeley: University of California Press.

Portes, Alejandro, and József Böröcz. 1989. "Contemporary Immigration: Theoretical Perspectives on Its Determinants and Modes of Incorporation." *International Migration Review* 23 (3): 606–30. https://doi.org/10.2307/2546431.

Portes, Alejandro, Patricia Fernández-Kelly, and William Haller. 2005. "Segmented Assimilation on the Ground: The New Second Generation in Early Adulthood." *Ethnic and Racial Studies* 28: 1000–1040.

Portes, Alejandro, and L. Hao. 2002. "The Price of Uniformity: Language, Family and Personality Adjustment in the Immigrant Second Generation." *Ethnic and Racial Studies* 25 (6): 889–912.

Portes, Alejandro, and Rubén G. Rumbaut. 1990. *Immigrant America: A Portrait*. Berkeley: University of California Press.

———. 2001. *Legacies: The Story of the Immigrant Second Generation*. Berkeley and New York: University of California Press and Russell Sage Foundation.

———. 2014. *Immigrant America: A Portrait*. 1990. Reprint, Berkeley: University of California Press.

Portes, Alejandro, and Julia Sensenbrenner. 1993. "Embeddedness and Immigration: Notes on the Social Determinants of Economic Action." *American Journal of Sociology* 98, no. 6 (May): 1320–50.

Portes, Alejandro, and Min Zhou. 1993a. "Gaining the Upper Hand: Economic Mobility among Immigrant and Domestic Minorities." *Ethnic and Racial Studies* 15: 491–522.

———. 1993b. "The New Second Generation: Segmented Assimilation and Its Variants." *Annals of the American Academy of Political and Social Sciences* 530: 74–96.

Posadskaya, Anastasia, ed. 1994. *Women in Russia: A New Era in Russian Feminism.* London: Verso.

Prasad, Vijay. 2000. *Karma of Brown Folks.* Minneapolis: University of Minnesota Press.

Radcliffe, S. A. 1999. "Latina Labour: Restructuring of Work and Renegotiations of Gender Relations in Contemporary Latin America." *Environment and Planning* 31: 196–208.

Radziłowski, John. 2001. "American Polonia in World War II: Toward a Social History." *Polish American Studies* 58, no. 1 (Spring): 63–80.

Ramos, Sandra. 2012. "Women's Labour Rights, Gender Equality and Economic Justice in Latin America and the Caribbean Development." *Development* 55 (3): 397–402.

Rangaswamy, Padma. 2000. *Namaste America: Indian Immigrants in an American Metropolis.* Philadelphia: Pennsylvania State University Press.

Ravage, M. E. 2009. *An American in the Making.* New Brunswick, NJ: Rutgers University Press.

Reading, Anna. 1992. *Polish Women, Solidarity, and Feminism.* London: Macmillan.

Reit, Rachel. 2009. "The Relationship between the Military's Masculine Culture and Service Members' Help-Seeking Behaviors." Master's thesis, Marquette University. https://epublications.marquette.edu/cgi/viewcontent.cgi?article =1411&context=theses_open.

Rick, Thomas E. 1997. *Making the Corps.* New York: Scribner.

Robila, Mihaela. 2004. "Families in Eastern Europe: Context, Change and Variations." In *Families in Eastern Europe*, edited by Mihaela Robila, 1–14. New York: Elsevier.

———. 2007. "Eastern European Immigrants in the United States: A Socio-demographic Profile." *Social Science Journal* 44 (1): 113–25.

Robila, Mihaela, and A. Krishnakumar. 2006. "The Role of Children in Eastern European Families." *Children & Society* 18 (1): 30–41.

Robinson, Fiona. 2011. *The Ethics of Care: A Feminist Approach to Human Security.* Philadelphia: Temple University Press.

Roceric, Alexandra. 1982. *Language Maintenance within an American Community: The Case of Romanian.* Grass Lake–Jackson, MI: Romanian-American Heritage Center.

Roediger, David R. 2005. *Working toward Whiteness: How America's Immigrants Became White; The Strange Journey from Ellis Island to the Suburbs.* New York: Basic Books.

———. 2007. *The Wages of Whiteness: Race and the Making of the American Working Class.* New York: Verso.

Romero, Mary. 1992. *Maid in the U.S.A.* New York: Routledge.

———. 1997. "Who Takes Care of the Maid's Children?" In *Feminism and Families*, edited by Hilde Lindemann Nelson. New York: Routledge.

Rose, Gilian. 2016. *Visual Methodologies: An Introduction to Researching with Visual Materials.* 4th ed. London: Sage.

Rosen, S., and P. Taubman. 1982. "Changes in Life-Cycle Earnings: What Do Social Security Data Show?" *Journal of Human Resources* 17: 321–38.

Rosman-Stollman, Elisheva. 2008. "Mediating Structures and the Military: The Case of Religious Soldiers." *Armed Forces & Society* 34 (615): 393–94.

Rudrappa, Sharmila. 2004. *Ethnic Routes to Becoming American: Indian Immigrants and the Cultures of Citizenship*. New Brunswick, NJ: Rutgers University Press.

Rueschemeyer, Marilyn, ed. 1994. *Women in the Politics of Postcommunist Eastern Europe*, Armonk, NY: M. E. Sharpe.

Ruggiero, K. M., and D. M. Taylor. 1997. "Why Minority Group Members Perceive or Do Not Perceive the Discrimination That Confronts Them: The Role of Self-Esteem and Perceived Control." *Journal of Personality and Social Psychology* 72 (2): 373–89. https://doi-org.ezproxy.cul.columbia.edu/10.1037/0022-3514.72.2.373.

Rumbaut, Rubén G. 1994a. "The Crucible Within: Ethnic Identity, Self-Esteem, and Segmented Assimilation among Children of Immigrants." *International Migration Review* 28 (4): 748–94. https:/doi.org/10.2307/2547157.

———. 1994b. "Origins and Destinies: Immigration to the United States since World War II." *Sociological Forum* 9 (4): 583–621.

———. 1996. "The Crucible Within: Ethnic Identity, Self-Esteem, and Segmented Assimilation among Children Immigrants." In *The New Second Generation*, edited by A. Portes. New York: Russell Sage Foundation.

———. 1997. "Paradoxes (and Orthodoxies) of Assimilation." *Immigration and Incorporation* 40 (3): 483–511.

Samora, Julian, Jorge A. Bustamante, and Gilbert Cardenas. 1971. *Los Mojados: The Wetback Story*. Notre Dame, IN: University of Notre Dame Press.

Sanchez-Hucles, J. V., and D. D. Davis. 2010. "Women and Women of Color in Leadership: Complexity, Identity, and Intersectionality." *American Psychologist* 65 (3): 171–81. https://doi.org/10.1037/a0017459.

Sanders, Jimy M., and Victor Nee. 1996. "Immigrant Self-Employment: The Family as Social Capital and the Value of Human Capital." *American Sociological Review* 61 (2): 231–49.

Sassler, Sharon. 2006. "School Participation of Immigrant Youths in the Early 20th Century: Integration or Segmented Assimilation?" *Sociology of Education* 79 (1): 1–24.

Saussure, Ferdinand de. 1959. *Course in General Linguistics*. New York: McGraw-Hill.

Sayles, Andrew. 1998. "On Diversity." http://www.au.af.mil/au/awc/awcgate/ssi/on_diversity.pdf.

Schatz, Edward. 2009. *Political Ethnography: What Immersion Contribute to the Study of Power*. Chicago: University of Chicago Press.

Schoeni, Robert F. 1998. "Labor Market Assimilation of Immigrant Women." *Industrial and Labor Relations Review* 51 (3): 986–92.

Schuster, Caroline. 2014. "The Social Unit of Debt: Gender and Creditworthiness in Paraguayan Microfinance." *American Ethnologist* 41 (3): 563–78.

Schwartz-Shea, Peregrine, and Dvora Yanow. 2011. *Interpretive Research Design: Concepts and Processes*. New York: Routledge.

Scott, James. 1985. *Weapons of the Weak: Everyday Forms of Peasant Resistance*. New Haven, CT: Yale University Press.

———. 1990. *Domination and the Art of Resistance*. New Haven, CT: Yale University Press.

Segal, David R., and Mady Wechsler Segal. 2005. "Army Recruitment Goals Endangered as Percent of African American Enlistees Declines." No longer available. Accessed October 12, 2007.

Segal, Mady Wechsler. 1995. "Women's Military Roles Cross-Nationally: Past, Present, and Future." *Gender and Society* 9 (6): 757–75.

Segal, Mady Wechsler, Meredith Hill Thanner, and David R. Segal. 2007. "Hispanic and African American Men and Women in the U.S. Military: Trends in Representation." *Race, Gender & Class* 14 (3–4): 48–64. www.jstor.org/stable/41675289.

Segal, Robert A. 2004. "The Place of Religion in Modernity." *History of the Human Sciences* 17, no. 4 (November): 131–49. https://doi.org/10.1177/0952695104048077.

Settersten, Richard A., Jr., and Robin S. Patterson. 2006. "Military Service, the Life Course, and Aging: An Introduction." *Sage Publications* 28 (1): 5–11.

Shaw, Henry I., Jr., and Ralph W. Donnelly. 1975. "Blacks in the Marine Corps." http://www.montfordpointmarines.com/BLACKS%20IN%20THE%20MA-RINE%20CORPS/BLACKS%20IN%20THE%20MARINE%20CORPS.pdf.

Shay, J. 2002. *Odysseus in America: Combat Trauma and the Trials of Homecoming*. New York: Scribner.

Shehata, Samer. 2006. "Ethnography, Identity and the Production of Knowledge." In *Interpretation and Method: Empirical Research Methods and Interpretive Turn*, edited by Dvora Yanow and Peregrine Schwatz-Shea. New York: Routledge.

Sherman, Janann. 1990. "'They Either Need These Women or They Do Not': Margaret Chase Smith and the Fight for Regular Status for Women in the Military." *Journal of Military* 54 (1): 47–78.

Sheth, Manju. 2006. "Asian Indian Americans." In *Asian Americans: Contemporary Trends and Issues*, edited by Pyong Gap Min. Thousand Oaks, CA: Pine Forge Press.

Sheth, Pravin. 2001. *Indians in America: On Stream, Two Waves, Three Generations*. New Delhi: Rawat.

Shibutani, Tamotsu. 1978. *The Derelicts of Company K: A Sociological Study of Demoralization*. Berkeley: University of California Press.

Shils, Edward A., and Morris Janowitz. 1948. "Cohesion and Disintegration in Wehrmacht in World War II." *Public Opinion Quarterly* 12: 280–315.

Shklar, Judith. 1998. *American Citizenship: A Quest for Inclusion*. Cambridge, MA: Harvard University Press.

Shoup, David M. 1969. *New American Militarism*. Boston: Atlantic Monthly.

Silberman, Roxane, Richard Alba, and Irène Fournier. 2007. "Segmented Assimilation in France? Discrimination in the Labour Market against the Second Generation." *Ethnic and Racial Studies* 30 (1): 1–27.

Silva, Jennifer M. 2008. "A New Generation of Women? How Female ROTC Cadets Negotiate the Tension between Masculine Military Culture and Traditional Femininity." *Social Forces* 87 (2): 937–60.

Silvestri, Lisa Ellen. 2015. *Friend at the Front: Social Media in the American War Zone*. Lawrence: University Press of Kansas. muse.jhu.edu/book/42326.

Smith, Rogers. 1997. *Civic Ideals*. New Haven, CT: Yale University Press.

Snider, Don M., Paul Oh, and Kevin Toner. 2009. *The Army's Professional Military Ethic in an Era of Persistent Conflict*. Philadelphia: Strategic Studies Institute.

"The Soldier's Guide (1)." n.d. http://www.defense.gov/about/#mission.

Sondern, Frederic, Jr. 1994. "U.S. Negroes Make Reds See Red." *Reader's Digest* (January): 37–42.

Song, Jingyi. 2001. "The Reconstruction of the Chinese Community in New York in the Years of the Depression and World War II." PhD diss., City University of New York.

Stahl, Roni Y. 2017. *Enlisting Faith*. Kindle ed. Cambridge, MA: Harvard University Press.

Sterba, Christopher M. 2003. *Good Americans: Italian and Jewish Immigrants during the First World War*. New York: Oxford University Press.

Stillman, Richard, II. 1969. "Negroes in the Armed Forces." *Phylon (1960–)* 30 (22): 139–59.

Stur, Heather Marie. 2011. *Beyond Combat Women and Gender in the Vietnam War I*. Cambridge: Cambridge University Press.

Sullivan, Jill. 2011. *Band of Sisters: U.S. Women's Military Bands during World War II*. Lanham, MD: Scarecrow Press.

Swamy, Padma. 2000. *Namaste America: Indian Immigrants in an American Metropolis*. University Park: Pennsylvania State University Press.

Swers, Michele. 2007. "Building a Reputation on National Security: The Impact of Stereotypes Related to Gender and Military Experience." *Legislative Studies Quarterly* 32 (4): 559–95.

Taylor, Charles. 1994. "Politics of Recognition." In *Multiculturalism: Examining the Politics of Recognition*. Princeton, NJ: Princeton University Press.

Taylor, William A. 2016. *Military Service and American Democracy: From World War II to the Iraq and Afghanistan War*. Kindle ed. Lawrence: University Press of Kansas.

Teachman, Jay. 2007. "Race, Military Service, and Marital Timing: Evidence from the NLSY-79." *Demography* 44 (2): 389–404.

Thorpe, Helen. 2015. *Soldier Girls: The Battles of Three Women at Home and at War*. New York: Scribner Press.

Threat, Charissa. 2015. *Nursing Civil Rights: Gender and Race in the Army Nurse Corps*. Urbana: University of Illinois Press.

Tichenor, Daniel J. 2002. *Dividing Lines: Politics of Immigration Control in America*. Princeton, NJ: Princeton University Press.

Titunik, Regina. 2008. "The Myth of the Macho Military." *Polity* 40 (2): 423–33.

Tonnelat, Stephane, and William Kornblum. 2017. *International Express: New Yorkers on the 7 Train*. New York: Columbia University Press.

"Top Women in the Military." 2014. *Women of Color Magazine* 13, no. 1 (Spring): 46–63. http://www.jstor.org/stable/43769498.

Tronto, Joan C. 2002. "The 'Nanny' Question in Feminism." *Hypatia* 17 (2): 34–51. www.jstor.org/stable/3810749.

Tucker, Philip Thomas. 2007. *God Help the Irish*. Abilene, TX: McWhiney Foundation Press.

Turner, Robin L. 2014. "Traditional, Democratic, Accountable? Navigating Citizen-Subjection in Rural South Africa." *Africa Spectrum* 49 (1): 27–54.

U.S. Congress. 2006. *Contribution of Immigrants to the United States Armed Forces Hearing before the Committee on Armed Services United States Senate.* 2nd ed. Washington, DC: U.S. Government Printing Office.

Vagts, Alfred. 1947. "The Foreigner as Soldier in the Second World War, II." *Journal of Politics* 9 (3): 392–416.

Van Creveld, Martin. 2000. "The Great Illusion: Women in the Military." *Millennium* 29 (2): 429–42.

Van Wormer, Nicholas. 2012. *The Ultimate Air Force Basic Training Guidebook.* New York: Savas Beatie.

Varvel, Todd K. 2000. "Ensuring Diversity Is Not Just Another BuzzWord." http://www.au.af.mil/au/awc/awcgate/acsc/00-180.pdf.

Wade, Peter. 2010a. *Race and Ethnicity in Latin America.* London: Pluto Press.

———. 2010b. "Rethinking Mestizaje: Ideology and Lived Experience." *Journal of Latin American Studies* 37:1–19.

———. 2014. "Race, Ethnicity, and Technologies of Belonging." *Science, Technology & Human Values* 39, no. 4 (July): 587–96. https://doi.org/10.1177/0162243913516807.

Waite, Linda J., and Sure E. Berryman. 1986. "Job Stability among Young Women: A Comparison of Traditional and Nontraditional Occupations." *American Journal of Sociology* 92 (3): 568–95.

Wakin, Edward. 1971. *Black Fighting Men in U.S. History.* New York: Lothrop, Lee, and Shepard.

Waldinger, Roger. 1999. *Still the Promised City? African-Americans and New Immigrants in Postindustrial New York.* Cambridge, MA: Harvard University Press.

Wang, Qingfang. 2008. "Race/Ethnicity, Gender and Job Earnings across Metropolitan Areas in the United States: A Multilevel Analysis." *Urban Studies* 45 (4): 825–43. www.jstor.org/stable/43197791.

Ware, Vron. 2012. *Military Migrants: Fighting for YOUR Country (Migration, Diasporas and Citizenship).* 1874. Reprint, Hampshire: Palgrave Macmillan.

Waters, Mary. 1994. "Ethnic and Racial Identities of Second-Generation Black Immigrants in New York City." *International Migration Review* 28 (4): 795–820.

———. 1999. "Black Identities." In *Economy and Society.* Berkeley: University of California Press.

Waters, Mary C., and Karl Eschbach. 1995. "Immigration and Ethnic and Racial Inequality in the United States." *Annual Review of Sociology* 21: 149–46.

Waters, Mary C., and Tomas R. Jimenez. 2005. "Assessing Immigrant Assimilation: New Empirical and Theoretical Challenges." *Annual Review Sociology* 31: 105–25.

Wedeen, Lisa. 2002. "Conceptualizing Culture: Possibilities for Political Science." *American Political Science Review* 96 (4): 713–28.

———. 2008. *Peripheral Vision.* Chicago: University of Chicago Press.

Weinstein, Laurie Lee, and Christie C. White, eds. 1997. *Wives and Warriors: Women and the Military in the United States and Canada.* Westport, CT: Bergin & Garvey.

Whites, LeeAnn, and Alecia P. Long, eds. 2009. *Occupied Women: Gender, Military Occupation, and the American Civil War.* Baton Rouge: Louisiana State University Press.

Wilcox, Clyde. 1992. "Race, Gender, and Support for Women in the Military." *Social Science Quarterly* 73 (2): 310–23.

Williams, S. W., and P. Dilworth-Anderson. 2002. "Systems of Social Support in Families Who Care for Dependent African American Elders." *Gerontologist* 42 (2): 224–36.

Williams, Terry. 1990. *The Cocaine Kids: The Inside Story of a Teenage Drug Ring*. Boston: Da Capo Press.

Williams, Terry, and Trevor Milton. 2015. *The Con Men*. New York: Columbia University Press.

Wilson, Kenneth L., and Alejandro Portes. 1980. "Immigrant Enclaves: An Analysis of the Labor Market Experiences of Cubans in Miami." *American Journal of Sociology* 86 (2): 295–319. www.jstor.org/stable/2778666.

Wing, A. K. 1990. "Brief Reflections toward a Multiplicative Theory and Praxis of Being." *Berkeley Women's Law Journal* 6 (1): 181–201.

Wittgenstein, Ludwig. 1953. *Philosophical Investigations*. New York: Macmillan.

Xavia Karner, Tracy. 1998. "Engendering Violent Men: Oral Histories of Military Masculinity." In *Masculinities and Violence*, edited by Lee H. Bowker. Thousand Oaks, CA: Sage.

Xie, Yu, and Emily Greenman. 2005. "Segmented Assimilation Theory: A Reformulation and Empirical Test." Population Studies Center, University of Michigan, Research Report 05-581. http://www.psc.isr.umich.edu/pubs/pdf/rr05-581.pdf.

Yanow, Dvora. 2003. *Constructing "Race" and "Ethnicity" in America: Category-Making in Public Policy and Administration*. New York: M. E. Sharpe.

———. 2006. "Dear Reviewer, Dear Author: Looking for Reflexivity and Other Hallmarks of Interpretative Research." Paper presented at the annual meeting of the American Political Science Association, "Interpretative Methods in Practice."

Yanow, Dvora, and Peregrine Schwartz-Shea, eds. 2006. *Interpretation and Method: Empirical Research Methods and the Interpretive Turn*. Armonk, NY: M. E. Sharpe.

Ybema, Sierk, Dvora Yanow, Harry Wels, and Frans Kamsteeg, eds. 2009. *Organizational Ethnography: Studying the Complexities of Everyday Life*. London: Sage.

Yin, Paul. 2012. "The Narratives of Chinese-American Litigation during the Chinese Exclusion Era." *Asian American Law Journal* 19 (1): 145–69. https://lawcat.berkeley.edu/record/1124971.

Yuval-Davis, Nira. 2006. "Intersectionality and Feminist Politics." *European Journal of Women's Studies* 13, no. 3 (August): 193–209. https://doi.org/10.1177/135050 6806065752.

Zellin, Thorsten, and Donald Young, eds. 1942. *Minority People in a Nation at War*. Philadelphia: American Academy of Political and Social Science.

Zetterberg, Pär. 2009. "Do Gender Quotas Foster Women's Political Engagement? Lessons from Latin America." *Political Research Quarterly* 62 (4): 715–30.

Zhao, Xiaojian. 1996. "Chinese American Women Defense Workers in World War II." *California History* 75 (2): 138–53.

Zhou, Min. 1997a. "Growing Up American: The Challenge Confronting Immigrant Children and Children of Immigrants." *Annual Review of Sociology* 23: 63–95.

———. 1997b. "Segmented Assimilation: Issues, Controversies, and Recent Research on the New Second Generation." In "Immigrant Adaptation and Native-Born Responses in the Making of American." Special issue, *International Migration Review* 31, no. 4 (Winter): 975–1008. https://doi.org/10.2307/2547421.

Zizek, Slavoj. 2007. "Resistance Is Surrender." *London Review of Books*, November 15. http://www.lrb.co.uk/v29/n22/slavoj-zizek/resistance-is-surrender.

Zolberg, Aristide. 1987. "Wanted but not Welcome: Alien Labor in Western Development." In *Population in an Interacting World*, edited by William Alonso. Cambridge, MA: Harvard University Press.

———. 1998. "International Migration, 1965–96: An Overview." *Population and Development Review* 24 (3): 429–68.

———. 2000. "The Dawn of Cosmopolitan Denizenship." *Indiana Journal of Global Legal Studies* 7 (3): 511–18.

———. 2006a. "Managing a World on the Move." *Population and Development Review* 32 (S1): 222–53. https://doi.org/10.1111/j.1728-4457.2006.tb00009.x.

———. 2006b. *A Nation by Design: Immigration Policy in the Fashioning of America*. Cambridge, MA: Harvard University Press.

ZurLippe, Captain J. C. 2009. "Allowing Undocumented/Illegal Immigrants to Enlist in the US Military." https://apps.dtic.mil/sti/pdfs/ADA508051.pdf.

Index

CRISTINA-IOANA DRAGOMIR is a clinical assistant professor in global liberal studies at New York University. She consults with the United Nations, Deutsche Gesellschaft für Internationale Zusammenarbeit (GIZ), and the International Organization for Migration. She is the author of *Power on the Move: Adivasi and Roma Accessing Social Justice.*

The University of Illinois Press
is a founding member of the
Association of American University Presses.

University of Illinois Press
1325 South Oak Street
Champaign, IL 61820-6903
www.press.uillinois.edu